Bitcoin

Bitcoin

2nd Edition

by Peter Kent and Tyler Bain

Bitcoin For Dummies®, 2nd Edition

Published by: **John Wiley & Sons, Inc.**, 111 River Street, Hoboken, NJ 07030-5774, www.wiley.com

For general information on our other products and services, please contact our Customer Care Department within the U.S. at 877-762-2974, outside the U.S. at 317-572-3993, or fax 317-572-4002. For technical support, please visit https://hub.wiley.com/community/support/dummies.

Wiley publishes in a variety of print and electronic formats and by print-on-demand. Some material included with standard print versions of this book may not be included in e-books or in print-on-demand. If this book refers to media such as a CD or DVD that is not included in the version you purchased, you may download this material at http://booksupport.wiley.com. For more information about Wiley products, visit www.wiley.com.

Library of Congress Control Number: 2022932288

ISBN 978-1-119-60213-2 (pbk); ISBN 978-1-119-60216-3 (ebk);
ISBN 978-1-119-60214-9 (ebk)

SKY10032738_022222

Contents at a Glance

Introduction 1

Part 1: Bitcoin Basics 5

CHAPTER 1: Bitcoin in a Nutshell 7
CHAPTER 2: Bitcoin Tech Explained 29

Part 2: Using Bitcoin 53

CHAPTER 3: Buying, Using, and Selling Bitcoin 55
CHAPTER 4: Taking Control of Your Wallet (and Hodling Your Bitcoin) 97
CHAPTER 5: Keeping Your Bitcoin Safe 139
CHAPTER 6: Investing in Bitcoin 165

Part 3: Getting Geeky 193

CHAPTER 7: Understanding the Bitcoin Network and Bitcoin Mining 195
CHAPTER 8: Bitcoin Adoption in the Real World 211
CHAPTER 9: Bitcoin Botheration 225

Part 4: The Part of Tens 237

CHAPTER 10: Ten Tips to Hodl and Stack Sats 239
CHAPTER 11: Ten Types of Bitcoin Resources 249
CHAPTER 12: Ten (Plus One) Thoughts about the Future of Bitcoin 257

Index 275

Table of Contents

INTRODUCTION . . . 1
About This Book . . . 1
Foolish Assumptions . . . 2
Icons Used in This Book . . . 3
Beyond the Book . . . 3
Where to Go from Here . . . 3

PART 1: BITCOIN BASICS . . . 5

CHAPTER 1: Bitcoin in a Nutshell . . . 7
In the Beginning, There Were . . . Digital Currencies? . . . 8
The Birth of Bitcoin . . . 10
But Who Is Nakamoto? . . . 12
Understanding What Bitcoin Actually Is . . . 13
Understanding Bitcoin Units . . . 16
Cryptocurrency or Cryptoasset? . . . 17
If There Is No Bitcoin, How Can It Be Valuable? . . . 18
Milton Friedman and the rai stones . . . 19
Money is belief . . . 22
Understanding Bitcoin Benefits . . . 23
Portability . . . 24
Verifiability . . . 24
Fungibility . . . 25
Durability . . . 25
Divisibility . . . 25
Open access . . . 25
Final settlement . . . 26
Borderless, stateless . . . 26
Pseudonymous . . . 26
Monopoly-resistant . . . 26
Debasement-proof . . . 27

CHAPTER 2: Bitcoin Tech Explained . . . 29
Understanding That There Is No Bitcoin! . . . 30
Discovering the Bitcoin Ledger . . . 31
So where is this "Bitcoin ledger"? . . . 32
Bitcoin uses a blockchain ledger . . . 32
Looking at the Bitcoin Distributed, Peer-to-Peer Network . . . 33

Using the Bitcoin Blockchain's Blocks of Business. 36
Hashing the blocks 37
The Bitcoin blockchain is "immutable". 39
Finding Out How the Ledger Functions. 40
Your address: Where your money is stored in the ledger . . 41
What's the crypto in cryptocurrency?. 41
Public key encryption magic 44
Messages to the blockchain. 46
Signing messages with the private key 47
Sending a transaction message to the Bitcoin ledger 47
Unraveling the message. 49
But you'll need a wallet. 50

PART 2: USING BITCOIN 53

CHAPTER 3: **Buying, Using, and Selling Bitcoin** 55
Finding the Price of Bitcoin 56
Your Options for Acquiring Bitcoin 57
Bitcoin ATMs 58
Retail Bitcoin 72
Person-to-person trading. 73
Bitcoin exchanges 75
"Bitcoin Back" on Credit and Debit Cards 90
Earning Your Bitcoin. 91
Mining Bitcoin 92
Finding Bitcoin Everywhere. 92
Selling Your Bitcoin. 93

CHAPTER 4: **Taking Control of Your Wallet (and Hodling Your Bitcoin)** 97
What Is a Wallet?. 98
Wallets store private keys 98
Wallets create and store keys and addresses. 99
Wallets communicate with the Bitcoin network. 100
Wallets can be hot or cold 100
Exploring Wallet Hardware 101
Brain wallets. 101
Paper wallets 102
Metal wallets 102
Hardware wallets 104
Web wallets 105
Dedicated full nodes. 106
Software wallets 107

Finding a Wallet. 107
Setting Up a Bitcoin Wallet 110
Creating and securing your first wallet 110
Creating a 24-word seed 113
Increasing security with a fake account. 115
Receiving Bitcoin 116
Getting those notifications. 118
Checking your addresses. 119
Sending Bitcoin 120
Following the money 123
Backing up your wallet. 124
Importing (or recovering) a wallet 125
Creating a watch-only wallet 127
Exploring multiple-signature wallets 129
Using the Lightning Network 136

CHAPTER 5: **Keeping Your Bitcoin Safe** 139
Understanding How You Can Lose Control of Your Bitcoin . . . 140
Grasping the Goal: Private Key and Seed Protection 142
Making a Choice: Custodial or Private Wallet? 144
Devising Your Cryptocurrency Safety Plan 145
Producing powerful passwords 145
Protecting passwords with password programs 147
Protecting your computer 149
Watching out for sophisticated phishing. 151
Employing two-factor authentication. 154
Exploring More Ways to Protect Your Bitcoin
(and Everything Else) 158
Knowing What Happens When You Kick the Bucket 161
Choosing the multi-sig solution 162
Scheduling future transactions 163
Using a digital inheritance feature 163

CHAPTER 6: **Investing in Bitcoin** 165
Bitcoin: Valuable Asset or Bubble About to Burst? 166
Bitcoin's got to rise in value! 167
Bitcoin's bound to bust! 169
Understanding stock-to-flow. 170
Bitcoin: digital gold 173
So You Want to Buy Bitcoin. 175
The basic strategy — buy and hodl 176
Dollar cost averaging 177
Timing the market. 179

Arbitrage....180
Other Bitcoin-related investment vehicles....181
Don't forget your retirement....182
Hodling II — An Even Better Strategy....184
The New Frontier — Other Cryptocurrencies....185
NFTs — What's It All About?....187

PART 3: GETTING GEEKY....193

CHAPTER 7: **Understanding the Bitcoin Network and Bitcoin Mining**....195
The Bitcoin Network....196
Submitting Transactions....200
Looking at transaction fees....200
Change address....202
Verifying the transaction....203
Mining for Bitcoin — the 10-minute contest....204
Winning the Bitcoin....208
Bitcoin Presets....209

CHAPTER 8: **Bitcoin Adoption in the Real World**....211
Bitcoin in the Boardroom....212
Bitcoin in Nations....212
When governments love Bitcoin....214
Nations promoting crypto....217
It's not just the rich....219
When the nation collapses....221

CHAPTER 9: **Bitcoin Botheration**....225
Bitcoin Is Too Volatile....226
Governments Ban Bitcoin....227
Bitcoin: A 21st-Century Ponzi Scheme....229
The Bitcoin Bubble....230
Bitcoin Costs Too Much to Use....231
Bitcoin Security Risks....233
Bitcoin Energy Usage....234

PART 4: THE PART OF TENS....237

CHAPTER 10: **Ten Tips to Hodl and Stack Sats**....239
Invest in Knowledge, Do Your Homework....239
Get Off Zero (₿)....240
Lower Your Cost Basis, Buy the Dip....241
Dry Powder, or Get on Zero ($)?....242

Run Your Own Bitcoin Node 242
Secure your Keys, Test Seed Backups 243
Bitcoin Price-Prediction Models 244
Bitcoin Technical Analysis, Market Indicators, and Other Tea Leaves 245
Slow and Steady Wins the Race 247
Tell Everyone, or Speak Softly? 248

CHAPTER 11: **Ten Types of Bitcoin Resources** 249
Bitcoin Documentaries 249
Bitcoin Books 250
Bitcoin Guides and Walkthroughs 251
Bitcoin Block Explorers 252
Bitcoin Data Aggregators 252
Bitcoin Forums 253
Bitcoin Volatility Charts 253
Bitcoin Foundational Documents 254
Bitcoin Wikis 255
Bitcoin Data Visualizations 255

CHAPTER 12: **Ten (Plus One) Thoughts about the Future of Bitcoin** 257
Bitcoiners Love Lindy's Law 258
Bitcoin's Limited Supply Drives Price 259
Bitcoin Adoption Coin Rush 261
Bitcoin Adoption by Corporations 262
Bitcoin Is Dead! 263
Bitcoin Boom-and-Bust Cycles 264
The Halvening and Bitcoin Price 265
New Bitcoin "Layers" 267
    Bitcoin Lightning Network 267
    Bitcoin sidechains 268
Bitcoin Will Get Easier 269
Bitcoin Development and Bitcoin Improvement Proposals 270
What *Is* the Future of Bitcoin? 272

INDEX 275

Introduction

Welcome to *Bitcoin For Dummies*, 2nd Edition, a book that tells you everything you need to know to get started with the original blockchain-based cryptocurrency (including what *blockchain* and *cryptocurrency* mean).

This is a very strange subject. Bitcoin is perhaps the most valuable asset (there's about a trillion dollars' worth right now) that almost nobody understands. How can you invest in something if you don't understand *what it is?* And make no mistake, most people, even some with thousands of dollars' worth of Bitcoin, don't know what it truly is. Read this book, and that won't be you.

We're firm believers that if you want to be involved in Bitcoin in some way, you need to understand it. Two huge problems come with *not* understanding it:

- **Thousands of Bitcoin owners have had their Bitcoin stolen.** We explain how that happens and how to avoid it.
- **Thousands of Bitcoin owners have "lost" their Bitcoin.** We explain how, how to avoid this, and why the Bitcoin isn't *really* lost (it's just out of reach).

Our job is to break it all down into intelligible, easy-to-digest, bite-sized pieces that ordinary folks like yourself can understand.

About This Book

This book explains, simplifies, and demystifies the world of Bitcoin. You find out what you need to know and do in order to decide if and how you're going to begin stepping into the beautiful world of Bitcoin.

In this book, we explain the following:

- Where Bitcoin came from (who's this person Satoshi Nakamoto?)
- What Bitcoin actually *is* (and *isn't*)
- The various Bitcoin units, down to the smallest (one-hundred millionth of a Bitcoin)
- How money works (yep, you think you know, but *do you?*)
- How the crypto in cryptocurrency works
- The best places to buy Bitcoin and *how* to do so
- Working with your own crypto wallet (no, this is not where your Bitcoin is stored, but it's critically important nonetheless)
- How to keep your Bitcoin safe from theft and loss
- How to invest in Bitcoin (and maybe other cryptocurrencies)

And plenty more!

Foolish Assumptions

We don't want to assume anything, but we have to believe that if you're reading this book, you already know a few things about the Internet. Bitcoin is a technology that depends on the Internet — no Internet, no Bitcoin. So you need to be tech-aware enough to use some kind of Internet-connected device: a desktop PC or laptop, or maybe just a smartphone. You need to be able to navigate to websites, and download and run software (not necessarily much software, maybe just a simple crypto wallet you can run on your smartphone).

We explain how to keep your Bitcoin safe, so you'll also need to be able to carry out processes such as loading a password-management program, installing anti-virus software, and doing backups. This isn't rocket surgery or brain science, but if your idea of using a computer is asking your grandkid to find something on the interwebs for you, this book may not be for you!

Icons Used in This Book

This book, like all *For Dummies* books, uses icons to highlight certain paragraphs and to alert you to particularly useful information. Here's a rundown of what those icons mean:

TIP

A Tip icon means we're giving you an extra snippet of information that may help you on your way or provide additional insight into the concepts being discussed.

REMEMBER

The Remember icon points out information that's worth committing to memory.

TECHNICAL STUFF

The Technical Stuff icon indicates geeky stuff that you can skip if you really want to, although you may want to read it if you're the kind of person who likes to have background info.

WARNING

The Warning icon helps you stay out of trouble. It's intended to grab your attention to help you avoid a pitfall that may harm your investment.

Beyond the Book

In addition to what you're reading right now, this product also comes with a free access-anywhere Cheat Sheet that covers quick tips and info to help you along the Bitcoin road. To get this Cheat Sheet, simply go to `www.dummies.com` and search for "Bitcoin For Dummies Cheat Sheet" in the Search box.

Where to Go from Here

Like all good reference tools, this book is designed to be read when needed. It's divided into several parts: background information on what Bitcoin actually *is*; how to actually *use* Bitcoin (buying, selling, and investing); some more details on how the technology functions; and the Part of Tens.

We recommend you start at the beginning and read through sequentially, but if you just want to know how to use wallets, read Chapter 4. If you need to understand where to buy Bitcoin, read Chapter 3. If all you need to understand is what the crypto in cryptocurrency is and how it works, Chapter 2 is for you.

However, Bitcoin is a complex subject. All the topics covered in this book are interrelated. We strongly recommend you read everything in this book before you dive deep into Bitcoin investing. It's essential that you have a strong understanding of everything involved before you start. Don't join the thousands who have lost their Bitcoin. A little knowledge goes a long way!

1 Bitcoin Basics

IN THIS PART . . .

Discovering where Bitcoin comes from

Understanding how money works

Learning how Bitcoin uses cryptography

Sending messages to the Bitcoin blockchain

Using private keys to prove Bitcoin ownership

» Finding out about early Bitcoin and its creator

» Understanding what money (and Bitcoin) is and is not

» Exploring the benefits of Bitcoin

Chapter 1 Bitcoin in a Nutshell

For a mere teenager, the Bitcoin network has certainly had a big impact on the world, transacting more than US$12.4T in 2021 alone. As we write these words, Bitcoin has a *market capitalization* (total value) of $918,705,395,133, which is almost a trillion dollars. (The market cap is the total number of Bitcoins in "circulation" multiplied by the current market price of a single Bitcoin.)

But that's a current low price; just a few weeks prior, it had a combined value of almost 1.3 trillion dollars. By the time you read this, the value may be higher, lower, or the same. That's one of the things about Bitcoin: Its market price can be very volatile, as you'll soon learn if you spend a little time watching the markets.

But the impact we're talking about is not just referring to Bitcoin's current market value. In fact, the market cap of Apple, Inc. is more than three times that of the Bitcoin network. However, a comparison with Apple might be apropos right now.

Figure 1-1 shows how much Bitcoin would be needed to buy a single share of Apple stock, from 2010 through 2021. The value of a single Bitcoin has been increasing against the Apple stock (just as it has, of course, against the U.S. dollar and other governmental currencies).

FIGURE 1-1: How much Bitcoin is needed to buy a share of Apple?

The launch of Bitcoin set off a revolution in blockchain and cryptocurrency. There are now more than 13,000 different cryptocurrencies. (Most, be warned, are essentially valueless and will remain that way.) At the time of writing, the top five cryptocurrencies have a combined market cap of almost 1.7 trillion dollars, and a number of cryptocurrencies have genuinely useful functions beyond merely being used as money or a store of value. It's likely that some of these cryptocurrencies will endure, even if most won't.

But we're here to talk about Bitcoin, so let's begin with a little history. Where did Bitcoin come from, and how did it develop?

In the Beginning, There Were . . . Digital Currencies?

Blockchain-based cryptocurrencies are pretty new, but digital currencies designed for use online have been around for quite a while. (Don't worry about this *blockchain* thing for the moment;

we explain that in not-too-mind-numbing detail in Chapter 2. Just understand for now that a blockchain is a special kind of database, a store of digital data.)

As people started flooding online — the process began in the early 1980s, but really took off in 1994 with the advent of the commercial Internet — it became clear that they were going to need some way to spend money in cyberspace (the first Internet stores opened in that year). Of course, most online transactions today use credit and debit cards — even PayPal and Venmo are essentially enabling such transactions, along with bank transfers — but that wasn't the case in the early days. Many people were concerned about credit-card theft and thus wary of using their numbers online, for instance. (When co-author Peter opened an online store in 1997, he did have a functioning credit-card gateway, but many customers would print out a paper order form and mail a check!)

There was also the issue of *microtransactions*. Surely, in the digital world, it should be possible to pay someone, say, five or ten cents for something, such as access to a video or article. The microtransaction problem has still not been solved (though one might argue that the Bitcoin Lightning network, which we discuss in Chapter 4, almost gets us there), but nonetheless, that's one of the ideas that drove the development of digital currencies.

And develop they did. In 1983 David Chaum wrote a research paper on the concept of digital currency (*Blind Signatures for Untraceable Payments*), suggesting the use of cryptography to create and manage a digital currency. So even back then, cryptography had a role in digital currencies, although they weren't known as cryptocurrencies back then. When you hear people talk about cryptocurrencies, they are generally talking about this new generation of blockchain-based cryptocurrencies that started with Bitcoin. (We explain more about cryptography and how it relates to cryptocurrencies in Chapter 2.)

Chaum actually launched a cryptography-based digital currency, known as *DigiCash*, in 1990, but these were still very early days. Very few people were online in 1990, and the currency died out by around 1998. What likely hurt digital currencies by the end of the '90s was that the credit-card companies wanted a piece of the online action, and thus went out of their way to assuage consumers' fears of using credit cards online.

Still other digital currencies came along. There was e-gold, a currency backed by real gold, and Millicent, a currency created by a major computing company, Digital Equipment Corporation (DEC). (If you're younger than, say, mid-thirties, you probably won't remember DEC, but it was a big deal. In fact, even IBM had a micropayments division working on digital currencies at the time.)

Then there was NetBill, a project of Carnegie Mellon University, which was later merged into another system, CyberCash, which eventually ended up in the clutches of PayPal. There was Beenz, which had a partnership with MasterCard at one point, First Virtual, CyberCoin, Flooz (promoted by Whoopi Goldberg, no less!), and various others.

But nothing much *stuck*. Lots of great ideas, but nobody could quite make it all *work*. By the early 2000s, most of these endeavors were moribund (probably ushered along by the dotcom crash of late 2000). There were exceptions. Liberty Reserve, based in Costa Rica, ran from 2006 until 2013, but was shut down after accusations that it was being used to launder billions of dollars of criminal proceeds. And closed systems that work on particular networks, such as China's QQ Coins, are mostly used on the Tencent QQ Messaging service.

But then, there was Satoshi Nakamoto and his magical blockchain.

The Birth of Bitcoin

On November 1, 2008, someone named Satoshi Nakamoto posted a message to a cryptography forum, titled *Bitcoin P2P e-cash paper* (archived at `https://www.mail-archive.com/cryptography@metzdowd.com/msg09959.html`). In his message, Nakamoto announced that he had "been working on a new electronic cash system that's fully peer-to-peer, with no trusted third party."

In other words, he'd created a currency system that worked on a network of peers — computers working together with each equal to the other. With no central power required, no bank or government to act as a "trusted third party" was required.

A comment he made in the post explained his view of the problem with the earlier cryptocurrencies. "A lot of people automatically dismiss e-currency as a lost cause because of all the companies that failed since the 1990s," he said. He believed that these other digital-money systems had a critical weakness, an Achilles heel. "I hope it's obvious it was only the centrally controlled nature of those systems that doomed them. I think this is the first time we're trying a decentralized, non-trust-based system."

Nakamoto had previously set up a domain name and a simple website, bitcoin.org, and there he posted a document explaining how all this would work: `https://bitcoin.org/bitcoin.pdf`. You might want to take a quick look, though it's not essential for your understanding of Bitcoin (it's pretty geeky stuff).

The whitepaper he posted describes how a *blockchain* (a special form of database) could be used to manage the currency. Essentially, the blockchain records a ledger, a record of currency transactions, and because the blockchain is duplicated over numerous computers (the *peers)* and because these peers are all equal, no trust in a central party is required. You may hear Bitcoin described as a "trustless" system. That doesn't mean it can't be trusted; it means that a trusted third party is not required. The trust, in effect, is baked into the system. The mathematics — or mathemagics, as Peter likes to call it — which powers the system means that Bitcoin transactions *can* be trusted, even without a central "power" overseeing the system. (See Chapter 2 for an explanation of why.)

Satoshi Nakamoto (whoever he, she, or it is) didn't use the words *cryptocurrency, blockchain,* or *trustless* anywhere in the whitepaper. Those are terms that others applied to the system later.

The idea of blockchain had actually been around for a while — at least since 1991 — in fact, remember David Chaum of DigiCash fame? He had been working with the idea of a blockchain since the early 1990s.

Anyway, Nakamoto didn't stop there. In January of 2009, he/she/it launched the Bitcoin network. Nakamoto released some thirty-thousand lines of code that defined the network protocols and processes necessary to operate this peer-to-peer, decentralized money system. And Bitcoin was born.

Of course, in January of 2009, Bitcoin had essentially no value. Still, the *genesis block* created by Nakamoto (the very first block of data in the blockchain creating the first 50 Bitcoins), along with subsequent blocks of data "mined" by Nakamoto (see Chapter 7), comprise perhaps a million Bitcoins: At current prices, that's $47,369,000,000. Yes, close to 50 billion dollars!

But Who Is Nakamoto?

So who is this Satoshi Nakamoto? Nobody knows. Well, somebody must know, but either they're not saying or they've been unable to convince anybody. In fact, it's not even clear *what* Satoshi Nakamoto is. A man? A woman? A group of collaborators? An organization or firm? We don't know for sure, though most assumptions seem to be that it's a man or a group of two or three people. Perhaps not surprisingly, the most cited targets are generally cryptographers and mathematicians.

There's the actual Satoshi Nakamoto, of course — that was an obvious choice. A Japanese-American resident of California who was born Satoshi Nakamoto, and now goes by the name Dorian Prentice Satoshi Nakamoto, seems to have some of the skills needed to be *the* Nakamoto, but he denies being the founder of Bitcoin.

Then there's Nick Szabo, a digital-currency enthusiast who has been tagged as Nakamoto but denies it. Elon Musk has been "accused," too, but he denies it (and we personally think he was probably too busy to find the time!). There's Japanese mathematician Shinichi Mochizuki (he denies it), Finnish economic sociologist Dr. Vili Lehdonvirta (denies it), and Irish cryptography student Michael Clear (yep, denies it).

One of the loudest candidates is Craig Wright, an Australian computer scientist. He certainly claims he is Nakamoto, though he's accused by many of carrying out an elaborate fraud. As we write these words, a jury found Wright liable to pay the estate of David Kleiman, a deceased friend and colleague, $100 million for misuse of funds in a joint venture they worked on. But separately, the jury also found that David Kleiman was not a partner in the creation of Bitcoin.

The jury didn't find that Craig Wright *is* Nakamoto, though — only that *if* he is, he doesn't have to share his $50 billion with Kleiman's estate. Not a bad deal. In fact, it's such a good deal that Wright stated that he was *relieved* that all he has to pay is $100 million! Still, the case is not over. Whether Kleiman's estate actually has ownership in the joint-venture company is unclear, and Wright might owe $100 million to his ex-wife. It doesn't settle the question of whether or not Wright actually is Nakamoto. (Wright says that the jury found that he *is* Nakamoto; they didn't.) That won't be settled until Wright — or the *real Satoshi Nakamoto* — moves some of the Bitcoin out of the blockchain addresses owned by Nakamoto.

Regardless, the Bitcoin network has continued to function as designed long after Satoshi Nakamoto mysteriously stopped participating in the network, shortly after claiming Julian Assange and Wikileaks had "kicked the hornets' nest" once they began accepting Bitcoin for donations for their controversial reporting in 2010.

Understanding What Bitcoin Actually Is

So what is Bitcoin? Well, we can tell you what it isn't very quickly. It's not tangible — there's nothing you can touch or hold. You can't taste it or smell it. You can't even see it. In fact — and we explain this in more detail in Chapter 2 — Bitcoin really *isn't*. That is. . .*there is no Bitcoin.*

What there is, though, is something known as the Bitcoin *ledger* (another word, by the way, that Satoshi Nakamoto didn't use in his famous Bitcoin whitepaper, but that is what the data stored in the Bitcoin blockchain has come to be popularly known as). A ledger is a written record of transactions; your checkbook's little account register is a form of ledger, for instance. (For those of you under 30, a check is a piece of paper you can write a number on, sign your name, and give to someone, and that someone can then give it to their bank and the bank gives them money. . .an amazingly efficient system.) Or consider a bank statement, showing money coming into and leaving your account. (All too often *leaving*.) That's a form of ledger, too.

So, when Satoshi Nakamoto created the first ever Bitcoin, how did he create it? Well, when we talk about Bitcoin being "created," we're really talking in shorthand. No Bitcoin *thing* was created. When Nakamoto first "created" Bitcoin, what he really did was to create a set of rules for a ledger in which he *recorded* the creation of Bitcoin. The ledger says, in effect, "50 new Bitcoin were created today." And there you go, Bitcoin exists.

When Nakamoto minted that first "genesis block," the nature of the network was set in computational stone. Buried in the first block of data was a little additional text, words from the front page of that day's *New York Times* (January 3, 2009): "Chancellor on Brink of Second Bailout for Banks." Perhaps this was a hint at Nakamoto's reason for creating the network, as an alternative to what he felt were the corrupt government-managed monetary systems.

The ledger essentially records two things. The first is the *creation* of Bitcoin, which is done through a process called "mining." Nakamoto "mined" those original 50 Bitcoins (however, the first 50 Bitcoins are unspendable due to the nature of the code). Mining continues, and in fact, new Bitcoins are created each time a new block of transactions is added to the Bitcoin blockchain, every ten minutes or so. (Chapter 7 explains how this "mining" process works.)

However, there is a mathematical arrangement to all this: Bitcoins are created on a steady schedule, and every four years or so (during an event quaintly called *the halvening*), the number of Bitcoins created every ten minutes is halved. Right now, 6.25 Bitcoins are created every ten minutes, but sometime in 2024, that will be reduced to 3.125, then again halved four years later, and so on (every four years) until around the year 2140, when the maximum number of Bitcoins will finally be in circulation.

The second thing that the ledger records is what happens to the Bitcoin once it has been created. As we discuss in Chapter 2, all

Bitcoin is associated with "addresses" in the blockchain, and as people buy and sell Bitcoin, or use Bitcoin to buy something (essentially the same as selling Bitcoin), the coins get sent from one address in the blockchain to another. The Bitcoin ledger keeps track of where the Bitcoin flows, from address to address to address. Each address is under the control of someone, and thus the blockchain is, in effect, keeping track of who owns what. If the Bitcoin blockchain ledger says the address you control has 2 Bitcoins associated with it, then you control those 2 Bitcoins. (In Chapters 3 and 4, we explain how to exercise this control — that is, how you can transfer your Bitcoin to other addresses in return for governmental fiat currency or for goods and services.)

FIAT CURRENCY?

Hang around in the Bitcoin community long enough and eventually, you'll hear people talking about *fiat* currency, usually disparagingly. A fiat currency is currency by decree, by official order. A fiat currency is one that is issued by a government, without being backed by a commodity such as gold. (To quote Nobel-prize winning economist Paul Krugman, "fiat currencies have underlying value because men with guns say they do.") Most currencies these days are fiat currencies; the "gold standard" generally fell out of favor in the 1930s, during the Great Depression. (Great Britain dropped the gold standard in 1931.) The U.S. dollar used to be pegged to silver, but in 1900, a law was passed linking it to gold. It remained linked to gold through most of the century, until being completely de-linked from gold in 1971 and becoming a fiat currency. (However, in 1934 the U.S. did devalue the dollar against gold; that is, they reduced the weight of gold per dollar.)

The advantage of fiat currency is that it gives governments more control over the money supply. Many economists, probably most, believe that adherence to the gold standard prolonged the Great Depression, as governments were not able to stimulate their economies by increasing the money supply. The disadvantage, according to many true believers in Bitcoin, is that it provides governments with too much control over the money supply!

Now, if this all sounds a little flakey, a bit like a con game — and there are certainly plenty of people who will tell you that Bitcoin *is* a con game — we're going to explain in a few moments what *money* is. You may think you know what it is, but you probably don't, and without understanding what money is, it's hard to understand how Bitcoin *can be* money. But first, a little more about Bitcoin.

Understanding Bitcoin Units

To begin with, you need to understand that Bitcoin can be broken down and bought and sold in pieces. A Bitcoin is not like a gold coin; if you buy, for instance, a US$10 Liberty Gold Coin (for around $1,000, by the way), you're buying the whole thing. You're not buying half or a quarter.

But with Bitcoin, which can sell at $50,000, $60,000, or whatever *per coin*, most people can't afford to buy in if they have to buy the entire thing. And in any case, there is no *coin*. It's just an entry in the ledger.

So that entry in the ledger can say whatever we want it to say. It can say that you bought half a Bitcoin, or a tenth or hundredth, or a ten thousandth, all the way to a single one hundred millionth. That is, you can buy partial coins — fragments of a Bitcoin. Table 1-1 offers a quick look at Bitcoin units.

TABLE 1-1 Bitcoin Units

Unit	Unit Name
1; one	Bitcoin, BTC, ฿
1/10; one tenth	deci-Bitcoin, dBTC
1/1,000; one thousandth	milli-Bitcoin, millibit
1/1,000,000; one millionth	micro-Bitcoin, µBTC, bit
1/100,000,000; one hundred millionth	Satoshi, sat

The table doesn't show all the units, but these are the units you're most likely to see and hear about. Because Bitcoins are divided into Satoshis — one hundred million Satoshis in each Bitcoin — you can divide a Bitcoin into tenths: deci-Bitcoin, centi-Bitcoin, milli-Bitcoin, micro-Bitcoin, and so on. (In fact, there is even a theoretical way to divide a Bitcoin down below the Satoshi level into *milliSatoshi*, using a special ancillary network called the Lightning Network, which we talk about in Chapter 4.)

Is there enough of the smallest Bitcoin unit to go around? Well, let's take a look. There will only ever be 21 million Bitcoins; that means there will only ever be, at its maximum, 2,100,000,000,000,000 Satoshis in circulation.

Today, though, around 19 million Bitcoins are in circulation, and somewhere around 1,900,000,000,000,000 Satoshis.

With around eight billion folks living on the planet, today, about 237,500 Satoshis are in circulation per person (the number fluctuates; see the Satoshi clock at `https://satoshisperperson.com/`). Today, that's valued at around US$110.

To put this into perspective, roughly US$2,500 are in circulation ("M1" money supply) per person on the planet today (according to the Federal Reserve website at `https://fred.stlouisfed.org/series/M1SL`). That's 250,000 cents per person, similar to the number of Satoshis.

All this means is that you don't need a huge sum of money to get started with Bitcoin. You can buy small pieces of a Bitcoin, but beware the fees. Buying small quantities at a traditional exchange (see Chapter 3) can be expensive; in some cases, you'll likely be paying more in fees than the price of the Bitcoin. Some exchange sites now have fee-free transactions. See, for instance, Strike (`https://strike.me/en`).

Cryptocurrency or Cryptoasset?

Bitcoin is commonly described as a cryptocurrency. Is it really a currency? We would argue that it is not. We provide more detail about this in Chapter 3, but for the moment at least, you can think of Bitcoin as more like an asset than a currency. It's more like gold than dollar bills. It's hard to spend Bitcoin, just as it's hard to spend gold. Sure, you can do it, but it's not always simple, and most places where you'd want to spend your Bitcoin won't accept it.

And furthermore, why would you want to spend your Bitcoin when it might double or triple in value over the next few months? No, Bitcoin is not a true currency, though it was originally intended to be one (and perhaps in the future, it will become one).

Google and the Oxford Languages dictionary describe *currency* as "a system of money in general use in a particular country." Bitcoin is certainly not a currency in, say, Europe or North America. Perhaps the only country in which it comes anywhere close to being a currency is El Salvador, the government of which launched Bitcoin as a secondary currency. But for most of us, Bitcoin is a *store of value*, not something we're going to use to buy groceries.

Still, we will be talking about how you can buy and sell Bitcoin — and selling Bitcoin is, of course, essentially the same as exchanging it (you swap it in return for goods or services) — in Chapter 3.

If There Is No Bitcoin, How Can It Be Valuable?

As we write these words, anyone owning a Bitcoin can sell it for around US$48,000. But we've just told you *there is no Bitcoin*. . .that all there is, is a ledger stating that the Bitcoin exists, and who (which address in the blockchain) owns it. How can that possibly hold value!?

To understand that, we need to understand a little about money and how it works. As with *any* form of money, Bitcoin is all about *belief*. If enough people believe a form of money has value, then it has value. It can be exchanged for goods and services with other people who believe it has value. Once people stop believing, though, the money no longer holds value. And that does happen sometimes. There have been around 60 *hyperinflation* events in human history, in which people lost faith in the currency, and it precipitously dropped in value until it was essentially worthless. Most recently, it happened in Zimbabwe; in 2008, the country actually abandoned its currency in favor of using foreign currencies. (Ironically, Zimbabwean dollar bills then rose in value, as collectors worldwide started snapping them up.)

So, again, as long as people *believe* in a particular form of money, that form of money has value. Let's say you own half of a Bitcoin; in other words, the Bitcoin blockchain *says* that you own half of a Bitcoin. (Remember, there is no actual physical Bitcoin, just a record of Bitcoin transactions.) You want to cash out, to convert that Bitcoin into your local currency. The Bitcoin blockchain says you own the address in the blockchain with which that coin is associated (we explain how that works in Chapter 2), and so you can transfer it to *someone else's* address.

Currently you can find someone who sees value in having that Bitcoin associated with their address in the blockchain. Why? Because people believe in this form of money, and so potential buyers know that when they are ready to sell it, there will be *someone else* who believes in it enough to pay for it or exchange goods and services for it. (Plus, they are hoping the money will go up in value, something we discuss more in Chapter 6.)

Belief is what makes Bitcoin work. That may sound a little woowoo or weak. You may think that's not much on which to base a form of money, but in fact, that's pretty much what *all* money is based on. Let us tell you a story.

Milton Friedman and the rai stones

Eminent, Nobel Prize–winning economist Milton Friedman wrote a paper in the 1990s about *rai stones* — a form of money once used on the Yap islands — comparing this system to the use of gold by Western nations to back their currencies.

The Yap islands are a group of four small islands in the middle of the Pacific Ocean, about 800 miles east of the Philippines. With a population of around 12,000, Yap isn't known for much, except perhaps, most notably, for an unusual form of money it used to have, known as *rai* (or *fei*) *stones*.

Rai stones were "coins" made of limestone. You couldn't carry these coins around in your pockets because they were large, sometimes very large. The stones had holes in the middle for a log to be threaded through so they could be carried! (If you'd like to see what we're talking about, do a quick image search online for rai stones.)

They mostly weren't carried, though; in fact, they sat where they were long enough to gather moss. Anyway, here's how these things worked. Let's say you wanted to buy a bunch of coconut copra (the dried kernels from which coconut oil is extracted, which is big business in the Yap islands). You would go to the seller and say something like, "You know my rai stone in the woods by the river? Well, I'll give you the rai stone in exchange for the copra." Assuming the price was right, you and the other party would then tell everybody that you no longer owned that particular rai stone, that it was now in the possession of the seller.

Note, by the way, that there was a degree of rarity to these stones. You couldn't simply grab a piece of limestone and make your own money. Apart from the amount of work required to create one of these things, there was an additional problem: There *isn't* any limestone on the Yap islands! Instead, limestone has to be quarried in Palau and brought back, a round trip of about 600 miles. (This is known in currency circles as *proof of work*, something you can learn more about in Chapter 7.)

There's even a famous story (well, famous for people who know about rai stones!) about a large rai stone falling overboard during a journey back from Palau. One can imagine the conversation.

Sailor 1: "Oh, no, we've lost that huge stone, that was valuable!"

Sailor 2: "Oh, boy, we're going to be in trouble! Oh, but wait, we know more or less where it *is*, right?"

And thus, that particular rai stone remained in circulation as long as the owner could say, "You know that rai stone I own, the one that sunk?"

Now, back to Milton Friedman. In his paper about this form of currency, he discussed what happened when the islands were occupied by Germany. (Rai stones were in use right up until the early 20th century.) The German authorities, he writes, were unable — not surprisingly — to get the local population to provide labor (to improve roads and paths on the islands, for instance).

But the German administrators had an idea. They sent someone out to paint black crosses on the rai stones, telling the locals this meant that they — the Germans — now owned them! They were, in effect, fining the local population for not providing labor.

This actually worked, which shows that the Yapese — perhaps like some readers of this book — didn't really understand what money was (a belief) and how it functioned (carried value only as long as people believed in that value). The local population provided labor to get their money back (the crosses were erased).

Now, Friedman took the story further. He discussed an event that occurred in 1932, far from the Yap islands. France asked the Federal Reserve Bank of New York to convert some of its dollar assets into gold. Rather than shipping gold to France, the bank employees simply went into its vaults and moved the gold around a little, putting the appropriate amount of gold bars into particular drawers, and marking those drawers to show they were owned by France. (This event actually led to a banking panic in the U.S., as newspapers decried the loss of gold to France.)

Friedman compared the marking of the rai stones with the marking of the gold; he explains that Federal Reserve officials set apart the amount of gold required and marked the gold to indicate that it belonged to France. As Friedman explains, "For all it matters, they could have done so by marking them 'with a cross in black paint' just as the Germans did to the stones."

You can read this paper at `https://miltonfriedman.hoover.org/internal/media/dispatcher/215061/full`. It is actually helpful, a way to shake up your thinking about money and what it really is. Let's just see how Friedman finished up his paper:

> What both examples—and numerous additional ones that could be listed—illustrate is how important "myth," unquestioned belief, is in monetary matters. Our own money, the money we have grown up with, the system under which it is controlled, these appear "real" and "rational" to us. The money of other countries often seems to us like paper or worthless metal, even when the purchasing power of individual units is high.

REMEMBER

Money does not actually exist. It's merely an idea. Yes, we have coins and bills that *represent* money, but they are not the actual money itself, and they have little or no intrinsic value. Without the belief in the underlying promise behind money, the physical representation has no value, as the people of Zimbabwe discovered in 2008.

Money is belief

Money, then, is all about belief. The physical representations of money that we grow up with make perfect sense to us. Other representations feel like "play money."

Marco Polo was stunned to discover, on his journey to China, that the Great Khan used *alchemy* — magic, in effect — to (as one chapter title in Polo's book puts it) "*Causeth the Bark of Trees, Made Into Something Like Paper, to Pass for Money All Over his Country.*" That's right, surely only magic could turn paper into money!

In fact, even most of your own fiat currency is made of nothing more than an idea. Historian Yuval Noah Harari, in his book *Sapiens*, explains that money is merely an idea, a human concept, not an actual thing you can see or touch.

In fact, he says, "the total value of money worldwide is $60 trillion dollars, of which a mere $6 trillion is in cash or coins 90 percent of all money is nothing more than entries in a computer server. Money is a faith-based object, whose value is derived by the shared narrative about its worth."

You can see this for yourself. If you do an Internet search for "money supply" and dig around a little, you'll find different measures of money supply: M0, M1, M2, and so on. M0 is cash — coins and bills. M1 also includes deposits in checking accounts. M2 includes all that, but also includes savings accounts, mutual funds, and so on. Dig around a little more, and you'll find that what you think of as money — the coins and bills — actually represents only around 10 percent of all the money in circulation!

So, here's a quick question for you. What's the difference between Bitcoin and U.S. dollars, or pounds sterling, or euros? With those fiat currencies, 90 percent of the money is "nothing more than entries in a computer server." With Bitcoin, it's 100 percent!

REMEMBER

There are other differences, of course (some of which we cover in Chapter 2). But our goal here is to show you that Bitcoin and fiat currencies share an important characteristic: They all rely on belief to function. As long as people believe in *any* currency, the currency holds value.

That's not to say any particular currency — including Bitcoin — will hold peoples' beliefs forever. What we are trying to do here is explain how something as ephemeral as Bitcoin can be valuable.

Understanding Bitcoin Benefits

Now that you understand how Bitcoin *can* have value — and clearly it does right now, as millions of people are willing to pay for it — let's take a look at some of the benefits of Bitcoin, characteristics that set it apart as a form of money.

First, consider the roles that money plays:

- Money can act as a **medium of exchange**. That is, you can use it to buy things. Bitcoin currently doesn't do well on this account, because it's not widely accepted, transactions are generally slow and expensive, and most people are still buying and accumulating Bitcoin for speculative purposes, to see if the value will go up.

- Money can also be a **measure of value** or a **unit of account.** We use it to assign a value to things, from sugar to motor cars. Bitcoin also doesn't do well in this area at the moment because its price is so volatile.
- Money can also act as a **store of value**, a way to take value you have saved and store it away safely. You should be able to buy Bitcoin and let it store your wealth for you, then retrieve it when you need it. Bitcoin has actually done very well in this way over the long term. Certainly, there are short-term fluctuations, but over the long term, due to significant appreciation in value, it's acted very well as a store of value.

Here then, are various characteristics and benefits that set Bitcoin apart.

Portability

Money needs to be portable. If you can't move it around, how can you use it? It may seem that rai stones, from our example earlier in this chapter, were not physically very portable, but in fact their value was definitely portable. The residents of Yap communicated and transferred ownership via word of mouth. Bitcoin is likewise very portable, as you'll discover in this book. You can transmit it across the Internet to anywhere or anyone in the world at nearly the speed of light.

Verifiability

As you see in Chapter 2, your ownership of Bitcoin is most definitely verifiable. Because an entire copy of the Bitcoin blockchain transaction history lives on each computer running the Bitcoin software, the thousands of nodes on the network must verify each and every transaction and block based on the rules of Bitcoin. These are rules that everybody has to follow or they can't function within the network. The structure of the Bitcoin blockchain ensures that you can, and in fact must, prove you own your Bitcoin, and have total control over it before you can transfer it (assuming you don't lose your private keys; see Chapter 2).

Fungibility

An important characteristic of money is that it has to be *fungible*. That is, one dollar is the same as another, my dollar is just as valuable as your dollar. Like every good form of money, Bitcoin is fungible; every Bitcoin has, in general, the same value as another Bitcoin. (Okay, this isn't 100 percent true. Some people like to own Bitcoin that cannot be traced back through the blockchain to a particular owner. They are willing to pay a bit of a premium for Bitcoin created and transferred without being subject to the kind of Know Your Client banking rules discussed in Chapter 3.)

Durability

Bitcoin won't rot if left out in the weather or burn if your house burns down. Bitcoin is just information, pure money without the vulnerable tangible material. As long as the Bitcoin blockchain and Bitcoin network endure, your Bitcoin will remain where it's always been: in the blockchain. You just have to understand how to protect your access to the blockchain address associated with your Bitcoin, which we discuss in Chapter 5.

Divisibility

Bitcoin can be divided into tiny, tiny parts — one hundred millionths, known as Satoshis. This means you can spend a Bitcoin or any fraction of a Bitcoin. At the current price, the smallest fraction of a Bitcoin is worth about a twentieth of a U.S. cent.

Open access

The Bitcoin network, like the rai stones of the past, is an openly accessible network that cannot be censored. While Bitcoin may not be for everyone, it is for anyone who chooses to use it; no one can limit another's access to the network.

Final settlement

Monetary networks of the past have achieved settlement well; even in the case of the sunken rai stone, the ledger was updated and settlement occurred — albeit via word of mouth. With Bitcoin, transactions can be mathematically irreversible within six confirmations (explained in Chapter 3), which takes about an hour. Compared to other methods, the Bitcoin network provides fairly fast finalized settlements that cannot be charged back.

Borderless, stateless

Bitcoin is international. Any citizen of any country that has open access to the Internet can own and trade Bitcoin. Even if a country tries to ban Bitcoin, the cryptocurrency will continue elsewhere, and knowledgeable citizens would likely be able to bypass restrictions and hide their tracks. A Bitcoin transaction can even be transferred via ham radio, local mesh networks, and satellites.

Pseudonymous

Bitcoin is not, contrary to popular belief, anonymous. But it is *pseudonymous*. The blockchain itself has no account names, for instance. Your Bitcoin is not labeled with your name or any identifying information. (You learn how the blockchain works in Chapter 2.) But the blockchain is open to viewing by the public. Anyone can get in and dig around, and trace transactions from one address to another, to another. This means that if information exists identifying your "entry" into the blockchain — for instance, when you buy Bitcoin from an exchange following KYC (Know Your Customer) banking regulations — your transactions can be traced.

Monopoly-resistant

Bitcoin resides in the peer-to-peer Bitcoin blockchain, which is run by tens of thousands of people. No one person or group of people can seize control.

Debasement-proof

To *debase* means to "reduce (something) in quality or value; degrade." In the context of currency, it originally meant to lower the value of the metal used in coinage. Today, currency debasement typically refers to a government printing more of it, thus making each bill or coin worth less.

An undercurrent of libertarianism runs through the Bitcoin community. One of the big benefits of Bitcoin touted by Bitcoin true believers is that Bitcoin is *not* under the control of any particular government. It's money for the people, by the people.

This means no government — or other form of governing body — can "print" more Bitcoin. In fact, the mathematics that define how Bitcoin works have "baked in" a regular flow of Bitcoin coming into circulation (6.25 Bitcoins every ten minutes currently); every four years, that rate will drop by half, until eventually, the flow of new Bitcoin will dribble away to nothing. Bitcoin cannot be "debased" by flooding the market with more Bitcoin.

» **Finding out about public-key cryptography**

» **Sending messages to the Bitcoin ledger**

» **Understanding how cryptography proves you own your Bitcoin**

Chapter 2
Bitcoin Tech Explained

How Bitcoin works is a mystery to most of the world. *Don't let it be so to you!* If you're going to get involved with Bitcoin — perhaps invest in it — then you really should know what you're working with.

Understanding the specifics of how Bitcoin functions as "money" — as well as other aspects of this cryptocurrency — is important. First, it's always nice to sound intelligent when someone asks you, "*So what is Bitcoin, anyway?*" (It's *so* embarrassing to admit that you've just invested in something and have no idea what it is!) But more importantly, if you don't understand how Bitcoin works, it's hard to keep it safe. Thousands of people have had their Bitcoin stolen from them, or have simply lost access to it, primarily because they really don't understand how it works. (It's *so* sad to know exactly where your Bitcoin is, but never be able to touch it!)

So in this chapter, we explain just that. How Bitcoin really works at a high level. We explain the specifics of securing your Bitcoin in Chapter 5. But for now, let's start with a high-level, Bitcoin-101 explanation of what's actually going on when you buy, sell, and store Bitcoin.

Before we get started, though, be prepared. This is complicated stuff that you don't need to remember in order to buy and sell Bitcoin. We've tried to simplify it as much as we can, and we believe that grasping this information is necessary to your understanding of a few important points, which are themselves valuable in helping you keep your Bitcoin safe. We want you to understand, at the very least, the background information that explains these critical issues:

- Bitcoin is stored in the blockchain, *not* in your Bitcoin wallet.
- The Bitcoin wallet stores information about your addresses in the blockchain.
- The wallet stores the private and public keys that allow you to control your address (and thus control your Bitcoin).

Understanding That There Is No Bitcoin!

The first thing to understand is that *there is no Bitcoin*! Bitcoin as a "physical thing" doesn't exist, of course. There is no tangible object, no "thing"; no coins, no bills or notes. But more than that, if you were to dig into the programming source code that makes Bitcoin work, you wouldn't even see a "digital representation" of Bitcoins. That's because Bitcoin is, plain and simple, information about transactions.

That's okay, though. There is no physical or digital representation of most of your everyday money, either, whether you use dollars, pounds, euros, yen, or whatever. As historian Yuval Harari has said, "90 percent of all money is nothing more than entries in a computer server." You can confirm this for yourself;

do an Internet search for information about different money supply numbers — M0, M1, M2, and so on — and you'll find that only around 10 percent of a major currency's value is represented by actual, physical money (M0) by bills and coins. Instead, the great majority of money is nothing more than entries in a computer server — entries in what we may term a *ledger*.

Discovering the Bitcoin Ledger

Spend some time around Bitcoin folk, and you'll start to hear talk of the *Bitcoin ledger*. So let's back up a moment. What is a ledger? The Merriam-Webster online dictionary defines a ledger as "a book containing accounts to which debits and credits are posted from books of original entry." Wikipedia defines a ledger as "a book or collection of accounts in which account transactions are recorded."

So a ledger is a record of transactions. You've seen ledgers. Your bank statement, on paper or on your computer screen, is a form of ledger. Your checkbook register is a form of ledger (does anyone still use a checkbook register?). If you use Quicken or Mint or some other form of accounting program, you've seen ledgers.

Well, there's also a Bitcoin ledger, and inside that ledger is a record of Bitcoin transactions. There is no actual Bitcoin, but there is a record of Bitcoin coming into your account and leaving the account. Which is pretty much what you see when you look at your bank statement, which is a record of currency transactions, too, payments to and from your account. It's generally not, however, a record of actual, *physical* money transactions. In fact, in the U.S., only one-quarter of transactions are cash (mostly under $25), and more than one-half of transactions are plastic (credit and debit cards). The rest are various electronic payment methods (and a few checks).

Here's a quick question for you: What's the difference between U.S. dollars and Bitcoin? With U.S. dollars, 90 percent of all the money is nothing more than entries in a computer server. With Bitcoin, it's 100 percent!

Now, the Bitcoin ledger is often described as being *immutable*. The word *immutable* means "not capable of or susceptible to change," and of course the Bitcoin ledger *can* change; hundreds of thousands of transactions are added to the ledger every day. But what *immutable* means in this context is that once a transaction has been committed to the ledger, that's it; it can't be changed. The ledger can't be "hacked" and modified, for instance. (You'll find out why in a few moments.)

So, because the ledger is immutable, it means that whatever is recorded in the ledger is the truth. If the ledger says that you own, say, half a Bitcoin, then the fact is *you own half a Bitcoin!*

So where is this "Bitcoin ledger"?

Well, there is another very important difference between everyday money and Bitcoin. The transactions are not mere entries in a computer server. Rather, they are entries in a duplicated, distributed ledger spread across a network of thousands of servers.

Bitcoin is sometimes known as a "trustless" system; not because it can't be trusted, but because trust in a single person or company isn't required. In a sense, trust is already *baked into* the system. It's "trustless" because you don't have to trust any particular individual, or any particular organization. This is because of the way the mathematics behind Bitcoin functions (keeping participants honest, in effect): It ensures that many servers are involved, and that the *system itself* can be trusted.

So we have Bitcoin transactions stored in the Bitcoin ledger. Where and how is that ledger stored? To understand that, we have to take another step back, and understand a little about blockchains.

Bitcoin uses a blockchain ledger

The Bitcoin ledger — the record of Bitcoin transactions — is saved in the Bitcoin blockchain. What's a blockchain, you ask? A *blockchain* is a very special type of database. So once again, we need to step back — very quickly this time — to ask, what's a database?

Quite simply, a *database* is an electronic store of information, that is being stored in a structured format on a computer. If you open a word-processing file and type a bunch of names and addresses into a document and save it, that's not really a database; it's just a jumble of information. But if you open a spreadsheet document and save the names and addresses — first name in the first column, last name in the second column, street address in the third, and so on — then you are creating a form of simple database where the information is stored in an organized, structured format.

Blockchains are a form of database; more specifically, they are specialized, sophisticated databases with special features that make them immutable unchangeable and unhackable.

The first significant characteristic is (and perhaps once we've said this, it may not be a surprise) that the blockchain uses blocks of data that are, um, chained together in a manner that makes it impossible to change any piece of data — a particular transaction, for instance — without changing the entire chain of blocks (we'll explain how that works in a moment).

The other important characteristic is that the blockchain database is duplicated and distributed. Let's look at these two issues one by one, starting with the duplication and distribution.

Looking at the Bitcoin Distributed, Peer-to-Peer Network

Without the Internet, there's no Bitcoin. Bitcoin is an Internet technology, just as email and the World Wide Web are Internet technologies. And all three of these technologies require *networks*. (You might think of the Internet as the road system, and the different networks as different types of traffic — cars, trucks, buses — running over those roads.)

The Bitcoin ledger is stored on Bitcoin "nodes" on what is known as a *peer-to-peer* network: thousands of computers spread across the world. Each of these nodes contains a full copy or a portion of the blockchain, and so in effect thousands of copies of the ledger exist. Because of this, if you wanted to hack into the ledger and change a transaction, you'd have to convince all these computers to agree. By *peer-to-peer*, we mean that every one of these nodes is "equal"; there is no central server (or central group of servers) that manages the process, as there is with, say, a bank's or credit-card network's transactions. Rather, the process is managed according to a set of rules by which the entire community abides (again, the rules are baked into the mathematics that runs the system).

The nodes make the entire Bitcoin system function; they add transactions — including your transactions when you buy and sell Bitcoin — to the blockchain. Some of these nodes are also *mining* nodes, by the way, the nodes that are part of the process that brings new Bitcoin into existence (in the form of what is known as a *coinbase* transaction in the blockchain, a transaction in which new Bitcoin is added to the ledger).

However, having said that the Bitcoin network is a *peer-to-peer* network, it also works in some ways like a *client-server* network. Consider, for instance, the email system. Computers throughout the world exist that can manage email (we call them *email servers*). And what we call *email clients* (*servers* provide services to *clients*) also exist. An email client is a program such as Microsoft Outlook that sends email to a server — or the web program you see when you log into Gmail or Yahoo! Mail; that's a client, too. These programs communicate with the *servers*. So, for instance, when you send email from, say, your Gmail account to, perhaps, grandma, that message first goes from your Gmail account to one of the Gmail system's email servers, which then sends the email across the Internet to the server that manages gran's email. Gran then uses her client program — Outlook, Gmail, Yahoo! Mail, or whatever — to get the email from that server.

The Bitcoin network is very similar. For example, it's a *peer-to-peer* system of *nodes* that communicate with each other, each storing a copy of part (or all) of the blockchain ledger. But most Bitcoin owners don't run one of these nodes. Instead, they have *wallets*. Now, different types of wallets exist, including what are known as *cold wallets*, wallets that are not connected to the Internet (see Chapter 4 for more). And while some of these wallets are offline most of the time, but online when needed, other wallets are never connected to the Internet at all (such as paper wallets, brain wallets, and metal wallets).

However, *hot wallets* also exist, which are essentially wallet software programs connected to the Internet (and the program might be running on a personal computer, a tablet, a smartphone, or even a dedicated computer, known as a *hardware wallet*). These hot wallets can be regarded as client programs, and the Bitcoin nodes as servers.

You, the Bitcoin owner or buyer or seller, communicate with the servers that validate transactions using your Bitcoin client program (your wallet). (Wallets, by the way, are also a form of node — a device connected to the network — but typically when someone is talking about a Bitcoin node, they are talking about more than a simple wallet.) Let's say you want to sell some Bitcoin, or buy something with Bitcoin (which is essentially the same thing, right? You give some Bitcoin to someone and in return get something back.). You use your wallet to send a message to the Bitcoin network, asking the nodes to add your transaction to the blockchain, showing a transfer from your address in the blockchain to someone else's address (don't worry, we'll get to addresses in a moment!).

With us so far? There's a network of computers — the Bitcoin network — all talking to each other to manage the processing of Bitcoin transactions. Nodes exist that add transactions to the blockchain ledger, some of which are also mining, and wallets are used by individuals to manage their Bitcoin, acting as clients sending messages to the server nodes to move Bitcoin around in the ledger.

How many servers are there? It's hard to tell. Servers come, servers go, and in fact, one can run a server privately, so it can't be seen on the network. The number of active nodes fluctuates greatly, in particular based on the price of Bitcoin; as the price rises, more nodes come online, because mining becomes more profitable (remember, some nodes, but not all, are also mining Bitcoin).

Thus, estimates for the number of active nodes vary greatly; and the number you end up with also depends on what exactly you are trying to measure. Some surveys are looking for all nodes, both *full nodes* and *listening* nodes, while others are looking for only full nodes or only listening nodes.

TECHNICAL STUFF

Full nodes — or more properly, *fully validating nodes* — are those that are involved in the process of validating and adding transactions to the ledger (some of them are mining, too). A subset of these fully validating nodes are also *listening nodes* (also known as *super nodes*), which are full nodes that are publicly connectable, not behind a firewall or locked port.

When we did a quick Google search on the subject, we found sources claiming anywhere from 13,000 to 47,000 to 76,000 to 83,000 to 100,000 nodes but it doesn't really matter. Just be aware that thousands of Bitcoin servers exist that contain a partial or full copy of the ledger. And, by the way, those nodes are in scores of different countries — certainly more than 100. As a result, no single government can stop Bitcoin, should it decide to do so.

Using the Bitcoin Blockchain's Blocks of Business

So now you know about the Bitcoin network — thousands of nodes holding a copy of the ledger, along with wallets owned by ordinary Bitcoin owners (like you) which send transactions to the network. Now let's look at the actual ledger.

You found out earlier why a blockchain is known as a *blockchain*: because it chains blocks of data together. What does that mean, though? *How* are blocks chained together? Let us explain. (By the way, we're focusing here on the Bitcoin blockchain; blockchains can be used for many different purposes, and may have different characteristics, but they generally follow the same overall structure.)

First, we start with blocks of data. In the case of the Bitcoin blockchain, each block of data contains information about transactions. We'll explain *addresses* in a moment, but suffice it to say that a transaction is a record of a transfer from one address in the blockchain to another address.

Wallets send transactions to the network, and the nodes add them to a list of transactions that need to be added to the blockchain. Every ten minutes, more or less, these transactions are gathered together into a block of data, and added to the blockchain. But remember, these blocks are not merely connected to one another; they are *chained together*. In a sense, they are *locked together*, and this is done using a complicated piece of mathematics called *hashing*.

Hashing the blocks

All these blocks of data containing a record of transactions are, as you've discovered, stored on multiple computers — thousands of them, in scores of countries. That's a powerful thing in itself; how can you hack all those computers? But there's more; the chaining of the blocks from which blockchains get their name further complicates any attempt at hacking. Here's how it works.

The Bitcoin network uses a *hash* to identify each block of transactions. The block is passed through a special hashing algorithm, a bit of complex mathematics that has very useful characteristics.

- When you hash a block of information, you end up with a very large string of characters.
- This string of characters is unique, and only matches that particular piece of hashed data. It acts like a fingerprint, uniquely identifying a particular block of data.
- Every time you hash the data, you will always end up with the same unique hash number.

» If you were to change a single character in the list of transactions, the hash would no longer match. That is, should you hash the modified data *again*, you would end up with a completely different hash.

How does this hashing mathematics do all this? *You don't need to know!* We don't know, after all, so why should you? Just accept that the mathematics does all this (it does), and don't worry about *how* (just as you accept how your smartphone works do you really know how it functions?).

So here's how the overall process works:

1. **A node puts together a block of transactions.**
2. **The hash — the long string of characters acting as a "fingerprint" — copied from the *previous block* is also added to the block of transactions.**
3. **The node then *hashes* the block, previous-block's hash and all. That is, it passes the combination to the hashing algorithm, which reads it and then creates the "fingerprint" the hash.**

   Here's a real example, taken from the Bitcoin blockchain:

   ```
   00000000000000000012b707bf6d172f0de94cfb31111
      3c5d26dfe92764acc95
   ```

4. **The hash is added to the block of transactions.**
5. **The block of transactions is added to the blockchain.**

So, as the process moves along, and more transactions are added, we have a series of blocks of data, each containing two hashes: the hash identifying the previous block, and the new hash identifying the current block (including the current transactions *and* the previous block's hash).

That's how blocks are chained together into the blockchain (see Figure 2-1). Each block contains the previous block's hash — in effect, a copy of the previous block's unique fingerprint. Each block is also, in effect, identifying its position in the blockchain; the hash from the previous block identifies the order in which the current block sits.

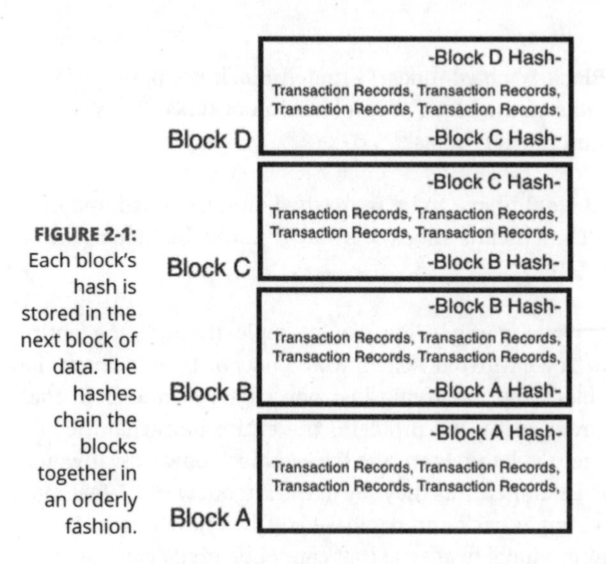

FIGURE 2-1: Each block's hash is stored in the next block of data. The hashes chain the blocks together in an orderly fashion.

The Bitcoin blockchain is "immutable"

Remember when we said earlier that the Bitcoin blockchain is *immutable* that once created, it can't be changed? It's the hashes that make it immutable. If the Bitcoin blockchain says you own *x* Bitcoin, then you do own *x* Bitcoin, and there can be no disagreement. . .and nobody can go into the blockchain and hack it or somehow change or alter it.

Imagine what would happen if someone went into a block (we'll call it Block A) and changed a little bit of data — for example, they went in and showed that instead of sending someone one Bitcoin, you sent nine.

Well, the hash in Block A would no longer match its data. Remember, a hash is a fingerprint that identifies the data, so if you change the data, the hash no longer matches.

Okay, so the hacker could rehash Block A's data and then save the "corrected" hash. But wait, now the next block (Block B) would not match because Block B is carrying Block A's original hash, and they just changed that. So now, the hacker needs to change the Block A hash stored in Block B.

But now Block B's hash doesn't match Block B's data, because that hash was created from a combination of Block B's transaction data and Block A's hash!

So, Block B would have to be re-hashed, and the hash updated. But wait! That means Block B's hash stored in Block C now doesn't match!. . .

See where we're going? This would ripple through the entire blockchain. The entire blockchain would now be broken above the "hacked" block, by modifying just one single character in that block. In order to fix the problem, the entire blockchain would have to be recalculated. From the hacked block onwards, it would need to be "re-mined," as they say in the Bitcoin world. What may look like a simple hack and database edit has now turned into a major computational headache that cannot be easily completed.

So, this hashing function, combined with the fact that thousands of other nodes must be in sync with identical copies of the blockchain, makes the blockchain virtually immutable; it simply can't be hacked.

Nobody can change it or destroy it. Hackers can't get into the peer-to-peer node network and create transactions in order to steal crypto, governments can't close it down (China, for example, could attempt to shut down Bitcoin within its borders, as they have tried recently, but the blockchain would continue to exist in many other countries, and even in China for people managing to get through the Chinese "Great Firewall"), a terrorist group can't destroy it, one nation can't attack another and destroy its blockchain, and so on. Because so many copies of the Bitcoin blockchain prevail in so many countries, and as long as enough people want to continue working with the blockchain, it's practically immutable and indestructible.

Finding Out How the Ledger Functions

So what do we have so far? You found out that Bitcoin is stored as a history of Bitcoin transactions in a ledger and that ledger is stored in a distributed, "immutable" blockchain, with blocks of transactions chained together, spread across scores of countries and tens of thousands of nodes. Now it's time to look into the ledger and see how it works. The first thing to know about is the *address*.

Your address: Where your money is stored in the ledger

Every Bitcoin or fraction of a Bitcoin is "stored" in the ledger associated with a particular "address." An address is a unique string of letters and numbers. Here's an example of a real one I just grabbed from the Bitcoin blockchain using the blockchain explorer at `www.blockchain.com`:

```
1L7hHWfJL1dd7ZhQFgRv8ke1PTKAHoc9Tq
```

Trillions of different address combinations are possible, so this address is fundamentally unique. All your Bitcoin is associated with one or more addresses. There's nothing in the blockchain identifying you specifically, which is why Bitcoin is called *pseudonymous* it's partly anonymous. Nothing in the blockchain says who owns what. However, the blockchain is also open and public. Anyone can look into the blockchain and see, within the ledger, how Bitcoin is being transferred from one address to another. So if you know who owns a particular address (as Bitcoin exchanges do, for instance; you'll find out more about those in Chapter 3), you can see what that person did with their Bitcoin. That's why it's not completely anonymous.

Now, where do addresses come from? They come from *wallets*, which are software programs that generate addresses mathematically from a public key, which in turn was generated from a private key. In fact, wallets contain at least one private key, one associated public key, and one associated blockchain address. Which brings us to another subject you're going to have to discover (just a little) about.

What's the crypto in cryptocurrency?

The *crypto* in cryptocurrency refers to *cryptography*. So, what exactly is cryptography?

According to The Oxford English online dictionary, cryptography is "the art of writing or solving codes." Wikipedia's explanation is more complicated and more digital: "The practice and study of techniques for secure communication. . .cryptography is about constructing and analyzing protocols that prevent third parties or the public from reading private messages."

The history of cryptography goes back at least 4,000 years. People have always needed to send secret messages now and then, and that's what cryptography is all about.

Today's cryptography, with the help of computers, is far more complicated than the ancient ciphers of the classical world, and it's used more extensively. In fact, cryptography is an integral part of the Internet; without it, the Internet just wouldn't work in the way we need it to work.

Almost every time you use your web browser, you're employing cryptography. Remember the little lock icon, shown in Figure 2-2, in your browser's Location bar?

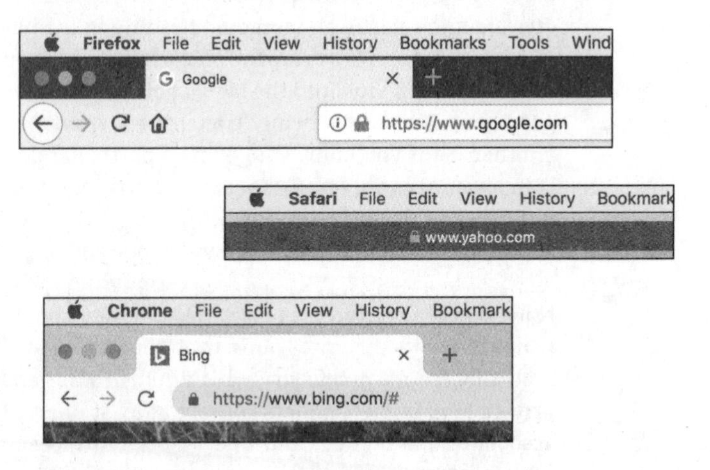

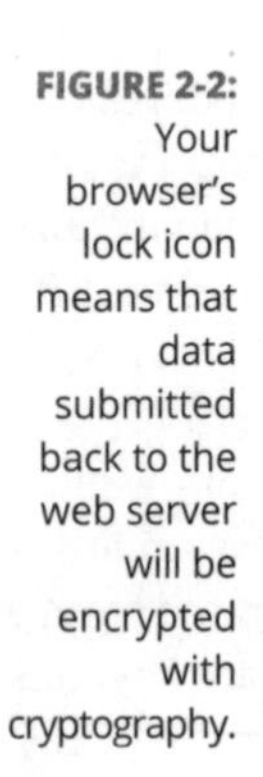
FIGURE 2-2: Your browser's lock icon means that data submitted back to the web server will be encrypted with cryptography.

The lock icon means the page is secured. When you send information from your browser to the web server (and receive information back), that information is *encrypted* — scrambled — so that if it's intercepted on the hundreds or thousands of miles of

Internet transmission between the two, it can't be read. When your credit card number is transmitted to an ecommerce site, for example, it's scrambled by your browser, sent to the web server, and then unscrambled by the receiving server.

Ah, so, the blockchain is encrypted, right? Well, no. Cryptocurrency uses cryptography, but not to scramble the data in the blockchain. The Bitcoin blockchain is plain text which is open, public, and auditable. Figure 2-3 shows you an example of a blockchain explorer designed for Bitcoin. Using a blockchain explorer, anyone can investigate the blockchain and see every transaction that has occurred since the genesis block (the first block of Bitcoin created).

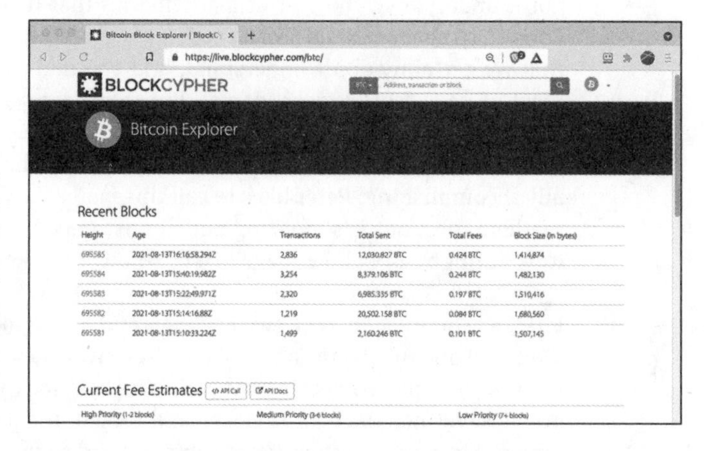

FIGURE 2-3: An example of a blockchain explorer tool, found at `https://live.blockcypher.com/btc/`.

ENCRYPTED BLOCKCHAINS

It is possible to build encrypted blockchains and encrypt data within a blockchain. For example, it is possible to create encrypted blockchains that obscure the transaction data, such as the Zcash blockchain, and some blockchains used for purposes other than cryptocurrencies may be encrypted. In general, though, cryptocurrency blockchains are not encrypted — the Bitcoin blockchain is not — so anyone can read the transactions stored within them.

No, the cryptography in cryptocurrency isn't used to encrypt the data in the blockchain, it's used to sign messages that you send to the blockchain. These messages are the ones that trigger transactions and updates to the blockchain ledger. We'll explain this signing process in a moment, but to understand that, you have to understand a little about the magical keys.

Public key encryption magic

Public key encryption is a clever little trick created using digital cryptography. This type of encryption is all accomplished using hugely complicated mathematics — the sort of mathematics that even most people with advanced degrees in mathematics don't understand, the sort of mathematics that has names like *Carmichael numbers* and *Goppa codes*, the sort of mathematics that we certainly don't understand, and you don't either (well, most of you, dear readers, don't). But that's fine; gravity isn't well understood either, but we all use it every day. So, forget *how* this amazing stuff works, and consider instead what it is actually accomplishing. Peter likes to call this *mathemagics*; sure, it's mathematics, but it's amazing and almost nobody understands it, so it might as well be magic! Here's how it works.

First, imagine a safe, with two keyholes and two associated keys. We'll call one the public key, and one the private key. Now imagine that you put something into the safe and lock it using the public key. Once the door is closed and locked, the public key no longer has access to the safe; it can't be used to unlock the safe and extract the item. The private key, however, will work. In fact, once the safe is locked, the only way to open it is to use the private key.

That's weird enough, but it gets even stranger. This magical mathematical safe actually works both ways. You can also lock it with the *private* key, but after you lock it, you can't use the private key to open the safe. Only the public key will open a safe locked with a private key.

Oh, and these two keys are magically associated. They work only with each other and no other keys. Private Key X will work only with Public Key X, and vice versa. You can't lock the safe with

Public Key X and then unlock the safe with Private Key W or Private Key K, for example.

Okay, same principle, but now think of electronic messages. You can lock an electronic message with a public key — that is, you can use a key to scramble, or encrypt, the message. That message may be an email or information being sent from your browser to a web server.

After that locked (encrypted) message is received at the other end (by the email recipient or the web server), only the private key can unlock it; the public key is useless at this point. And again, the private key must be the mathemagically associated key (okay, mathematically associated), and no other.

Encryption is a handy tool. It means Peter can give you a public key, and you can write him a message and encrypt it using the public key; once it is encrypted, nobody in the world can read it unless they have the private key. So, if Peter carefully protects his keys, he's the only person in the world who can read it.

The names of these keys aren't arbitrary. The private key should be truly private — only you, and nobody else in the world, should have access to it. The public key can be truly public. You can give it away. For example, if you want to have people email encrypted messages to you, you could publish your public key — on your website, in the footer of your emails, on your business card, or whatever — so that anybody who wants to send a message to you can encrypt it with your public key knowing that you are the only person in the world who can read it (because you keep the private key secret).

This process is essentially what your web browser uses when you send your credit card information online; the web browser uses the web server's public key to scramble the data so that only the web browser, with the associated private key, can decrypt and read the credit card information. (Okay, that's a simplification. Browser-to-server communication is more complicated than this description, involving temporary session keys and so on; but the basic principle still applies.)

HOW DO YOU ENCRYPT EMAILS?

Email encryption has been around for decades, but it simply never caught on with the public at large. Still, you can encrypt email from most email systems, such as Outlook, Gmail, and Yahoo! Mail, and systems, such as ProtonMail, can encrypt it by default. If you're interested, you can dig deep into the Help pages.

Messages to the blockchain

That's public key encryption, then. But if the blockchain is not encrypted, what does it have to do with Bitcoin? Well, you use public-key encryption when you send transactions to the blockchain. When you want to send Bitcoin to someone else, you send an encrypted message to the blockchain saying, "Send *x.xx* of my Bitcoin to this address."

But wait. We just told you the blockchain isn't encrypted, and now we're telling you a message to the blockchain is encrypted! So why do you care if the message going to the blockchain is encrypted if you're just going to decrypt it anyway?

Well, remember that we told you this lock-and-unlock mechanism works both ways. You can lock with the public key and unlock with the private key or lock with the private key and unlock with the public key. Either way, the data is scrambled. The difference is in who has the ability to unscramble it. If you scramble something with the public key, the only person in the world who can unscramble it is the person with the private key. But if you scramble it with the private key, the only person in the world who can open it is. . .everybody! Anybody and everybody can get to the public key. It's public, remember!

So, what's the purpose of encrypting a message with the private key? Not to secure it, obviously, because anybody can decrypt it. No, the purpose is to *sign* the message (transaction) and prove ownership of the associated public key.

Signing messages with the private key

Let's go back to the concept of encrypted email for a moment, to help you understand. Let's say that Peter publishes his public key on his website, in his emails, and on his business cards. Now, one day you get a message that seems to come from Peter. But how can you be sure it's from him? Well, he encrypted the message using his private key. So, you take his public key (which is publicly available) and use it to decrypt the message. If the message really is from Peter, his public key will decrypt it, and you'll be able to read it. If it isn't, the decryption won't work, because it came from someone else.

So, by encrypting the message with the private key, Peter has in effect *signed the message*, proving that it came from him. The recipient knows that the message was created by the person holding the private key that is associated with the public key that opened the message up and made it readable.

Okay, back to Bitcoin. Remember that these three things are mathemagically associated with each other. Your address in the blockchain was created by your wallet software, which has a private key that was used to create a public key, and which then used the public key to create an address. All done with the magic of mathematics.

Thus, the private key is associated, through the public key, with the address. Remember also that these elements are all unique and operate with each other. The address is associated with just one private key and one public key, each of which are uniquely associated with each other.

Sending a transaction message to the Bitcoin ledger

So, here's how cryptography is used when you want to send a transaction to the blockchain, to transfer a Bitcoin balance within the ledger to another person. Let's say you own the address `1L7hHWfJL1dd7ZhQFgRv8ke1PTKAHoc9Tq`. This is a real

Bitcoin ledger address, by the way; when we checked, it had a balance of 0.10701382 Bitcoin.

TIP

You can see this address for yourself in a blockchain explorer. (Use this link to get to it: `https://blockstream.info/address/1L7hHWfJL1dd7ZhQFgRv8ke1PTKAHoc9Tq`.) By the time you see it, of course, the balance associated with the address may be different.

Now, let's say this is your Bitcoin, and you want to send, perhaps, 0.05 Bitcoin to a friend, an exchange, or a merchant from whom you are buying goods or services.

You send a message to the blockchain saying, essentially, "I own address `1L7hHWfJL1dd7ZhQFgRv8ke1PTKAHoc9Tq`, and I want to send 0.05 Bitcoin to address `1NdaT7URGyG67L9nkP2TuBZjYV6yL7XepS`."

If you just sent a plain text (unencrypted) message to the blockchain, there would be a huge problem of verification and validity. How would the Bitcoin node receiving this message know that you do indeed own this address and the money associated with it? You could just be spoofing this information and making it up, right?

What we do is use the wallet to sign the message using the private key associated with the address. In other words, we use the private key to encrypt the message. Then we take the public key, add it to the encrypted message, and send it all out across the Bitcoin network.

MESSAGE TO THE BLOCKCHAIN

How do you send a message to the blockchain? That's what your wallet software does. In fact, wallet software is less like a wallet — your wallet contains no Bitcoin — and more like an email program. Your email program sends messages across the email network. Your wallet sends messages (about transactions) across the Bitcoin network. More on wallets soon.

Unraveling the message

So, the node — a computer containing a copy of the Bitcoin blockchain — receives the message. It takes the public key that has been attached to the encrypted message, and decrypts the message. The node "learns" something: "This message must have been encrypted — signed — by the private key associated with the public key." Of course, that's not really saying much. It's virtually a tautology! By definition, if the public key can decrypt a message, the message must have been encrypted with the matching private key. Whoop-de-doo.

But remember, the public key must be mathematically associated with the address `1L7hHWfJL1dd7ZhQFgRv8ke1PTKAHoc9Tq`. So now the node can examine the address specified in the message, along with the public key sent with the message, asking, in effect, "Is the public key associated with the address?" If the answer is yes, then the node also knows that the private key held by the person sending the message is associated with the address (all three are uniquely associated with each other).

So, what does the node tell itself? It says, in effect: "This message, sending money from the address `1L7hHWfJL1dd7ZhQFgRv8ke1PTKAHoc9Tq`, was sent by the private key that was used to create this same address so the address must have been sent by the person who owns the address and therefore owns the money associated with the address."

TIP

We know this concept can be confusing and hard to "get your head around." So here's another way to think about it: The only person who could have sent an encrypted message with transaction instructions for this address, along with the public key that originally created the address, is the person controlling the associated private key — that is, the owner of the address and the money associated with it. Thus, they are verifying ownership and validating the transaction.

So that's the crypto in cryptocurrency! You can control money in the Bitcoin blockchain ledger anonymously through the use of cryptography, using public and private key pairs and associated addresses, by cryptographically signing messages.

THE HOLDER OF THE PRIVATE KEYS OWNS THE MONEY

Okay, so maybe more people have access to the key. But as far as the technology is concerned, it doesn't matter. Whoever has access to the private key has the cryptographic right to control the money assigned to the blockchain address associated with the key. You may hear the phrase, "whoever has the private key owns the money" or "not your private key, not your Bitcoin." They may not have acquired the private key legitimately or legally own it, but they can control it nonetheless. So, protect your private keys!

The public key is associated with the private key; in fact, it's created from the private key. The address is associated with the public key; in fact, it's created from the public key. So, all three are mathematically, and uniquely, associated with each other.

But you'll need a wallet

As we mention earlier, it's the wallet that sends messages to the blockchain. But it's more than that. The *wallet* is where everything begins as far as your Bitcoin is concerned. When you create a wallet file, the wallet software creates a private key. That private key is used to create a public key, and the public key is used to create an address. The address has never before existed in the blockchain and still doesn't exist in the blockchain yet.

After you have an address, you have a way to store Bitcoin. You can give the address to someone from whom you're buying Bitcoin or to an exchange, for example, and they can send the Bitcoin to that address — in other words, they send a message to the blockchain saying, "Send *x* amount of Bitcoin from address *x* to address *y*." Now the address exists in the blockchain, and it has Bitcoin associated with it.

A *wallet program* is a messaging program that stores your keys and addresses in a wallet file. The wallet program does these primary things:

- It retrieves data from the blockchain about your transactions and balance.
- It stores your private and public keys.
- It sends messages to the blockchain transferring your crypto from your addresses to other addresses, such as when you make a purchase using your Bitcoin.
- It uses your public keys to create addresses you can give to other people when they need to send Bitcoin to you.

There's lots more to find out about wallets; you can discover more about them in Chapter 4.

REMEMBER

Here's a quick summary and an image (see Figure 2-4) to reiterate the wallet's role and to help you put it all together:

1. Bitcoin is stored in the blockchain.
2. Your Bitcoin is associated with an address in the blockchain.
3. That address is mathematically associated with a public key.
4. The public key is mathematically associated with a private key.
5. Those keys are stored in your wallet.

FIGURE 2-4: The Bitcoin is associated with an address in the blockchain; the address is derived from the public key, which is associated with a private key . . . which is kept safe in a wallet.

Using Bitcoin

IN THIS PART . . .

Making your first small Bitcoin purchases

Understanding how to work with exchanges

Setting up and managing your own Bitcoin wallet

Learning the secrets to keeping your Bitcoin safe

Investing in Bitcoin and other cryptocurrencies

» Looking at the different marketplaces and exchanges

» Using a Bitcoin ATM

» Buying from a Bitcoin exchange

» Doing things with your coin

» Sending and receiving Bitcoin

Chapter 3

Buying, Using, and Selling Bitcoin

Chapter 2 shows you how this Bitcoin thing works; hopefully by now you have a good idea of how Bitcoin, merely a record in a ledger of transactions, can hold value. That chapter also shows how advanced mathematics and cryptography identify you as the owner of your Bitcoin, and how important private keys are. In this chapter, you begin to understand how to buy and sell Bitcoin.

WARNING

We suggest that you not buy a lot of Bitcoin until you really understand what you're doing because of the risks involved: the risk of having your Bitcoin stolen, of "losing" your Bitcoin, or even of being sold fake Bitcoin. We explain these risks as we go, so our recommendation is that for the moment, you do nothing more than small "test" transactions until you have a better understanding of what's going on. In particular, make sure you read through Chapter 5 to find out how to keep your Bitcoin safe, before going beyond small transactions.

Finding the Price of Bitcoin

Before we start, a quick note about pricing per coin — that is, the *exchange rate* between Bitcoin and dollars (or whatever local currency you're using). *Where* you buy your Bitcoin affects the price you'll pay; and in fact, pricing can range dramatically, as you find out in this chapter. So how do you know how much you *should* pay? Of course, you'll want to pay as little as possible, although if the price is too low, something fishy is going on; you may be in the middle of getting scammed in some way, and scams abound in the cryptocurrency markets. We talk a little later in this chapter about how to compare pricing and find the best rates. But a few benchmark sites can give you an idea of the ballpark you should be playing in.

First, there's Google. Go to Google and type **1btc** into the search bar; Google shows you the current price, which it gets from Coinbase, in dollars, *unless* it recognizes your computer as being in a different location. If you are in Germany, for instance, you see the price in euros. (We cover Coinbase later in this chapter, in the section, "Bitcoin Exchanges.")

TIP

You can pick a different currency conversion from the drop-down list box and even specify in your search query what you want. For instance, *1btc in pounds sterling* gets you the price in British pounds.

These search strings work on Bing.com, too, but Bing gets its pricing from a company called Refinitiv, a financial news service. The Refinitiv price of Bitcoin is lower than Google's Coinbase-derived price because it's closer to the "wholesale price" than Google/Coinbase; thus, Bing.com may be a better place to check pricing. Coinbase is an exchange, so it feeds Google the price at which it is currently selling Bitcoin. And as we show you in this chapter, it does not have the best price.

Of course, the Bitcoin exchanges, where you can buy Bitcoin, also have their own published exchange rates. So, here's the pricing for one Bitcoin at four different pricing sources (all at the same moment), from lowest price to most expensive. (You need to set up an account at BlockFi.com to see their pricing.)

Bing.com/Refinitiv	$46,422.19
BlockFi.com	$46,435.73
CoinMarketCap.com	$46,488.10
Google.com/Coinbase	$46,529.20

The reason we include BlockFi.com in this list is because, as we touch on in the section, "How to find the best exchange rate," later in this chapter, it has a pretty good price compared to other exchanges. The Bing.com price from Refinitiv is still better (slightly). This is perhaps closer to the wholesale than the retail price. That doesn't mean you can buy at this price, but at least it gives you a solid benchmark.

REMEMBER

The differences in these prices are minimal; the Google price is only 0.23 percent higher than the Bing price. Oh, and one more thing: You may be charged fees to purchase Bitcoin (you usually are), so you have to consider that when comparing sources; it's not all about the exchange rate.

Your Options for Acquiring Bitcoin

You have numerous ways to get your metaphorical hands on Bitcoin. We begin by giving you a quick list of a few options, and then show you the quickest and easiest ways for a Bitcoin newbie to get started.

TIP

You may actually be able to run out and buy a little Bitcoin at your local supermarket, liquor store, or drugstore. These are not locations where you should make significant investments, but they are pretty good ways to "get your feet wet" while you follow through the instructions in this chapter.

Here are a few options for obtaining Bitcoin:

- Buy at an ATM
- Buy at a retail store
- Buy from another individual (person-to-person trading)
- Buy at an exchange
- Earn it from credit or debit card transactions
- Work for it
- Mine it
- Find it all over the place

In the sections that follow, we cover each of the first three options in the preceding list in more depth, starting with the method that many people in North America can use very quickly and easily: buying from a Bitcoin ATM.

Bitcoin ATMs

The fastest and easiest way to grab a little Bitcoin is through a Bitcoin ATM. If you live in a major city in the United States, there is likely a Bitcoin ATM somewhere close by; the same is true in many other countries.

We want to say up front that buying from Bitcoin ATMs is most certainly *not* the best — or most economical — way to buy Bitcoin. But as a fast-learning experience, we think it can be worthwhile. And once you have a wallet set up by an ATM company, you can move on to other forms of purchase — such as through an exchange — and then send funds to and fro between the wallets to get familiar with using Bitcoin.

Buying Bitcoin from Coinme

To help you get a feel for how you can buy, here's a quick look at one Bitcoin ATM network. In this example, we use the Coinme network, which is the largest Bitcoin ATM network in North America, thanks to their partnership with Coinstar. In fact, they claim to be the "largest cash to Bitcoin network in the world."

You may have seen the Coinstar kiosks in grocery stores, at which you can convert large quantities of loose change into cash or gift cards. (Not into Bitcoin, ironically! You can only use bills for Bitcoin.) They have 60,000 kiosks around the world, though at the time of this writing, they are only selling Bitcoin at their kiosks in the United States (at many, though not at all of them, so check the website before you rush off to buy).

We are going to use this network because it's big and, well, there's a kiosk less than a mile from co-author Peter Kent's house. We're willing to bet that you're more likely to find a Coinme ATM near *you*, too, than one from another network.

Peter bought 20 bucks' worth of Bitcoin — wait, no, $19.20 worth after they took out a 4 percent commission — at a Coinme/Coinstar kiosk. After the purchase (we'll show how this works in a moment), he checked pricing against CoinMarketCap.com, Google/Coinbase, and ATM Coiners, an ATM competitor, and discovered the following:

Coinme/Coinstar	1 BTC = $54,182.50
CoinMarketCap.com	1 BTC = $50,592.81
Google/Coinbase	1 BTC = $50,592.60
ATM Coiners	1 BTC = $50,552.77

So that means it would take $54,182.50 to buy a full Bitcoin at Coinme (before their 4 percent fee), but only $50,573.99 through Coinbase (without considering the fee). Or $50,552.77 from ATM Coiners, a smaller Bitcoin ATM network, though we don't know what fees they charge. (Bitcoin pricing fluctuates quickly, of course, but all four of these prices are from the same point in time, almost to the second.)

Interestingly, once you own Bitcoin and it's controlled by a Coinme wallet, all of a sudden Coinme shows you the *real* Bitcoin price. Peter installed a Coinme wallet on his phone, and the wallet had a price "ticker," showing a price remarkably close to that shown by Google. It also showed the day's high price: $50,997.43, apparently despite the fact that they sold the Bitcoin at the $54,182.50 price less than three hours earlier!

PARTIAL BITCOIN?

Yes, you can buy a fraction of a Bitcoin. As we explain in Chapter 2, just as dollars are made up of cents, and pounds are made up of pence, Bitcoin are made up of Satoshi. The major difference is that there's a whole lot more Satoshis in a Bitcoin than cents in a dollar. One hundred million, in fact.

So, when Peter purchased $19.20 worth of Bitcoin from Coinme, at a price of $54,182.50 per BTC, he got 0.0035424 BTC um, $19.20 divided by $54,182.50 is actually 0.0003543579569, not 0.0035424, but that's what Coinme gave him. Anyway, he got 0.0035424, which is 354,240 Satoshi, or *sats*, as they say in the Bitcoin world.

But wait, we're not finished. How about that fee? Coinme also takes a 4 percent transaction fee. That is, it's going to take 4 cents out of every dollar you put into the machine, before that money is used to buy Bitcoin. Buying a full Bitcoin wouldn't just cost $54,182.50; it would cost $56,440.10 — that is, almost 12 percent more than the Coinbase price! (Hidden deep within the small print on the Coinme.com website is a note that they have both the 4 percent "transaction fee" and an additional "cash convenience fee," which they build into the Bitcoin price, for a total of what they say is 11 percent. It's more like 12 percent compared to Coinbase.)

Buying from Coinme is not the cheapest way to get Bitcoin. But hey, with the way Bitcoin fluctuates so wildly in price, you stand to make a lot of money or potentially lose it all, so what does it matter!?

Quite frankly, as we've already told you, Bitcoin ATMs are not a great way to buy Bitcoin due to the higher fees and worse exchange rate compared to other sellers. You may still want to use them just to get your feet wet. Get your hands on some Bitcoin, see a wallet in action, and you can always transfer your coin to another wallet later (we show you how). We actually think Bitcoin ATMs are a really good way to start: buy 20 bucks' worth — or ten, or less — and consider the small amount you'll lose in fees as the price of education.

So, if you don't mind the overpriced Bitcoin with a "cash convenience fee," the 4 percent commission, and the weird math apparently programmed into Coinme's machines, and you just want to get your hands on some Bitcoin, we show you how in the following steps.

You can use a different Bitcoin ATM network if you want, which may or may not be cheaper. We've seen fees of 10 percent, and they reportedly go as high as 25 percent with some networks, so be careful!

In any case, read this Coinme walkthrough to get an idea of the process, and then read the note at the end of the steps about the other Bitcoin ATM networks.

1. **Find an ATM.**

   You can check using a locator page at `https://www.coinstar.com/findakiosk` or `https://CoinMe.com/locations`.

2. **Go to the ATM (okay, obviously).**

   Here's the process Peter used at the local Coinme/Coinstar kiosk.

3. **Read a bunch of small print and agree to various conditions.**

   Understand that once your cash is in the machine, you're not getting it back, it's not an anonymous transaction (that's a big misunderstanding among Bitcoin newbies), the transfer is permanent, and so on.

4. **Provide a phone number.**

   This needs to be a phone that can receive text messages. (You won't get one right now, but later in the process you'll have to enter your phone number again, and you will get a text message in response.)

   The next screen shows the exchange rate; in Peter's case, it told him that a dollar would get 0.00001845 BTC; as we're sure you quickly figured out, that's 1,845 sats.

5. **Put in as much cash as you want to change (bills only, at least $1).**

   Peter chose $20, mainly because he only had $20 bills in his wallet.

6. **Click the Buy button.**

   A few moments later, out pops a "voucher." Apart from background information, the voucher contains a few really important pieces of information.

   - **A redemption code:** The process isn't finished yet, as you still have to set up an account with Coinme. You'll need that redemption code to transfer the record of the purchased Bitcoin to the new wallet Coinme gives you.
   - **A PIN number:** For some obscure reason.
   - **A URL for the account setup webpage:** `https://coinme/redeem` (Note that the Coinme service — and thus these Coinme URLs — may not function outside the US; perhaps you can experiment with a Bitcoin ATM service that functions in your country.)

   At this point, you can complete the process in front of the kiosk, using a smartphone, or return home to use a laptop, which is what Peter opted to do.

7. **Go to http://coinme/redeem to create an account.**

   It's the usual thing, you've done it a thousand times before: enter an email address and a password, click a couple of approval buttons, and then click the Create Account button.

REMEMBER

   Save the login information into a password-management program! You have one, don't you? You really should! Find out more about protecting your information in Chapter 5.

8. **Enter a phone number.**

   Coinme confirms the number by sending it a text code; enter the code into the Coinme page.

9. **Follow the instructions to log into `https://account.coinme.com/login` on the mobile phone.**

   Coinme provides a QR code that you can photograph on your phone to take you to the login page, or you can type the link into your smartphone's browser, or have Coinme text you the link. (There is an alternative process if you don't have a smartphone.)

QR WHAT?

By the way, a quick note for those of you who have never used a QR code (we know there are many of you). The cameras in smartphones are often set up to read these codes automatically. You can often simply point the camera at the square — what's known as a "matrix barcode" — and within a split second the camera recognizes the barcode, reads the URL (the web address) embedded into the code, and asks if you want to load the URL into your phone's web browser. As we discuss later in this chapter, most Bitcoin wallets also have QR codes and QR code readers, which you use when sending Bitcoin to the wallet. In this case, when the camera on the sending device sees the QR code, it grabs the blockchain address provided by the recipient wallet and drops it straight into the sending wallet's To Address box.

However, sometimes smartphone cameras do not automatically recognize QR codes. There should be a setting somewhere to turn this feature on. This has been a problem with many iPhones; QR scanning may require that you turn it on in the camera settings.

Finally, a little trivia for you, something your friends don't know: QR means *quick response*.

10. **Log into the page on the smartphone.**
11. **Go through the process to identify yourself.**

    Any reputable company in the United States buying and selling Bitcoin has KYC (know your customer) and AML (anti-money-laundering) regulations they have to comply with. For Coinme, this process involves copying the front and back of your driver's license, taking a selfie, and confirming the information scanned from the license. (See Figure 3-1. And you thought Bitcoin was anonymous, eh?)

    Get used to this process if you're going to play in the Bitcoin pond a while. Every company in the U.S. selling Bitcoin, that's trying to stay on the right side of the law, has these processes. You'll provide a picture of your driver's license, front and back — through your smartphone camera, through your laptop's webcam, or by scanning and uploading the images — and often take a selfie, too. You may even have to provide "proof of life," by taking a video of your head and face and moving it around a little!

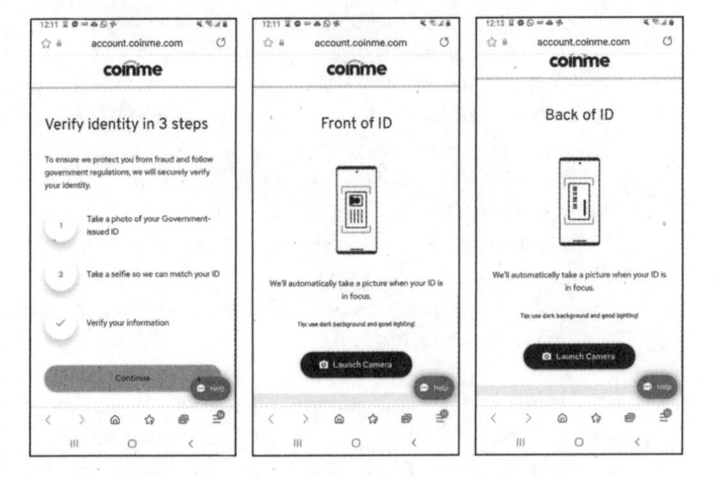

FIGURE 3-1: You're going to have to prove who you are.

At this stage, you have your new Coinme wallet (as shown in Figure 3-2). This is a *custodial wallet,* which is in the custody of Coinme. In other words, they manage the wallet for you, and all you need to remember is your login information.

This wallet has not seen any Bitcoin transactions yet. But Peter purchased $19.20 worth (well, $19.20 in Coinme/Coinstar valuation, which is more like $17 worth in real-world Bitcoin valuation).

FIGURE 3-2: The Coinme wallet.

12. **Locate the voucher from the kiosk, enter the redemption code and the PIN number, and click the big green Redeem button.**

    Why both a redemption code *and* a PIN number? Hmmm, we'll think about that and get back to you

    Coinme sets aside in its ledger some of the Bitcoin it owns, 0.0035424 BTC (354,240 Satoshi), assigning it to you. The Bitcoin purist would say you don't really own the Bitcoin, and indeed you don't, at least not directly. Essentially, you now have an IOU from Coinme for that amount of Bitcoin.

13. **Click HOME to go back to the wallet.**

    The kiosk purchase has been assigned to this wallet.

The Coinme wallet is pretty basic; obviously it's designed to be very simple for non-expert users. (As we've explained, ATMs are not an ideal way to buy Bitcoin.) What the wallet doesn't show is the *status* of the transaction; this is relevant because Bitcoin transactions don't happen immediately.

Understanding your custodial Coinme wallet

The Bitcoin purist will tell you that you should never allow anyone else to control your wallets, but A: hey, it's only 20 bucks, B: realistically, large quantities of Bitcoin are stored in custodial wallets, so you're by no means alone, and C: unless custodial wallets become safe and easy to use, there's really no glowing future for Bitcoin. Not everybody can be a Bitcoin expert, but not everyone has to be.

REMEMBER

Wallets *do not contain Bitcoin!* Wallets contain your address in the blockchain, and the private and public keys that control that address. The Bitcoin itself — at least, the record of the transaction — is in the blockchain associated with your address. At least, this is how wallets usually work: Each wallet controls one or more addresses, your addresses. In this case, however, your Bitcoin is being held by Coinme, in combination — commingled — with all its other clients' Bitcoin holdings. So you don't own the Bitcoin *directly*; rather, Coinme owns the Bitcoin and you are, in effect, holding an IOU from Coinme to you for the amount of Bitcoin you bought. (We show you later how to "collect on the IOU" by sending Bitcoin from Coinme to another wallet that's in your direct control.)

Notice the long, strange string of letters and numbers in the bottom-left corner of the Coinme wallet window (under the words *Bitcoin Receive Address* in Figure 3-2); that's an address to which you can send Bitcoin from another wallet, an address in the blockchain that's managed by this Coinme wallet. Click COPY, and the address is copied to your computer's clipboard. You may be wondering where this address came from, and how it got to be yours. Wallet software can create addresses as needed. When a new address is required, the software simply creates it based upon the private key.

That may sound dangerous — there are millions of wallets, so if wallets make up addresses randomly, duplicates happen, right? Well, if Bitcoin addresses were just numbers from, say, zero to a million, then yes, duplicates would occur now and then. But in fact, there are 1,461,501,637,330,902,918,203,684,832,716,283,019,655,932,542,976 possible combinations of Bitcoin addresses! That's enough for everybody on earth to have 196,385,600,286,334,710,857,791,565,804,391,698,421 addresses each!

There are so many possible combinations of these 34-character addresses that even *millions* of wallets, creating new addresses at random, are quite simply not going to create the same address twice. Okay, yes, it is *theoretically possible* (such an event is known as a *collision*). But with so many possible combinations, and the chance being so low, it is more or less impossible for it to happen — perhaps once or twice in the lifetime of the universe. (Google this subject if you don't believe us!)

So that's your new address in the blockchain. In fact, let's peek into the blockchain and take a look. Figure 3-3 shows this address, in the Blockchain.com *blockchain explorer* (`https://www.blockchain.com/explorer`). Blockchain explorers let you look into the blockchain and see what's going on. In this case, you can see that address 3BgtadMBFAQBqwNJoVqWwsSHzCX5uEvVck has a balance of 0 Bitcoin. In fact, it's never received any Bitcoin; remember, this is not where the Bitcoin you bought at the ATM is held. That's assigned to a Coinme addresses, and this is simply an address belonging to Peter to which he — or anyone else — can send Bitcoin.

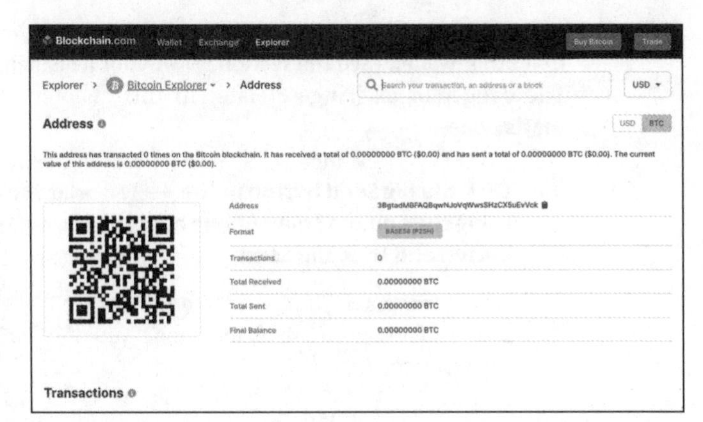

FIGURE 3-3: The new address shown in the Blockchain.com blockchain explorer.

Notice that QR code? That is the address encoded into the QR format; someone wanting to send Peter money could scan the code from their smartphone wallet and do so. Remember that addresses are *not* private, *not* secret. Peter can send the address to someone, and they can send him money. Or *you* could type it straight from the page here and send money! Go ahead, give it a try! (Make sure you get every character correct, please.)

3BgtadMBFAQBqwNJoVqWwsSHzCX5uEvVck

TIP

We're not suggesting that you send Bitcoin to your Coinme wallet, at least not beyond just playing around while learning. This is a super-simple wallet, managed by a third-party service that is not the optimal place to buy Bitcoin (and likely not the best place to store it, either).

If you do send Bitcoin to your Coinme account from another wallet, don't freak out if the sending wallet says it's gone but the Coinme wallet doesn't show the transaction right away. Until there are six "confirmations" that the transaction has been accepted into the blockchain, it's not regarded as completed, and so the Coinme wallet won't show it. That could take an hour or more.

Sending Bitcoin from your Coinme wallet

Later, once you have another wallet set up, you'll probably want to transfer control over your Bitcoin from your Coinme wallet to that other wallet. (See the section, "Not your keys, not your coins: The danger of exchanges," later in this chapter.) Here's how that's done:

1. **Click the big Send button in the wallet, or, if you're using the Coinme smartphone app, tap the big Transact button and then tap Send.**

   On the computer, you see a screen similar to what's shown on the left in Figure 3-4; on the phone, you see what's shown on the right.

FIGURE 3-4: Sending Bitcoin from the Coinme web console and smartphone app.

   The web app asks for a Bitcoin Address; the smartphone app asks for a Wallet Address same thing. They are both asking for the blockchain address to which you want to send your Bitcoin.

2. **Provide this information by scanning a QR code from the wallet that controls the address you're sending to.**

   Most wallets provide one. In fact, if you've been following along and have set up a Coinme account, you can see the Coinme receipt QR code by clicking the little square to the left of the *Bitcoin Receive Address*. The QR code pops up.

In this case we're sending money *from* the Coinme wallet, so it's the address from the *other* wallet we need, the wallet that manages the address to which we're sending the Bitcoin.

If you're using the smartphone app, tap the little QR icon in the top right and scan the other wallet's QR code from another phone or from your computer monitor.

If you're using the web console on your laptop or desktop and you have a webcam, click the big camera icon to scan through the webcam.

If you have both programs open on the same device — the Coinme wallet and the wallet that controls the address to which you are sending — the QR code isn't helpful. Instead, copy the address from the destination wallet and paste it into the Bitcoin Address/Wallet Address field.

3. **Enter the amount of Bitcoin (measured in dollars' worth) that you want to send to the other address.**

   You can't send all the Bitcoin, because there are fees to be paid. If you want to clear out the Bitcoin and send it all, you have to allow for those fees (the web console shows how much the fees are, while the smartphone app tells you what your "available balance" is after the fee). You can see the filled-out form in both the web console and smartphone app in Figure 3-4.

4. **Click the Send button and away it goes; you then see a confirmation message.**

The wallet software sends a message to the Bitcoin network. The first node picks it up, and sends it further into the network so that it also gets picked up by other nodes. This is a complicated process involving the mining of Bitcoin, but essentially, the transaction is bundled into a block of data containing a bunch of other transactions — how soon this happens depends on how much of a fee you paid — and added to the blockchain.

A few notes to keep in mind as you send Bitcoin:

- **Most wallet software allows you to pick the fees you want to pay.** The more you pay, the faster the transaction is added to the blockchain. The Coinme wallet is very basic, so they pick the fee for you. (See Chapter 4 for more details about wallets.)

WARNING

- **Make sure you get the address to which you are sending absolutely correct!** Either copy and paste the address, or use the QR code; if you really have to type it, check, check, and check again!

  If you get one character wrong, the Bitcoin will be sent to a different address and will be totally unrecoverable. In fact, what will happen is that a new address will be created in the blockchain, an address with no matching private key. This is like dropping a gold bar over the side of a ship; it will disappear into the depths. The only difference is that there's a chance that a scuba diver may one day find the gold bar; with Bitcoin, it's gone until the end of time.

TECHNICAL STUFF

- **Most wallets provide a different address each time you request the address or QR code, so wallets can end up controlling many different addresses in the blockchain.** This isn't totally necessary, but many people believe you should use a different address for every transaction for privacy reasons.

  As Satoshi Nakamoto said in his Bitcoin white paper, "a new [address] should be used for each transaction to keep [it] from being linked to a common owner. The risk is that if the owner of a key is revealed, linking could reveal other transactions that belonged to the same owner."

More Bitcoin ATM networks

There are other Bitcoin ATM networks, some of which may have better pricing. Some also allow the purchase of Bitcoin using debit cards (Coinme doesn't), though we don't believe any networks allow the use of credit cards. But, before buying — in fact, preferably before turning up at the ATM — you should ask these three questions:

- **What's the pricing?** Some networks actually display the Bitcoin price on their websites, so you can at least check the price against Google, Bing, and CoinMarketCap.com.
- **Do you need a wallet?** The process described earlier for Coinme provides a *custodial* wallet. Some ATMs want you to set up a wallet of your own first, and then, when you buy Bitcoin from the ATM, the Bitcoin is sent to the address in the blockchain managed by your wallet. In fact, Bitcoin purists would say it's far better for you to manage your own wallet, so they would regard these ATM networks as better than Coinme. (On the other hand, Bitcoin purists are almost certainly not buying Bitcoin from Bitcoin ATMs!)
- **What are the transaction fees?** Figuring these out isn't always easy because some fees are hidden. Before you make a very large purchase through an ATM, do your homework (figure out the wallet issue, the pricing, and the fees), and then make a small purchase and run the math to see what the actual costs are. You shouldn't be making large purchases through a Bitcoin ATM, because you can get more BTC for your money elsewhere.

Still, perhaps you like spending more than you need to. Here are a few other Bitcoin ATM networks you can check.

- ATM Coiners: `https://atmcoiners.com/`
- Bitcoin Depot: `https://Bitcoindepot.com/`
- Coinflip: `https://coinflip.tech/`
- DigitalMint: `https://www.digitalmint.io/`
- LibertyX: `https://libertyx.com/`
- XBTeller: `https://www.xbteller.com/`

You can find more ATMs at a Bitcoin ATM directory such as Coin ATM Radar (`https://coinatmradar.com/`) or by Googling. These things are proliferating like proverbial rabbits. You'll find them at gas stations, liquor stores, supermarkets, and even convenience stores. Not exactly hotbeds of finance, in other words.

Retail Bitcoin

Okay, now onto the number two easy (and not advisable) way to buy Bitcoin: over the counter at a Bitcoin "retail" location. There are plenty of places in which you can purchase Bitcoin from a real live person, but some of these are simply using the retail location as a place for you to deliver cash. That is, you set up an account online, then take your requisite cash to one of the retail locations and hand it over.

LibertyX, for instance, claims to have 20,000 "trusted stores" at which you can pay cash for Bitcoin. (The company has ATMs, too.) These guys have a partnership with CVS Pharmacy and Rite Aid. You can go to `www.LibertyX.com`, find locations on a map near you, filter to remove the Debit purchases (those are through their ATMs), and select the Cash locations. Once you pick a location, you have to set up an account with LibertyX, install the LibertyX app on your smartphone, scan your driver's license front and back, and take a selfie. (It may take up to two business days, in theory — more in practice — for the information to be approved before you can buy Bitcoin.)

Also, before you can buy from LibertyX, you need a wallet set up. Unlike with the Coinme ATM transaction described in the previous section, LibertyX does not provide a wallet for these cash transactions, and so you have to provide one yourself.

Coinme has a similar system (not requiring your own wallet; as with the ATMs, Coinme provides a custodial wallet). You create an account online, use your smartphone to set up a transaction, and then take your cash to a MoneyGram location. (MoneyGram is a money transfer service, with hundreds of thousands of offices in 200 countries and territories.) You give the clerk at the counter your cash and the transaction ID, and the Bitcoin is transferred to your wallet.

Azteco is another such company (`www.Azte.co`). Azteco sells "vouchers" you can take to a store along with your cash, and get Bitcoin in return, which is sent directly to your own wallet. It's very popular in Europe; less so in North America, though they do have a few locations in some major cities.

There are many other places, local stores such as pawn shops and coin dealers, that buy and sell Bitcoin. Just be very careful. These sorts of transactions are not for the newbie. You really must understand how the whole Bitcoin process works, and how to use a wallet (make sure you read and understand Chapters 4 and 5) before you risk such purchases.

Person-to-person trading

You can, of course, buy from, and sell to, individuals. But you need to understand two things:

- You have to have a wallet.
- Personal transactions are very risky!

Scams abound, so be careful. Here's one common trick. The seller gives you a wallet in some form — perhaps a hardware wallet — with Bitcoin already in the wallet. If the seller had control over the wallet when handing it over to you, the seller probably still has control after. Remember, the wallet contains the private keys that control the address in the blockchain. Just because you now have the private keys, doesn't mean the seller no longer has them — they may have kept a copy of the wallet, or even of the private keys themselves (or the "seed" used to create the keys; see Chapter 4). By the time you get home, the Bitcoin may have been moved from the wallet and your Bitcoin is gone!

You can also find sellers in the Craigslist classifieds site; some of these sellers are store owners, such as pawn shops. Some are individuals. Again, such transactions can be very risky, especially as the seller will likely want you to turn up in person with cash to fund the transaction. We would recommend that, if a physical exchange of goods or currency for Bitcoin is required, you select a safe, neutral public place, ideally in daylight. Better still, some police stations even provide safe spaces for the exchange of goods, for Craigslist transactions, for instance. See `http://www.safetradestations.com/safetrade-station-list.html` for a list of police stations in the U.S. that provide safe trade spaces. If you can't find something on this list, call your local police station and ask.

But again, there are lots of scams, and you should not do these kinds of transactions until you really understand Bitcoin well.

LocalBitcoins.com

LocalBitcoins.com is a long-established Finnish company that puts buyers and sellers together. Sellers accept a wide range of payment methods: Apple Pay, Zelle, Walmart2Walmart transfers, PayPal, cash deposits to bank accounts, and so on. The company holds the Bitcoin in escrow. That is, the seller sends the Bitcoin to LocalBitcoins.com, you pay, and then once payment is shown to have been received, LocalBitcoins.com transfers the Bitcoin to you.

However, while until recently LocalBitcoins.com operated throughout the U.S. (and many other countries; it's one of the biggest Bitcoin marketplaces in some African countries), in the spring of 2021 it stopped trading in all U.S. locations except Florida, Connecticut, Utah, Arkansas, Nevada, Nebraska, Mississippi, Iowa, the District of Columbia, North Dakota, Minnesota, Kentucky, and Vermont.

A number of businesses in the Bitcoin arena are only semi-legal, operating in a "gray area." Some LocalBitcoins.com sellers have been prosecuted for operating unlicensed MSBs (money service businesses) — one had sold $25 million worth of Bitcoin through the website.

One study (by a company called CipherTrace) showed that a huge proportion of illicit Bitcoin was being sold through LocalBitcoins.com. About 12% of all the Bitcoin flowing through the site, CipherTrace believed, was coming from criminal activity.

Bisq

Bisq (`https://bisq.network/`) is a unique decentralized person-to-person Bitcoin exchange. Bisq provides an app that facilitates the trading of Bitcoin for local (fiat) currency directly between individuals without them meeting in person, verifying identity, or needing a trusted third party to hold their Bitcoin in escrow. The Bisq network is a Bitcoin trading platform that removes the trusted third party from the equation, and is designed and operated a lot like the Bitcoin network itself.

WARNING

Bisq is an advanced system, and so perhaps only users comfortable with operating a Bitcoin node should attempt to use it.

Trusted sellers

Perhaps one of the best ways to buy Bitcoin is from a trusted friend or relative, someone who you know isn't out to rip you off. You'll need to understand how to use a wallet, of course, because you'll need a Bitcoin blockchain address to which your friend can send the Bitcoin.

Bitcoin exchanges

This section covers the places most investors are likely to use: the major Bitcoin exchanges. There are numerous exchanges, but we'll start by looking at Coinbase. We're not saying that everyone should use Coinbase, but it's a good place to start because it's the most popular exchange in the U.S. Since early 2021, it's been a public company, traded on Nasdaq (the ticker symbol is COIN). In an arena of more than 1,000 exchanges, some of which are less than reputable, the idea that Coinbase gets the kind of oversight that public companies in the U.S. are subjected to may be comforting.

They have been in business around a decade, and have literally millions of accounts, from over one hundred countries. Coinbase's holdings are also at least partially insured (rare in the cryptocurrency space!); however, their policy does not cover unauthorized access into your account. (So protect your password! See Chapter 5.) One more reason to go with Coinbase: At the time of this writing, when you sign up, you get $5 worth of Bitcoin to experiment with. So let's play with Coinbase, and then we'll reconvene and talk a little more about the different types of exchanges.

Buying from Coinbase

This section shows you how to set up a Coinbase account and buy a little Bitcoin.

TIP

When you visit cryptocurrency sites, make sure you type domain names carefully and check them after typing. Large companies such as Coinbase police their domain names, registering alternative versions that are close to their primary domain name — spelling mistakes, for instance — and suing "cybersquatters," people who have registered domain names using spelling mistakes and similar terms. For instance, in 2018 Coinbase filed a complaint against a company in Hong Kong that had registered the coinbae.com domain name, and was forwarding people accidentally using this domain name to Bitcoin.com and binance.com. So you're unlikely to end up at the wrong place when trying to get to Coinbase.com, but be careful. Scams abound in the cryptocurrency space.

1. **Go to Coinbase.com, and when the home page loads, click the signup button.**

   If you're in the United States, you may see a promotional message such as "Get $5 in free Bitcoin for signing up."

2. **Do the usual KYC (know your customer) exercise: enter your name, email address, state, and a password, click a checkbox, and click Create Account.**

3. **In the confirmation email, click the link in the email; another webpage loads.**

4. **Enter your phone number and click Submit; you're sent a text message with a verification code.**

5. **Enter the code into the text box that appears in your web browser, and click Submit.**

6. **On the next page, select your nationality from the Citizenship drop-down box.**

7. **Fill out the Verify Your Identity box: your date of birth, address, social security number, and so on.**

   You then see a box in which you have to answer a couple of questions: the amount of crypto you expect to trade each year, and the industry in which you work.

8. **Fill in your answers and click Submit.**

   And you're in, but you're not finished. Before you get your free $5 worth of Bitcoin (assuming they are still running that promotion), you need to finish verifying your ID.

9. **Click the Verify Your ID or equivalent button or link.**

   A screen appears asking you to verify your identity.

10. **Click to choose your driver's license or another form of state-issued ID card.**

    Depending on the type of device you're using, you can use your laptop's webcam or your phone's camera, or you can scan documents and upload them.

11. **Load your account with money by clicking Add Payment, choosing how to transfer funds, and following the directions.**

    You can choose a direct transfer from your bank account (surprisingly easy to set up for most banks), PayPal, debit cards (only for small amounts), and wire transfers (for large amounts).

After you are verified and have money in your account, you can buy a little Bitcoin by following these steps:

1. **Click the Buy Crypto button.**

   Up pops the transaction box, as shown in Figure 3-5.

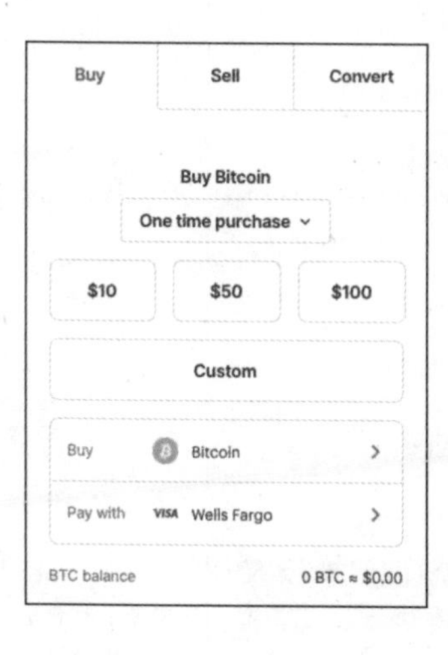

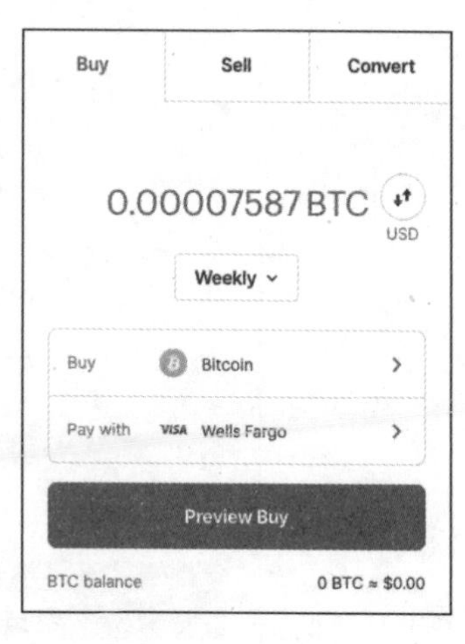

FIGURE 3-5: Let's buy!

2. **Click the $10, $50, or $100 button, or click Custom to enter a specific sum (a minimum of $1.99 for some reason).**

3. **Click the One Time Purchase drop-down menu if you want to set up timed purchases.**

   The choices are every day, once a week, twice a month, or once a month (you can always cancel these scheduled purchases later). The little button to the right of the value field, with the two up and down arrows, is for toggling the value between dollars and Bitcoin (on the right in Figure 3-5).

The two boxes at the bottom show what you're going to buy (Bitcoin) and where the funding is coming from.

4. **Click the Bitcoin box to see a list of cryptocurrencies bought and sold by Coinbase.**
5. **When everything's set the way you want it, click Preview Buy, and Coinbase shows you a confirmation box outlining your choices (Figure 3-6).**

   Notice that the fee is coming out of the sum entered in Step 2 — in this example, $5. Coinbase subtracts a 99-cent fee, and Peter gets to buy $4.01 worth of Bitcoin. (Larger transactions have much lower fees proportional to the purchase.)

   You see a box confirming the transaction, and you're done.

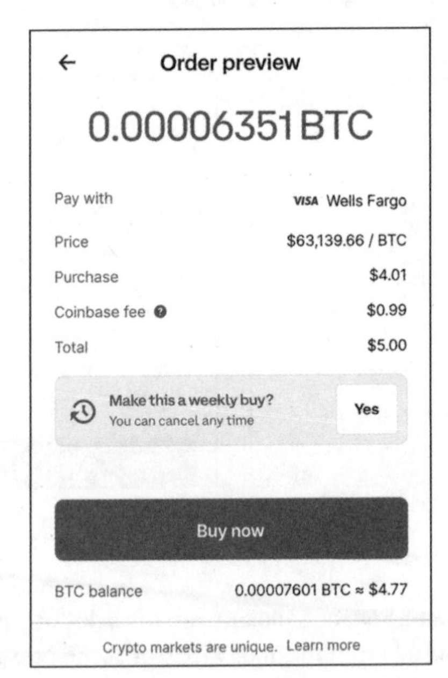

FIGURE 3-6: You're ready to buy; click Buy Now when you're sure.

What has just happened? Well, you purchased Bitcoin from Coinbase; that is, you have a custodial wallet within your Coinbase account, and Coinbase has set aside, in its own ledger, the purchased Bitcoin. You don't have an address on the Bitcoin blockchain, as all of this is internal to Coinbase; you just own legal claim to a small part of Coinbase's hundreds of millions of dollars' worth of Bitcoin.

You can find your transaction on the Assets page (sometimes called Portfolio) of the web app; on the smartphone app, you tap Assets, then tap Bitcoin in the list of currencies, and then tap the BTC Wallet.

Sending Bitcoin to another wallet

At some point you may prefer to manage your Bitcoin yourself, rather than leave it up to a third party (in this case, Coinbase) to look after it for you. You may want to send your Bitcoin to another wallet. Or you may want to use some of it to buy something. In this section, we show you how to send Bitcoin from Coinbase to somewhere or someone else. In fact, if you set up a Coinme account earlier in this chapter, you may want to play with sending a small sum to the Coinme wallet.

Go to the Coinbase web app, and follow these steps:

1. **Click the big Send/Receive button at the top. (In the smartphone app, tap the big button with two horizontal arrows at the bottom of the app, select Send, and in the screen that appears, tap the Bitcoin wallet.)**

   If you have other wallets from purchasing other cryptocurrencies, they are listed here.

   Figure 3-7 shows the Send box in the web app. (The smartphone app breaks some of these inputs into steps: the amount being sent first, then where the money is being sent, and so on.) These steps follow the web app process.

2. **In the To box, enter a mobile number, an email address, or a wallet address.**

   Coinbase has tens of millions of accounts, and someone you know may have an account there. If you need to send Bitcoin to another Coinbase account holder, instead of sending the transaction to the blockchain, you can enter the phone number or email address the recipient used for their Coinbase account, and Coinbase will transfer Bitcoin directly to that person's Coinbase wallet. If you know the recipient has a Coinbase wallet, use this method — it's faster than sending a transaction to the blockchain, and it's free. (Sending a transaction to the blockchain is not.)

Peter is sending to an address in the blockchain controlled by another wallet using the address from his Coinme wallet (refer to Figure 3-2).

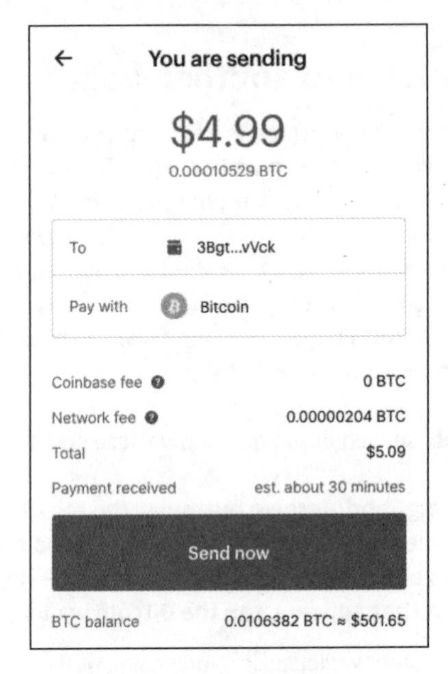

FIGURE 3-7: Sending money from Coinbase to somewhere else.

3. **Ignore the Note box unless you're sending to another Coinbase account holder and you want to add a message. The Pay With box should be set to Bitcoin.**

4. **Click Continue, and a summary box appears.**

   Notice that Coinbase isn't charging a fee for this withdrawal transaction, but a network fee does apply. This transaction is going to cost 0.00000204 BTC (204 Satoshi), a little over 9 cents at the time of the transaction (notice the rounding going on; we're getting charged $5.09, and sending $4.99 worth of Bitcoin). Notice also that Coinbase is estimating 30 minutes for the transaction to complete.

5. **Click Send Now.**

   You may see a warning about the dangers of sending people Bitcoin, and you get a verification code from Coinbase on your cell phone.

6. **Enter the code, and the Bitcoin is on its way.**

To see the transaction in the web app, go into the Portfolio screen (you may have to click on Assets in the left navigation column, or it may say Portfolio), and scroll down until you see Recent Transactions. Click on the most recent transaction, and you see the screen in Figure 3-8. In the smartphone app, tap Assets, scroll down and tap Bitcoin, then BTC Wallet, and finally tap your pending transaction to see information similar to what's shown in Figure 3-8:

- The amount sent, in Bitcoin and dollars, including the network fee.
- The blockchain address to which you are sending Bitcoin.
- The number of confirmations. We discussed this earlier; your transaction has to be added to all the nodes eventually, but once it's been confirmed as added by six nodes, it's regarded as irreversible. It may take a while to see all these confirmations.
- The portion of the sum you sent that is going to be paid as a fee.
- A View Transaction link. (We'll come back to that, but here's a clue: on the smartphone app, there's a button labeled View on Blockchain Explorer instead.)
- A line showing the date and time of the transaction, and a status; in this case, the status is Pending, because we haven't yet got our six confirmations.

Click the View Transaction link (or tap the smartphone's View on Blockchain Explorer button). A webpage opens, showing the transaction in the Blockchain.com blockchain explorer (see Figure 3-9).

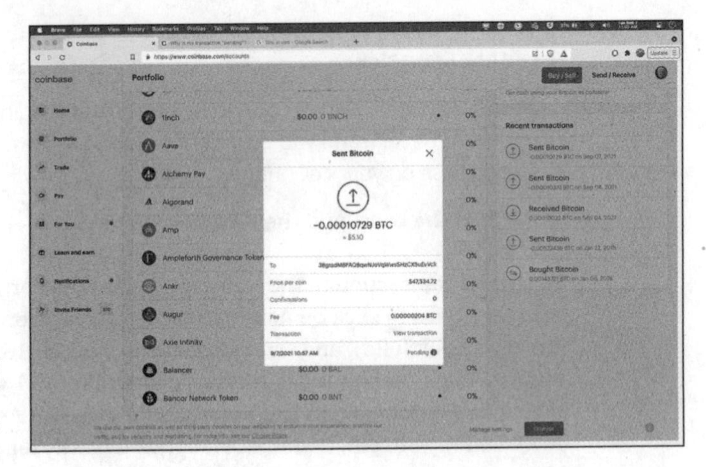

FIGURE 3-8: Your transaction, still pending.

And now, we're betting that you're saying, "Woah, what the &^%!! is that? Surely we're sending five bucks from one blockchain address to another, aren't we?" Well, not quite.

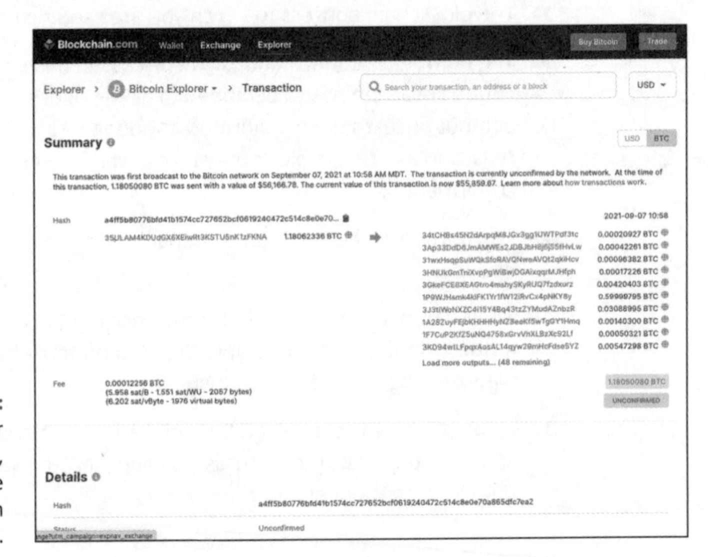

FIGURE 3-9: Your transaction, in the blockchain explorer.

On the left, you see the block's hash:

```
a4ff5b80776bfd41b1574cc727652bcf0619240472c514c8e
  0e70a865dfc7ea2
```

We introduce the hash in Chapter 2; it's a kind of fingerprint that uniquely identifies the block of transactions. Below that is an address:

```
35ULAM4KDUdGX6XEiwRt3KSTU5nK1zFKNA
```

This is where the Bitcoin is coming from; it's one of Coinbase's blockchain addresses. It can be interesting to dig around in blockchain explorers and see what you can find. Click on that address to see a page that shows the history of the address; it used to hold 1.18062336 BTC ($55,865.47), and in fact that's the exact sum "spent" in the current transaction, as shown on the right of the address in Figure 3-9.

On the left in Figure 3-9 is the input to the transactions. On the right are the outputs, the various addresses to which the Bitcoin is being sent. This is obviously more than a paltry five-dollar transaction (it's more than 11,000 times that).

In fact, if you look closely at the addresses on the right, you won't even see the address from Step 2 of the previous steps (3BgtadMBFAQBqwNJoVqWwsSHzCX5uEvVck). To see that, click the "Load more outputs" link several times until the list expands to include that transaction. (Click on the address to see information about that address.)

So, here's what's going on: When you set up a Coinbase wallet and buy Bitcoin, your Bitcoin is not associated with your own address in the blockchain. Rather, you own a small part of Coinbase's huge stash of Bitcoin, and Coinbase keeps track of how much of it is yours.

When you do a Send transaction, Coinbase bundles together your transaction with a bunch of other transactions, finds one of its addresses that has the sum of the addresses plus a little bit more, then sends a message to the blockchain with all the different transactions. For the money left over, part of the transaction returns the change. That is, the money left over after all those account holder transactions is sent to another address owned by Coinbase, which is known as, not surprisingly, a *change address.*

You can use this process to send your Bitcoin from Coinbase's combined account holders' stash to your very own Bitcoin address when you understand more about wallets.

Sending Bitcoin to the Coinbase wallet

You can also send Bitcoin from other wallets to Coinbase. We show you how with Coinme earlier in this chapter, and it's very similar for Coinbase.

Go to the Coinbase web app, and follow these steps:

1. **In the web app, click the Send/Receive button at the top and then click Receive. In the smartphone app, tap the two arrows at the bottom and then tap Receive.**

   The person sending you Bitcoin can scan the QR code directly into their wallet software. Clicking the Copy button in the smartphone app (in the web app, it's a small icon showing two overlapping rectangles) lets you copy the address and then email it or text it, or copy it directly into another program. The smartphone app also has a Share Address button that lets you drop the address into another app so you can send it directly through email, or text, or whatever.

   WARNING

   Don't type the address! One mistyped character and the Bitcoin is gone forever.

2. **Click Share Address and wait for your Bitcoin to come in.**

Now you own an address on the Bitcoin blockchain, right? Well, not so fast. Um, no this is an address under the control of Coinbase. It's Coinbase's private keys; whoever has the keys, owns the money! Legally, you own that Bitcoin — or at least a share of the Bitcoin that Coinbase owns, equal to the amount just sent to the address — but it's in the custody of Coinbase.

If you go to a blockchain explorer later in the day, you'll probably find "your" address is already empty. Coinbase bundles up Bitcoin from numerous individual account holders' addresses — hundreds at a time — and combines them into a larger bundle on a single address. Within minutes of his five-dollar receipt, Peter's address was empty and the five bucks ended up being combined with more than 400 other transactions, on an address holding a third of a million dollars' worth of Bitcoin.

How to find the best exchange rate

When you get started with Bitcoin, ease of use is really important. As you learn more, however, you may naturally want to focus on getting the very best deal when you buy your Bitcoin. After all, where you buy can have a huge effect on how much Bitcoin you get for your money. You've seen how expensive buying from an ATM can be, for instance, but even among the top, reputable exchanges, you'll get more Bitcoin for your buck at some than at others, though the difference is often not huge. Some of the smaller, less reputable exchanges, are expensive but some may offer a good deal.

Co-author Tyler Bain likes River.com, SwanBitcoin.com, Kraken.com, Coinbase.com, Strike.me, and Cash.app. How do you know which exchange provides the best deal? We haven't yet found a service that ranks exchanges by value for money. You can easily find lists of exchanges, perhaps even ranking them, showing how much they charge in fees. And BitcoinAverage has a handy list (`https://Bitcoinaverage.com/en/currency-markets/btc-to-usd`) comparing exchange rates between numerous exchanges. But you can't find the best deal by looking just at fees or just at exchange rates. How much Bitcoin you get for your buck is a function of two things:

- How much is charged as fees
- What the dollar/Bitcoin exchange rate is

Coinme "only" charges a 4% fee (you'll find that the exchanges have much lower fees), but they also adjust their exchange rate to take another seven or eight percent. That is, they sell Bitcoin at an inflated price. The Bitcoin exchanges also have varying exchange rates, with some exchanges being more favorable to you than others.

As mentioned, you can't just look at fees and ignore the exchange rate (after all, *most* of Coinme's earnings come from the exchange rate, not the fees). The only way to be sure about which exchange has the best price, is to compare carefully. Look at the exchange rate, and all the fees, based on the size of transaction you're going to make. Fees may vary depending on the value of the trade, with smaller trades being charged a higher percentage. For instance, a $100 trade may be charged $2.50 — 2.5%, of course — while a $500 trade may be charged $7.50 (1.5%). In some cases, *how* you pay the fees also affects how much you pay. For example, the Binance exchange has its own cryptocurrency, Binance Coin (BNB); if you pay your fees in BNB, you get a lower rate.

We checked trades at four major exchanges that are available to U.S. customers: Coinbase, Gemini, BlockFi, and Binance. We checked pricing at the exact same time, and then figured out fees for a $500 trade. (We assumed that we would have $500 to spend, and so subtracted the fees from the $500 and then converted the remainder into Bitcoin.) We then figured out how many Satoshi we'd get for our $500, sorted Table 3-1 from best to worst, and calculated the different percentages so that you can see how they compare against the best price.

TABLE 3-1 $500 Trades Compared

Exchange	1 BTC=Dollars	Fees	Satoshi	Percent of Best
BlockFi	$52,467.78	$0	952,966	100%
Binance.US	$52,470.51	$3.75	945,769	99.25%
Gemini	$52,477.51	$7.45	938,593	98.49%
Coinbase	$52,509.28	$7.34	938,234	98.45%

The difference isn't huge, about one-and-a-half percent from the top to the bottom. In other words, Coinbase, on a $500 trade, would provide you with 1.55% *less* Bitcoin than BlockFi. (At least at that particular time and day; things change.) One way to look at this is to consider that if we assume BlockFi, the best in the table, sold us $500 worth of Bitcoin, then Coinbase sold us only $492.25 worth of Bitcoin for $500.

Still, price isn't everything. Ease of use is important, and Coinbase has a special, unusual advantage: the Bitcoin is, at least partially, insured. (Note that if someone steals your Coinbase password from you, your Bitcoin is not covered! In other words, the insurance partially covers Coinbase getting hacked, but not *you* getting hacked.)

REMEMBER

When comparing exchange rates showing how many dollars it costs to buy a Bitcoin, you are, of course, looking for the lower numbers. Smaller dollar numbers mean more Bitcoin (or Satoshi) per dollar. An exchange rate of $52,267.78 to the dollar means each dollar is worth 1,913 sats; an exchange rate of $52,509.28 is 1,904 sats.

Different types of exchanges

We describe Coinbase and Coinme (which, in effect, is a form of exchange) in the previous sections. Exchanges come in essentially two categories (with lots of permutations).

- **Brokers:** At these exchanges, the exchange itself owns the Bitcoin, and sells it to you or buys it back from you. The exchange often holds the Bitcoin, and you own a portion of the holdings. Coinbase is a broker exchange.
- **Trading platforms:** These exchanges connect buyers with sellers. They facilitate the transaction, generally holding the funds in escrow while the transaction completes. Binance, Bitstamp, and ShapeShift are trading platforms.

Most of the brokers provide you with a wallet; some of the trading platforms expect you to have your own wallet (ShapeShift, for instance), while others (such as Bitstamp) provide a wallet, though, of course, they also allow you to transfer to your own wallet.

Exchange brokers make money through a combination of fees and the "spread" between the buy and sell prices. Just like the foreign-exchange desks at international airports, the price to buy Bitcoin from them is higher than the price to sell to them. For instance, we just checked Coinbase, and if we buy one Bitcoin from them, it will cost us $46,594.61. But if we sell a Bitcoin back to Coinbase, we'll earn $46,072.93. So, if they buy from us, and sell to you, they make about 1.1%, before their fees. (They charge fees for both buying and selling.)

As for the trading platforms, the price is set by you and the other party, and the platform makes money by taking a cut of the transaction: a fee.

You can find far more advanced exchanges and trading platforms than Coinbase, platforms designed for serious and professional traders. Here are a few well-known and reputable systems.

- Kraken: `www.kraken.com`
- Poloniex: `www.poloniex.com`
- Gemini: `www.gemini.com`
- BitMEX: `www.bitmex.com`
- Bitstamp: `www.bitstamp.net`
- Binance: `www.binance.com`
- FTX: `www.ftx.us`
- ShapeShift: `www.shapeshift.com`

Coinbase also offers one of these more complex trading platforms, which allows users to place market, spot, or limit orders: Coinbase Pro (`https://pro.coinbase.com/`).

Not your keys, not your coins: The danger of exchanges

Before we move on, a quick word about why Bitcoin purists believe you *should not* leave your Bitcoin to be controlled by an exchange, and why you should manage your own wallet.

In February 2014, the world's leading exchange, a Japanese company named Mt. Gox, filed for bankruptcy, claiming that it had somehow lost 850,000 Bitcoins — today worth somewhere around $42 *billion* (back then, about $450 million, still nothing to sneeze at)! Over time, it was revealed that someone had been siphoning Bitcoin out of the exchange for a couple of years. Almost a quarter of the Bitcoin was eventually retrieved, but seven years later, more than three quarters have not.

Mt. Gox is not alone. Bitfinex (120,000 BTC stolen), Zaif (5,966 BTC), Altsbit (6,929 BTC, as well as a bunch of other cryptocurrencies), and *dozens* of other exchanges have been hacked, some losing Bitcoin, some losing other cryptocurrencies, some losing both.

QuadrigaCX is a Canadian exchange that lost 26,500 BTC, but wasn't hacked. When the owner died under strange circumstances, however (taking the exchange's private keys with him), account holders lost access to their Bitcoin, and discovered that in any case, much of the Bitcoin had been transferred out of the exchange a few months before his death. (Now the big question is *is he really dead*?) ShapeShift lost hundreds of thousands of dollars' worth of Bitcoin to an "inside job."

"How can this happen?" we hear you asking. "If cryptocurrency is so darn crypto, how can it possibly be hacked? Isn't the blockchain unhackable?"

Yes, it is. But these exchanges aren't. As long as the private keys that control the addresses are safe, the addresses — and the Bitcoin assigned to those addresses — are safe, too.

But the private keys have to be kept somewhere, they have to be managed by software, and the software has to be under the control of someone. So if you hack into the systems that control the private keys, then that gives you control over the addresses and the Bitcoin, too. *Not your keys, not your coins!*

Now, exchanges are certainly getting better (though a dozen were hacked in 2019, and at least one in 2020). And some, of course, are better than others. It's likely that Coinbase, for instance, invests a lot in protection. Some exchanges save large amounts of their Bitcoin in "cold wallets," which cannot be hacked into because they are "offline." Coinbase claims that 98 to 99 percent of all its crypto is stored in such wallets. And a portion of the rest is insured.

But still, this is why, according to the Bitcoin purists, you need to have your own wallets and manage your own private keys. Managing your own keys may reduce the risk of hacking and theft — but it doesn't eliminate it. And it does dramatically increase the risk of *loss* — of losing your keys, and thus losing access to the blockchain address and your Bitcoin.

Coinbase states that "In case of a covered security event, we will endeavor to make you whole. However, total losses may exceed insurance recoveries so your funds may still be lost." This is an interesting situation. While you don't directly own Bitcoin at Coinbase — you own a portion of the overall Coinbase holdings — in the event of a big hack, you would lose "your" Bitcoin.

Chapter 5 can help you take total control and manage your own blockchain addresses, by managing your own wallet. We're not saying you *have* to do this; it's a choice you have to make. In some cases, leaving your Bitcoin on a well-managed, insured exchange may actually be safer than managing your own wallet, and the inherent problems with doing so.

"Bitcoin Back" on Credit and Debit Cards

You've seen credit cards that pay you bonuses in airline miles, or cash back. Well, how about Bitcoin? Every time you buy gas or go out for dinner, you can earn a few Satoshis. In fact, this is becoming popular with exchanges, some of which have their own credit cards. Consider the four big exchanges that we mention in the preceding sections. Gemini has a credit card coming soon, giving up to 3% Bitcoin back on purchases; BlockFi already has a Visa credit card, giving 1.5% back; Binance has a Visa card that supposedly gives up to 8% back on certain transactions; and Coinbase has a debit card paying up to 4% back when used through Apple Pay and Google Pay.

Some of these cards also allow you to *spend* your Bitcoin, too. When you buy something in dollars, the money is taken from your Bitcoin account and converted. Numerous other companies provide spending rewards. See, for instance, CoinCorner.com, FoldApp.com, Lolli.com, and Stekking.com.

Earning Your Bitcoin

One of the more recent trends in the Bitcoin market is folks demanding to be compensated for their work in Bitcoin instead of their local currency. From everyday workers, skilled laborers, and tradespeople to celebrities and professional athletes, everyone's getting in on the game. It was widely reported, late in 2020, that Russell Okung, an offensive lineman for the Carolina Panthers, was taking part of his salary — half of his $13 million! — in Bitcoin. Search Google or Twitter for *#paymeinBitcoin* and you'll find plenty of activity in this area.

In fact, a number of companies are offering the service of managing the Bitcoin payment of employees. If you want to get paid in Bitcoin, check with one of these companies.

- **Bitwage:** `https://www.bitwage.com/`
- **Strike:** `https://strike.me/`

You would have your employer submit your payments to the company you work with, which then converts to Bitcoin and sends the Bitcoin on to you. There are also companies that claim to help people work on freelance projects for Bitcoin, such as these.

- **FreelanceForCoins:** `https://freelanceforcoins.com/`
- **WorkingForBitcoins:** `https://workingforBitcoins.com/`

These freelance-directory companies are unlikely to last, though; it's a case of the tail wagging the dog. Other sites have a far greater inventory of freelance jobs listed, and if enough demand builds for payment in Bitcoin, those companies — the Upworks of the world — will do it, putting these two out of business.

WARNING

We must mention one teensy problem with this whole pay-for-Bitcoin thing: Paying employees in Bitcoin may not be legal. Certainly, demanding that employees accept Bitcoin as payment is not legal. But even if employees *want* to be paid in Bitcoin, it may still not be legal under the Fair Labor Standards Act, which specifies that wages must be paid "in cash or negotiable instrument payable at par." (And no, Bitcoin doesn't fit the definition of a "negotiable instrument" and obviously isn't cash.) Also, some states demand that wages be paid in "U.S. currency," though they often have exemptions. In Georgia, for instance, you don't have to pay your turpentine-industry employees with U.S. currency! (Turpentine is evidently a big thing in Georgia.) More usefully, Texas allows employees to opt out in writing and accept payment in another form.

Employers should only pay employees in Bitcoin if employees agree in writing (acknowledging awareness of the risks), and it's probably a good idea for employers to pay minimum base pay in U.S. currency. Having your pay submitted to an intermediary company, such as Bitwage or Strike, likely gets around these legal issues.

Mining Bitcoin

You've probably heard of the Bitcoin mines. Yep, Bitcoin is *mined*, not underground, but within computers. Bitcoin mining is very complicated, and most definitely not for the newbie. You really need to understand what you're doing, and to be pretty computer literate. To mine, you need advanced computer skills and the willingness to invest significant sums in equipment and electricity. If you want to become a mining master, check out Chapter 7.

Finding Bitcoin Everywhere

We went into depth with a couple of mechanisms through which you can buy Bitcoin: the ATMs and the major exchanges. But there's more. Bitcoin, it seems, is popping up everywhere. You can buy it through the Robinhood investment app. You can buy it through the PayPal app. You can buy it through the Venmo app. (These apps sell Bitcoin in the U.S. and not necessarily in your country.)

Your brokerage account may let you buy into Bitcoin funds (you're buying a share in a fund that invests in Bitcoin, not Bitcoin itself) or purchase Bitcoin futures. Very soon, you'll probably be able to buy it from your bank. Bitcoin is being picked up widely in the financial industry, which is why many people are confident that it will survive, thrive, and go up in value.

With most of these mechanisms, and with most of the "wallets" provided by such sources, you don't directly own any Bitcoin. Rather, you own a claim to a portion of that company's Bitcoin holdings. You don't have your own address in the blockchain. The wallet addresses belong to the company.

If you trust the organization you're working with to look after your concerns, and if the price of Bitcoin goes up, you will benefit. Bitcoin exchanges are doing their best to protect your Bitcoin, and the large companies are likely to "make customers whole" in the case of smallish hacks (as ShapeShift did in 2016). Still, hacks continue, in particular with the smaller, less-well-protected exchanges.

Selling Your Bitcoin

Selling your Bitcoin through an exchange where you bought it is generally easy. It's basically a matter of clicking the SELL button or tab and following the instructions.

But Bitcoin is money, and, of course, money can be used to buy stuff. We've shown you how to buy Bitcoin and also how to buy with it. For both Coinme and Coinbase, we'll now show you how to *send* Bitcoin to another party. That's essentially what you do when you buy something with Bitcoin. Generally, the process goes like this:

1. During the checkout process, the seller's software generates an address; this address "belongs" to your transaction, and none other.
2. You send Bitcoin to that address.
3. When the seller's software sees Bitcoin arrive at that address, it knows the payment has arrived and can complete the transaction.

There really aren't that many places you can buy things with Bitcoin. Not Amazon, not Starbucks, not Walmart. You could once buy Tesla cars with Bitcoin, but no longer. Many stores that jumped on the "buy with Bitcoin" bandwagon jumped off not long after. There's even the lovely story of the North American Bitcoin Conference in Miami, during January of 2018. With tickets at $1,000 each, the conference accepted cryptocurrency payments. . .until they didn't. They had to stop "Due to network congestion and manual processing." When it's too much hassle for a Bitcoin conference to take payments in Bitcoin, you know the problems are real!

The following list highlights three major problems with accepting Bitcoin for everyday transactions.

- **Volatility:** The value of Bitcoin can rise and fall very quickly, sometimes within minutes. Sellers don't like seeing payments suddenly drop in value during or soon after a sale.
- **Fees:** The buyer has to pay fees to the miners to have the transaction completed. While these fees are minimal for large transactions, they are a significant percentage of small transactions.
- **Time:** It can take time to process Bitcoin transactions, making it completely unworkable in many retail situations. If you can buy your coffee at Starbucks with a credit or debit card within about three seconds, you're not going to stand around while your coffee gets cold waiting for six Bitcoin confirmations! (However, see Chapter 4 for a discussion of the Lightning Network, which speeds up Bitcoin transactions and is growing dramatically.)

REMEMBER

The Bitcoin cryptocurrency is not a real currency, at least not yet. A *currency*, according to Google and the *Oxford English Dictionary*, is "a system of money in general use in a particular country." We would argue that Bitcoin is a system of money ("the assets, property, and resources owned by someone or something; wealth"), but it's by no means "in general use" in any country, let alone the United States.

Buying things with your Bitcoin doesn't make a lot of sense at the moment, any more than buying things with your gold makes sense. Currently, Bitcoin is a speculative asset, and there seem to be only two options: either Bitcoin survives and flourishes, in which case its price will rise as it gains acceptance by a wider swath of the public, or it won't. And thus:

1. If you believe Bitcoin will rise in value in the near future, then it makes sense to own some.
2. If it makes sense to own it — because you think it will rise in value — then why on earth would you use it to buy stuff?
3. If you don't believe Bitcoin will rise in value in the near future, it doesn't make sense to own it.
4. If you don't believe Bitcoin will rise in value in the near future, then why would you own it just so you can buy things with it, when other options for purchasing abound?

Most people who own Bitcoin see it as a way to make money. Buy it, hold it (*hodl* it, as they say in the Bitcoin world; see Chapter 4), and the price will go up. For this reason, most people who own Bitcoin don't want to use it to buy things. They already have plenty of ways to do that (cash, credit and debit cards, ACH, checks, PayPal, Zelle, Venmo, and so on).

We're reminded of the world's most expensive pizza. In 2010, when Bitcoin was worth next to nothing, Laszlo Hanyecz found a pizzeria willing to be paid in Bitcoin. He bought two pizzas from Papa John's — the particular style is lost to history, it appears — and paid *gulp* (if you excuse the pun!) 10,000 Bitcoin! As we write this, according to Google, those pizzas cost, in today's value, $468,368,000! At its peak price so far (and many believe it will go far higher), that pizza purchase was worth $640,000,000. (We'd love to know what happened to those 10,000 coins, and how much Mr. Hanyecz enjoyed his pizza!)

Certainly, there are Bitcoin enthusiasts who look forward to the day when Bitcoin takes over and everyone's using it for everything. But even most of these people still buy their beer and groceries with cash or credit cards. True believers are stockpiling Bitcoin, not using it for everyday purchases.

they do

» The different types of wallets, from brains to metal

» Where to find a wallet

» Working with BlueWallet

» Using the Lightning Network

Chapter 4

Taking Control of Your Wallet (and Hodling Your Bitcoin)

We show you how to buy and sell Bitcoin using other peoples' wallets — the *custodial wallets* of the exchanges — in Chapter 3. Here we show you how to manage your own wallet. Before we jump in, though, we start by talking about what a wallet actually *is* (because it's not entirely clear even to most Bitcoin owners).

HODL?

Okay, so it's a bit of Bitcoin jargon, a cryptocurrency joke. Instead of "holding" your Bitcoin, you — in Bitcoin parlance — *hodl* it. It all comes from a message posted in the Bitcoin talk forums (`https://bitcointalk.org/`) in 2013, from a forum member named GameKyuubi, explaining (reportedly while drunk) that he couldn't figure out the ups and downs of Bitcoin, and thus intended to simply hold (mistyped hodl) his Bitcoin for the long term. The long term has been good to GameKyuubi, if indeed he did hold long term. He created a widely used term in the Bitcoin community, and his Bitcoin went from an exchange rate of $716 per Bitcoin down to $438 and then, over the years, up to a peak (so far, at the time of this writing) of almost $64,000.

Bitcoin purists believe that unless you manage your own wallet, you don't truly own your Bitcoin. *Legally* you do own Bitcoin you buy from an exchange, for instance, even if it's held by the exchange and you use a custodial wallet provided by the exchange. That hasn't helped all the people who have had their Bitcoin stolen from exchanges! To really understand Bitcoin, and have total control over your Bitcoin, you need to understand wallets. You need to *hodl* (that is, hold) your own Bitcoin for yourself. (For more about hodl, see the sidebar, "Hodl?")

What Is a Wallet?

Physically, a wallet can be a number of things. It may be a piece of software running on a Windows PC, a Mac or Linux machine, or any number of other computer types. It may be a piece of software running on a web server or on a smartphone or tablet. But it may also be a small device similar to a USB thumb drive. It could even be a piece of paper, a piece of metal, or even a brain! What, then, defines a wallet?

Wallets store private keys

So here's the very basic thing about wallets (without this, they're not wallets): At the very least, a wallet holds one or more *private keys.* (Or at least a way to get to your keys. A wallet may hold a wallet *seed*, which allows you to rebuild a wallet and get to the private keys, as we'll explain in this chapter.)

Your Bitcoin is associated with an address (maybe multiple addresses) in the Bitcoin blockchain ledger. That address is mathemagically associated with a public key (see Chapter 5). And that public key is mathemagically associated with a private key.

The address is totally public, of course; anyone can see it. Remember the blockchain explorer from Chapter 3? You can dig around in the blockchain and see anybody's addresses. (You can't tell who each address belongs to, but you can see how much Bitcoin is associated with each address.)

But the associated public key is also totally public. It doesn't matter who has it or who sees it. In fact, as explained in Chapter 5, the public key is used to sign the messages that go to the blockchain, to prove ownership of the address.

So the single most important thing that a wallet does, is to store your private keys (or seed). As you'll learn reading this chapter, that's *all* some wallets do: store private keys. That's essential — lose the private key, and you've lost your Bitcoin. Lose your public key or address, and that's okay; you can always re-create them if you have the private key.

TIP

Although wallets store private keys, you may never see them. Some wallets, like the BlueWallet (which we look at later in this chapter), hide them from you. Others, such as Electrum, provide a way for you to find them.

Wallets create and store keys and addresses

Some wallets can be used to *create* private keys, public keys, and addresses, and to store these things. We're talking now about software wallets, of course.

Wallet software uses complex math to create your private keys — you'll see this in action later in this chapter — and from the private keys, it creates public keys, and then it creates addresses from the public keys; again, all three are mathematically associated.

Even if you have other forms of wallet, you need a software wallet to get started; that's where you'll get your private key to begin with.

Wallets communicate with the Bitcoin network

Software wallets are designed to help you communicate with the Bitcoin network, so you can adjust the Bitcoin ledger held in the blockchain. You do this by using your wallet software to send messages to the blockchain asking the network to transfer Bitcoin from your address to someone else's. If you sell some of your Bitcoin, for instance, you'll send a message to the network, saying, "Send a bit of my Bitcoin from my address to this other person's address."

Wallets provide a way for you to remember your address so someone else can send Bitcoin to your address, such as when you are buying Bitcoin. You don't really need a wallet to *receive* Bitcoin, of course; it's your address that receives the Bitcoin, not the wallet. So you can just store your address, or the QR code, outside the wallet, and tell people where to send money.

Wallets often create new addresses so that each time you receive Bitcoin, it goes to a different address. (Although not essential, this can be a good privacy practice; see Chapter 5, where we discuss security issues.)

Wallets can be hot or cold

There are two important classifications of wallets: hot and cold. The distinction is simple. A *hot wallet* is a software wallet of some kind operating on a computing device — a laptop, smartphone, or whatever — that is connected to the Internet.

A *cold wallet* is any kind of wallet — software, paper, metal, anything holding private keys — that is *not* connected to the Internet. If you have a smartphone with wallet software running on it, and your device is connected to a Wi-Fi hotspot, which in turn is connected to the Internet, that's a hot wallet.

A *paper wallet* is a piece of paper with a seed or private key written on it. It's a cold wallet because (obviously) it isn't connected to the Internet (and never will be).

Some people even use old computers to do nothing but run Bitcoin wallet software. Or they have dedicated hardware wallets that operate in conjunction with wallet software running on a computing device that is connected to the Internet. The hardware wallet itself stores the private keys, but is never connected to the Internet itself.

Why this distinction? It's all about the degree of security you want. A hot wallet can be hacked. For the moment, understand that cold wallets can't be hacked, because nobody can get to them across the Internet. (If you use weak passwords, perhaps a cold hardware wallet can still be "hacked" by someone who gets hold of the device, but at least it can't be hacked from afar.)

Companies with large amounts of Bitcoin often keep the bulk of it offline, in cold storage wallets. Coinbase, for instance, has something it calls the *vault*: cold wallets storing most of its Bitcoin (and probably in some kind of actual vault, too).

Exploring Wallet Hardware

So, any kind of wallet can be a cold wallet, and some can on occasion be hot wallets. But there's another type of categorization of wallets: the "hardware" the wallet is on. These are the different types of wallets you may hear about (and which we cover in this section): brain, paper, metal, hardware, web, dedicated full nodes, and software.

Brain wallets

The *brain wallet* is more theoretical than real or even practical. A brain wallet is a brain (your actual human brain) that stores (memorizes) a private key or a seed or mnemonic phrase.

(*Seeds* — a unique list of a dozen or a couple of dozen short words — are used to *create* private keys, so if you save the seed, you can always re-create the private key. This concept becomes clearer when you see it in action; see the section, "Creating and securing your first wallet," later in this chapter, for more information.)

Brain wallets are, quite frankly, a terrible idea. If you have the world's best memory — if you can lock this kind of thing into your "brain vault" and are able to retrieve it months or years later — then perhaps it's practical. But what happens if you're hit by the proverbial bus? If you're the only person who knows the private key or seed, the Bitcoin dies with you! So much for passing on an inheritance.

This is also a problem if you, and only you, have the passwords to your software wallets. In Chapter 5, we talk about how to get around the problem of lost passwords, seeds, and private keys after one's death. You want to be able to pass on the necessary info when you get hit by that bus, but keep it safe until you shuffle off this mortal coil.

Paper wallets

A *paper wallet* is, you guessed it, a piece of paper with the private key — or maybe just the *seed* — written down.

Here's the problem with paper wallets. Paper is vulnerable. It can be lost, it can burn, it can be ruined by water, it can be easily stolen. You can eliminate the physical vulnerability problems by using multiple paper wallets, of course, but then you increase the risk of theft. They are, quite frankly, not a great idea.

Metal wallets

One way around the physical vulnerability of a paper wallet is to replace the paper with metal! It won't burn, nor will it be destroyed when the pipes burst and your home floods. But it still has the problem that you need duplicates, which increases the likelihood of theft.

There are companies selling metal-wallet kits, generally designed to save the seed (see Figure 4-1), that come with a selection of characters that you can use to string together the mnemonic words. Still these are not a great idea. They are often expensive — some not so much, perhaps — and one is not enough, of course.

FIGURE 4-1: The Cryptotag metal wallet kit (`www.cryptotag.io`).

Here are a few options:

- Billfodl: `https://billfodl.com/products/the-billfodl`
- Blockplate: `https://www.blockplate.com`
- Coldbit Steel: `https://coldbit.com/product/coldbit-steel`
- Cryptotag: `https://www.cryptotag.io`
- Cryptsteel Capsule: `https://cryptosteel.com/`
- CypherWheel: `https://cyphersafe.io/product/cypherwheel/`
- Key Stack: `https://cryptokeystack.com`
- Seedplate: `https://bitcoinseedbackup.com`

Hardware wallets

A *hardware wallet* is a small, dedicated computing device that runs wallet software. You can create your own hardware wallet by getting a dedicated device — a laptop or desktop computer, a smartphone, or a tablet — installing wallet software on it, and using that device solely as a wallet. Keep it turned off most of the time, and it's a cold wallet, too. (You'll often hear the term *air-gapped* to describe these things, because there's a gap — nothing but air — between the device and the Internet.)

A number of companies make dedicated hardware wallets, too. Some more recent hardware wallets are designed with two parts: One part connects to the Internet to send a transaction message to the Bitcoin network, and the other part stores the private key. The part storing the private key is never connected to the Internet, and thus cannot be easily hacked. The Ellipal device shown in Figure 4-2 functions in this manner.

We don't describe these devices in this book, but we provide enough information for you to get a good understanding of what wallets are and how they work. So, if you do decide you want one of these hardware wallets, the vendor's instructions will be enough to get you started.

FIGURE 4-2: An Ellipal hardware wallet.

WARNING

Be careful where you buy your wallet. Scammers have bought hardware wallets, opened them up, replaced the instructions with their own, repackaged them, and then sold them on eBay and Craigslist. Unsuspecting and not-so-knowledgeable buyers have then followed the instructions, which direct the user to enter a particular "seed" that creates the seller's private key on the device. Then, when the buyer of the device sends Bitcoin to the address associated with the key, the seller quickly sweeps the Bitcoin away from the address! (This will all make sense when you understand what the seed is, which you will soon.)

Here are a few popular hardware wallets:

- BitBox02: `https://shiftcrypto.ch/bitbox02`
- Coldcard: `https://coldcardwallet.com`
- CoolWallet: `https://coolwallet.io`
- Ellipal: `https://www.ellipal.com`
- KeepKey: `https://shapeshift.io/keepkey`
- Ledger: `https://shop.ledger.com/products/ledger-nano-s`
- Trezor: `https://shop.trezor.io/product/trezor-model-t`

Web wallets

We show you how to set up a form of web wallet in Chapter 3, but that's a custodial wallet provided by an exchange, in this case Coinbase. What we're talking about here are websites where you can create an account and get a wallet that is accessible through your web browser.

WARNING

This is a pretty terrible idea. You *really* have to trust the website. Not only do the site owners need to be legitimate — and web-wallet sites have been set up to scam Bitcoin owners — but they also have to be extremely capable, providing wallet software that protects you against dishonest employees of the site and external hackers. An additional danger is that the site could go out of business, taking your private keys with it. We recommend you stay away from these.

Dedicated full nodes

Dedicated full nodes are full peers on the Bitcoin network running your own Bitcoin nodes. A node can be anything from a laptop running the Bitcoin core software (`https://bitcoin.org`), or as cheap and simple as a mini-computer Raspberry Pi running Raspiblitz (`https://raspiblitz.com/`).

This is not beginners' stuff, though, so it definitely shouldn't be your first step into the world of Bitcoin wallets. Just in case you want to learn more, though, we provide a few resources.

Dedicated hardware full nodes

Some companies sell dedicated hardware specifically designed to run Bitcoin node software right out of the box; here are a few options.

- Lightning in a Box: `https://lightninginabox.co/shop`
- myNode One: `http://mynodebtc.com/products/one`
- Nodl: `https://www.nodl.it`
- The Bitcoin Machine: `https://thebitcoinmachines.com`
- Embassy: `https://start9labs.com`

Full-node software

And here are a few software resources you may want to check out.

- Bcoin: `https://github.com/bcoin-org/bcoin/releases`
- BitcoinCore: `https://bitcoin.org/en/download`
- Blockcore: `https://github.com/block-core/blockcore/releases`
- Libbitcoin: `https://github.com/libbitcoin/libbitcoin-node/releases`
- RaspiBolt: `https://stadicus.github.io/RaspiBolt`
- Samourai Dojo: `https://samouraiwallet.com/dojo`
- Umbrel: `https://getumbrel.com`

Software wallets

A *software wallet* is simply a computer program — usually running on a Windows PC, Mac computer, Linux computer, iOS device, or Android device — that saves your keys and addresses, and enables you to communicate with the Bitcoin network. Even if you have a hardware wallet, there's a software wallet running on it.

Finding a Wallet

For the rest of this chapter, we focus on software wallets. If you like the idea of the other wallet types, you can do a little research to learn more about them. But, regardless of which wallet type you use, remember the following:

- **At some point, you must have a hot software wallet.** That's the device you're going to use to communicate your transactions to the Bitcoin network.
- **You must have a way to save the important information — private key or seed — in multiple locations.** If you save this critical information in one location, it can be destroyed, by fire, flood, computer failure, and so on. Many Bitcoin owners have lost their Bitcoin because they stored this essential information in only a single location and lost access to it. If they had just one more location, they could have recovered their Bitcoin. (Two more locations would be better.)
- **You must have a way to save the important information, so other people cannot steal it.** Many Bitcoin owners have lost their Bitcoin because they stored this essential information insecurely — on paper wallets, for instance — and had the information stolen by someone who stumbled upon it.

REMEMBER

Another quick technical issue. We're looking at two things: first, wallet *software*; and second, the actual wallet, which is a file opened and managed by the software program. People (even us) often use the term *wallet* to mean the software, but the actual wallet is the file holding your information — private keys, public keys, addresses, and so on. The wallet software we're going to use allows you to create multiple individual wallets, and the data in each wallet is stored in a separate file.

So where do you get a wallet? As with everything else Bitcoin, it's not a simple answer. We're recommending the BlueWallet — and using it here as an example — which is very well known, popular, and widely used. So you might start there. But many wallet programs are available, with different features and usability. You may have a friend who recommends something else, for instance.

TIP

Be careful that the software you use is safe, and widely reviewed and audited by the Bitcoin community. There have been many scams, such as Bitcoin-wallet software with "backdoors" that allow the software publisher to access your private keys. We recommend that you pick software that has been recommended by a reputable source. Not by your friend Joe, because he's just an individual who may himself have been tricked into picking something unsafe. Only use software that is, well, well known, popular, and widely used.

One good source is Bitcoin.org; this is the original Bitcoin website set up by Satashi Nakamoto, and it recommends a variety of wallet programs. It even provides a wizard that asks you various questions and lists the wallet programs that match your answers (`https://bitcoin.org/en/choose-your-wallet`). You might also check `https://bitcoin-only.com/wallets` and `https://www.lopp.net/bitcoin-information/recommended-wallets.html`.

Here are a few things you need to be concerned with, and some features you may find useful.

- **Operating system:** Wallet software is mostly available for Android devices, iOS devices, Windows, macOS, and Linux. Not all programs are available for all the operating systems, so decide which operating system you're going to use first.
- **Multiple operating systems:** You may want to run the wallet software on both a mobile device and your laptop or desktop, so it would be best to have a program that runs

on both your systems. (You can use different wallet software on different devices, but for simplicity's sake, you'll most likely want to use the same software.)

- **HD wallets:** Make sure you get an HD — hierarchical deterministic — wallet program. HD wallet programs use "seeds." Most wallet programs these days create HD wallets.

  A *hierarchical deterministic wallet* is the type of wallet that you really should use, because it adds a layer of security. If it has a *seed* — a list of words — then it's an HD wallet. And this seed can help you rebuild your wallet if you run into problems. You can even enter the seed into different wallet software on a different device and recover your transactions and access to your Bitcoin. If the device on which you installed your wallet is destroyed, or lost or stolen, as long as you have your seed saved somewhere, all is not lost! You can recover everything. (Try doing that with the money under your mattress when your house burns down! We said this cryptocurrency thing was magic, eh?)

- **Multi-sig wallets:** Some programs have a function that allows you to create *multi-sig wallets,* wallets that cannot be used to send transactions to the Bitcoin network unless two or more people, using two or more wallet programs, agree. That is, there must be multiple signatures to complete the transaction. Check out the section, "Understanding multi-sig wallets," later in this chapter, to learn more about them.

- **2FA:** A 2-factor authentication wallet program requires that you provide a code the software sends you (via text, or that you get from an authentication program) after logging in. Not all wallet programs have this, as it requires a 2FA server, and the programs that do have it — such as Electrum — may charge a fee to use the server.

- **Core wallets:** These are wallets that are full nodes on the blockchain; they contain much or all of the blockchain — a huge amount of data — but have a direct connection to the Bitcoin network and validate transactions. We don't recommend these for beginners and don't cover them in this book.

Setting Up a Bitcoin Wallet

In this section, we show you how to set up and work with a very popular wallet, the BlueWallet, which is available in various flavors. You can run it on your Android smartphone or tablet, your iPhone or other iOS device, or on a Mac, Windows, or Linux PC. So you can take your pick.

We're using the Mac app as an example, but the various versions work much the same way; the screen layout for each is slightly different, but your options are similar.

Creating and securing your first wallet

You can have multiple wallets; you may start with one wallet for testing and later create another wallet for your personal Bitcoin investments, another for Bitcoin you've invested for your children, and so on.

To create a wallet using BlueWallet, follow these steps:

1. **Go to `https://bluewallet.io/` and download and install the version you want to work with.**

   You can run it on multiple devices if you like; we show you how to duplicate your wallets on two or more devices, such as your laptop and your smartphone.

2. **Start the software; you see a screen like that shown in Figure 4-3 (in the Mac version).**

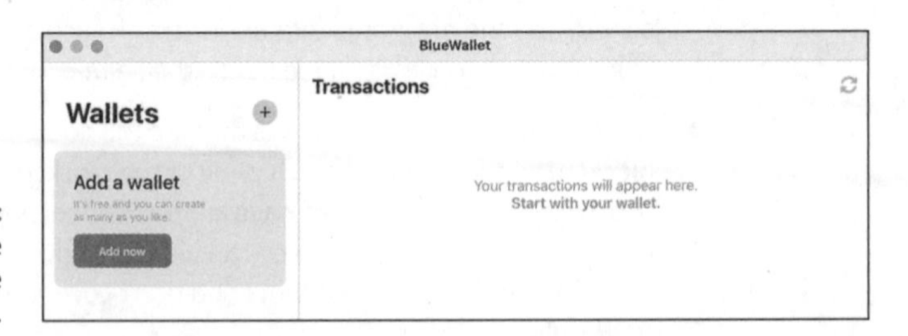

FIGURE 4-3: The Blue home screen.

3. **Click the + button (top right) or click the blue Add Now button.**

   The screen shown on left in Figure 4-4 appears, giving you three choices.

   - **Bitcoin wallets:** You know what these are, and this is the type we're going to work with right now.
   - **Lightning wallets:** These are for use on the Lightning Network, which interfaces with the Bitcoin network to help speed up transactions and reduce transaction fees. See the section, "Using the Lightning Network," later in this chapter, for more information.
   - **Vault wallets:** This option is used to create a multi-sig wallet, a wallet that works in combination with one or more other wallets. See the section, "Creating a multiple-sig wallet," later in this chapter, to learn more.

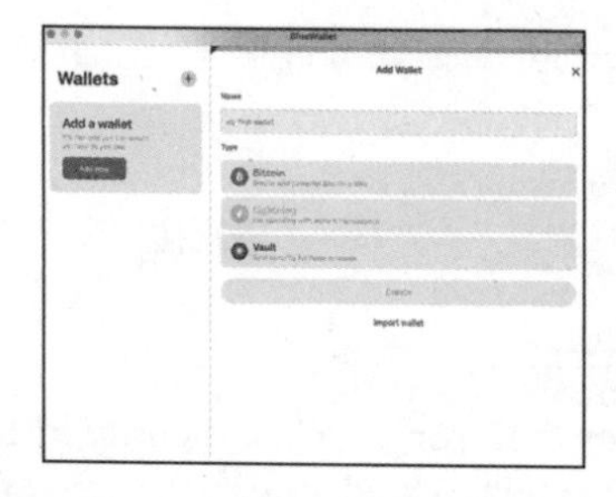

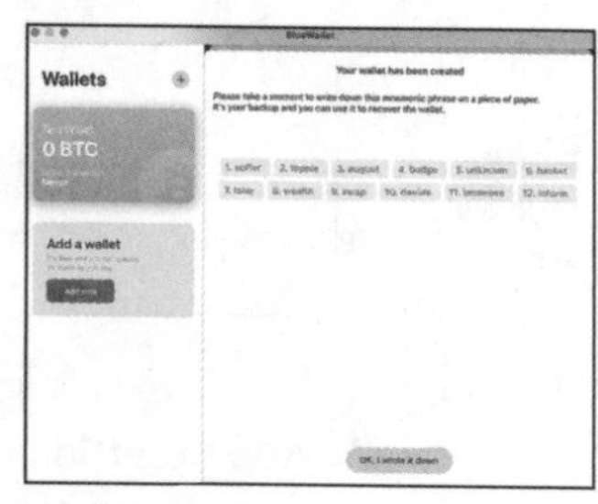

FIGURE 4-4: Picking your wallet type and saving your seed.

4. **Type a wallet name, click Bitcoin, and click Create at the bottom.**

   The screen shown on the right in Figure 4-4 appears. This screen contains your *seed:* a series of 12 words. The seed is as important to you as the private key, maybe *more* important. (Although this is generally called a seed in the Bitcoin world, Blue calls it both a *mnemonic phrase* and a *backup phrase.*)

   There are two critical things you must do with this seed:

   - *Do not forget or lose it!*
   - *Do not let it fall into the wrong hands.*

5. **Write down your seed and store it in a safe place; then click the OK I Wrote it Down button at the bottom.**

   You've created your wallet. An empty transaction screen appears (see Figure 4-5), and your wallet is ready to be used.

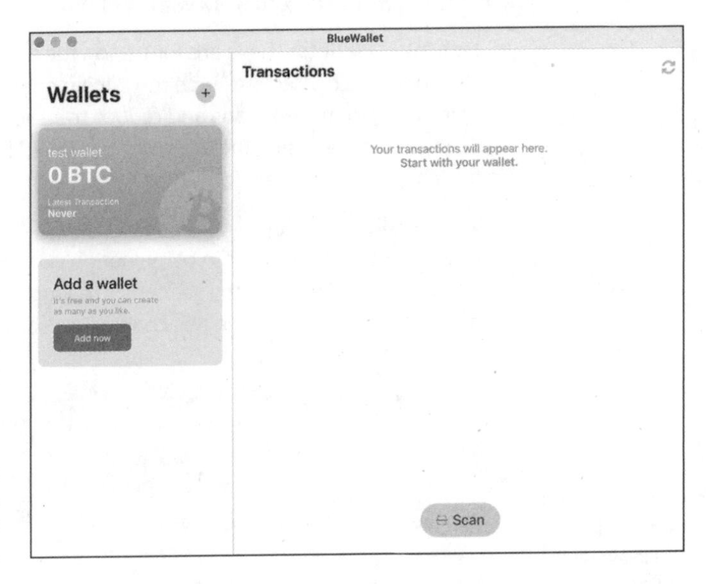

FIGURE 4-5: Your wallet, ready for work.

6. **Go to Settings or Preferences, click Security, click Encrypted and Password Protected, and enter the password twice.**

   You need to save that password carefully, too, along with your seed, in a password-management program (which you can read about in Chapter 5).

DIGGING INTO SEED ORIGINS

The seed is simply a list of words randomly taken from a particular dictionary of 2,048 terms. The program creates this list of terms and then runs the list through a mathematical algorithm that math-emagically creates your private key. Enough words are in the list that they can be combined in different orders, and the chance of you getting the same combination as someone else is essentially zero.

The seed is an important element, so here are a few more notes about it:

- **You must secure your seed.** The program advises that you write it down, and perhaps that's fine for a while. Ideally, it needs to be saved securely so you can't lose it, and nobody else can find it (unless you want them to have it).

  There are a couple of theories about this. Co-author Tyler suggests storing the seed in a metal wallet that you keep in a safe place. Co-author Peter likes the idea of using a password-management program. No solution is perfect, and both have problems. Metal wallets can't be hacked across the Internet, of course, but you'll need at least two, each stored in a different location. Password management programs are necessarily connected to the Internet, which Bitcoin purists don't like.
- **You need to decide how to pass these wallets to family members in the event of your incapacitation or death.** Password-management programs provide an easy way to pass on the information (we explain how in Chapter 5), and duplication is easy, too. But if someone figures out your master password, you could be in trouble.
- **Some wallet software hides the private key because the seed can be used to re-create the private key.** The theory is that you don't *need* to see it, so showing it to you simply raises an unnecessary security risk. BlueWallet does not provide a way for you to see the raw private key.

Creating a 24-word seed

In the previous section, we show you how Blue automatically generates a seed for you, and in fact all HD wallets do this — using complex mathematics and cryptographic techniques that have names like elliptic curve multiplication and hashing. They do a very good job at randomly picking a seed. The words are selected randomly from a dictionary of 2,048 words, and the order in which they appear in the seed is also random, which means there are 2^{132} possible combinations. (What's that? Well, it's 5,444,517,870,735,020,000,000,000,000,000,000,000,000 combinations. Enough for you?)

THE GEEKY STUFF

By default, your wallet is going to be what is known as a SegWit HD (BIP84 Bech32 Native) wallet. It's a hierarchical deterministic (HD) wallet, so it creates multiple addresses for incoming transactions and uses the latest format of blockchain address, which can actually save you money on transaction fees. You can actually pick a couple of other formats. In the BlueWallet Preferences or Settings, select General and then Advanced Mode. Now, when you create a wallet, you can choose a type. But there's no need to do this unless you have a good reason and know what you're doing.

HD wallets have a single master private key, from which *child keys* can be created. Many wallet programs create a new address each time you want to receive Bitcoin. To do this, the wallet has to create a child private key, from which it then creates a public key, from which it creates the address. So, HD wallets have a single master private key, and numerous child private keys with associated public keys and addresses.

If you're working with popular wallet software or hardware, you can rely on the random generation of this seed as being unique, but some Bitcoin purists want a bit more. The wallets have defined ways to introduce randomness into the seed-generation process. In the past there have been concerns that if someone was able to duplicate the exact same conditions present in the device at the very moment the seed was created, it may be possible to regenerate the seed. This is essentially impossible, but some Bitcoin purists prefer the possibility to be *absolutely* impossible.

If you want to be *really* sure the seed generation is completely random, in a way that could not possibly be duplicated, you can, on many wallets, introduce *entropy* to the system before the seed is generated. Doing so sometimes results in not just a 12-word seed, but a 24-word seed (which you really don't need because your 12-word seed is just fine). Here's how to do this in Blue:

1. **On the Mac, select Preferences from the BlueWallet menu (in the Android app, tap the ellipsis ( ) menu in the top-right corner).**

2. **In Settings or Preferences, click General and then click the Advanced Mode switch to turn it on.**

   Now, when you create a new Bitcoin wallet, you see the additional options shown on the left in Figure 4-6.

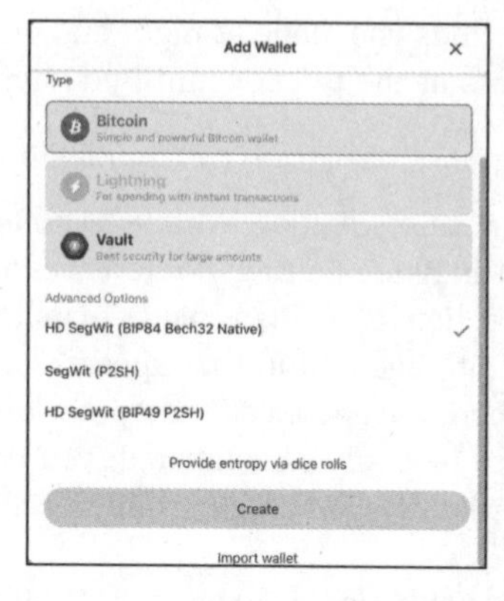

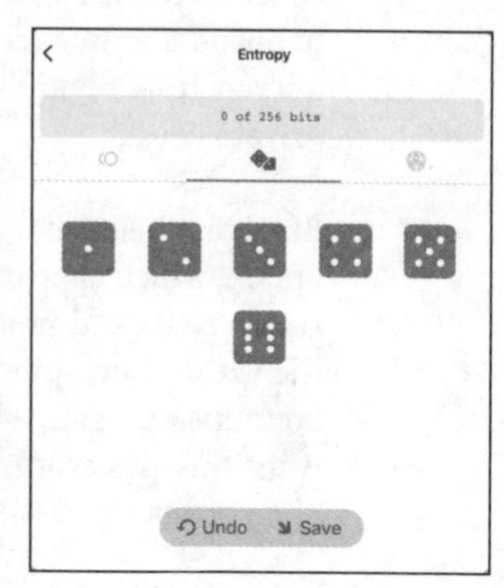

FIGURE 4-6: Advanced options enable you to add more randomness.

3. **Click the "provide entropy via dice rolls" link.**

   The screen shown on the right in Figure 4-6 appears.

4. **Click on these dice randomly, and you see the measure at the top (0 of 256 bits) increment each time you click.**

   You can also click on the little coin icon to the left of the dice icon under the count line, to see two coins, a head and a tail, on which you can randomly click as well. And there's also an icon to the right of the dice icon; click this, and you see 20 numbered boxes that you can click on.

5. **When you get to 256 of 256 bits, click Save.**
6. **In the Add Wallet box, click Create.**

   This time, a 24-word seed appears.

Increasing security with a fake account

One of the problems with Bitcoin is that it is very liquid, far more liquid than bank deposits. Suppose you have a few million dollars' worth of Bitcoin, managed by your BlueWallet program. And you also have a few million dollars in a bank account. Which can you move faster? Right, your Bitcoin.

Of course, the primary concern is hacking, and that's how most Bitcoin has been stolen over the years. But some folks have been concerned with what has been termed a *$5 wrench attack*: What happens if a mugger finds you alone at night and beats you with a wrench — regardless of the price — until you hand over your private keys?

Blue can help you in this situation with a *Plausible Deniability* option, which appears in Blue's Settings/Preferences area after you set up password protection. Click Plausible Deniability, then click the Create Encrypted Storage button that appears. The password box appears again, where you enter a *different* password, twice. You want this password to be easily remembered; you don't want to open up your password-management program to get to it.

Now, suppose one day you're forced to open BlueWallet. You enter your Plausible Deniability password, and the wallet opens, but it opens into the fake account. If you want to use this feature, you have to create a fake wallet with a little Bitcoin in it, so your deniability looks plausible!

Receiving Bitcoin

Until you have Bitcoin associated with one of your wallet addresses, it's actually not much of a wallet. So here we give you a quick look at how to send Bitcoin from another source to the wallet address. If you created a Coinme or Coinbase account — or both — you might send a little Bitcoin across just to experiment. Follow these steps:

1. **If the wallet you've created isn't already open, open it by clicking on the big Wallet icon.**

   The Transactions screen appears, as shown in Figure 4-7.

2. **Click the Receive button.**

   A QR code and notification question box appears, as shown in Figure 4-8.

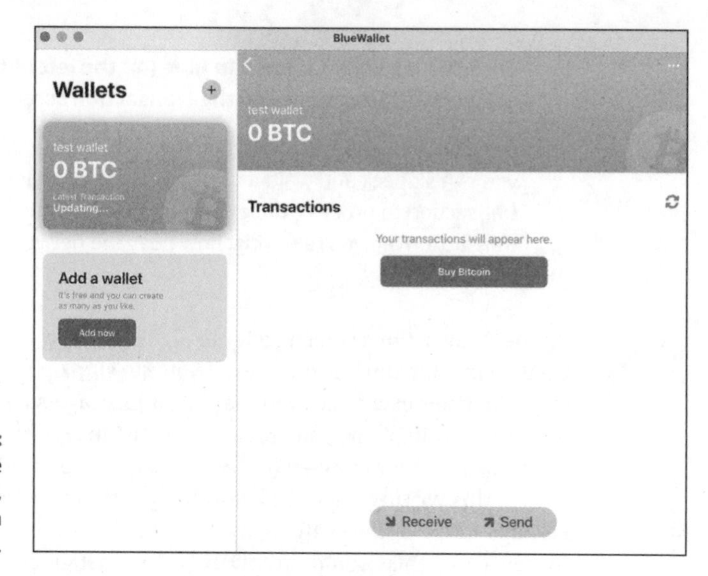

FIGURE 4-7: The BlueWallet, ready for a transaction.

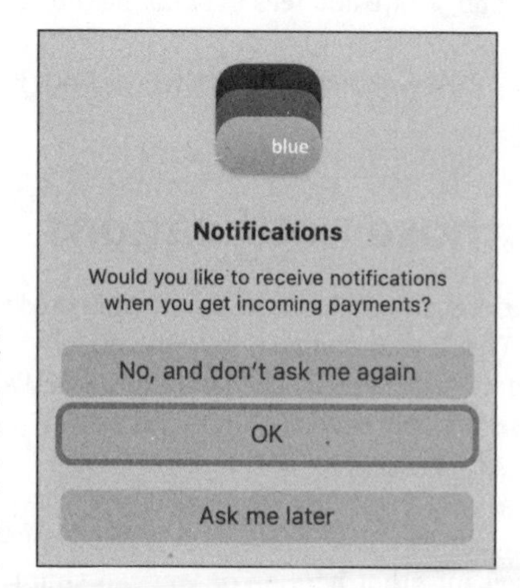

FIGURE 4-8: Tell Blue if you want to receive a notification when your Bitcoin arrives.

3. **Choose OK to have Blue check the blockchain now and then to see when the Bitcoin has arrived, and notify you.**

   Find out more about this issue in the next section, "Getting those notifications."

4. **Take a snap of the QR code with the wallet software from which you're going to transmit your Send message.**

   Alternatively, you can click on the address shown below the QR code to copy the address to your device's clipboard, and paste it into the other wallet.

5. **Click the big wallet button in Blue (on the left of the screen in Figure 4-7) to go back to the transaction screen.**

   Once you've sent the transaction from the other wallet, you can sit back and wait. It can take a little while for the transaction to process, depending on how much of a transaction fee you're paying, how busy the network is, and so on.

TIP

On the Transactions screen (refer to Figure 4-7), you can click the big blue Buy Bitcoin button to see if you can sign up for an account with a partner exchange; you may see a message saying the feature isn't available in your region. For instance, Blue may allow you to work with MoonPay (`https://www.moonpay.com/`). At the time of this writing, MoonPay won't sell within the United States. Perhaps a U.S. option will be available by the time you read this. In any case, this would simply be an exchange purchase, and MoonPay's exchange rate and fees may not be the best.

REMEMBER

As we caution you in Chapter 3, you need to check exchanges to find a good deal.

Getting those notifications

To get notifications, the wallet needs to be connected to an "Electrum server." That's your connection to the Bitcoin network, and through that network to the blockchain. Your BlueWallet talks to the Electrum server, and sends and receives information through that server.

You can set up your own Electrum server if you want — but we're not going to get into that here — or you can simply use Blue's own, default Electrum server. However, you may want to check the settings, because sometimes Blue has an intermittent problem with the connection.

Go to the wallet's Settings or Preferences, and click Network. Then click Electrum Server; the screen shown in Figure 4-9 appears. Under status, it shows the server is Connected. If it's not, try clicking the Offline Mode button to turn off the connection, then click it again to turn it back on, and the connection should reestablish. If that doesn't work, check your Internet connection.

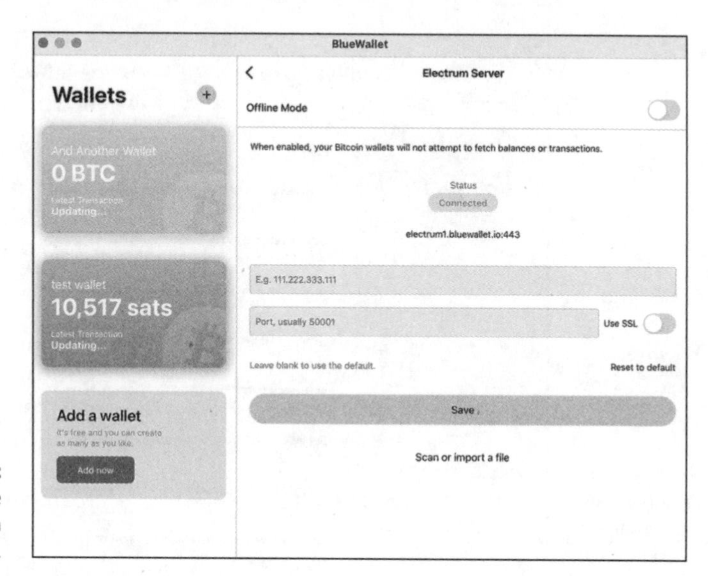

FIGURE 4-9: The Electrum connections.

You can ignore the text boxes. Those are for people who want to run their own Electrum server, which some Bitcoin fanatics do. Again, that's an advanced subject we don't cover in this book.

TIP

If you don't have notifications turned on, click the refresh button to the right of the Transactions heading in the wallet's main screen (the little circle created by two curved arrows). Clicking this button updates the transaction to show the number of confirmations received so far.

Checking your addresses

You can look at your wallet's addresses to see where in the blockchain your Bitcoin is stored. While viewing the wallet's main screen, click the little ellipsis ( ) menu in the top right to display the wallet's information screen. Click the "Show addresses" link just above the Export/Backup button, and you see the screen in Figure 4-10. You may enjoy checking the addresses page after sending Bitcoin to your wallet the first time. You'll see exactly where it is stored.

This screen shows you the addresses that have been created — more will be created as needed — and how much Bitcoin has been associated with each.

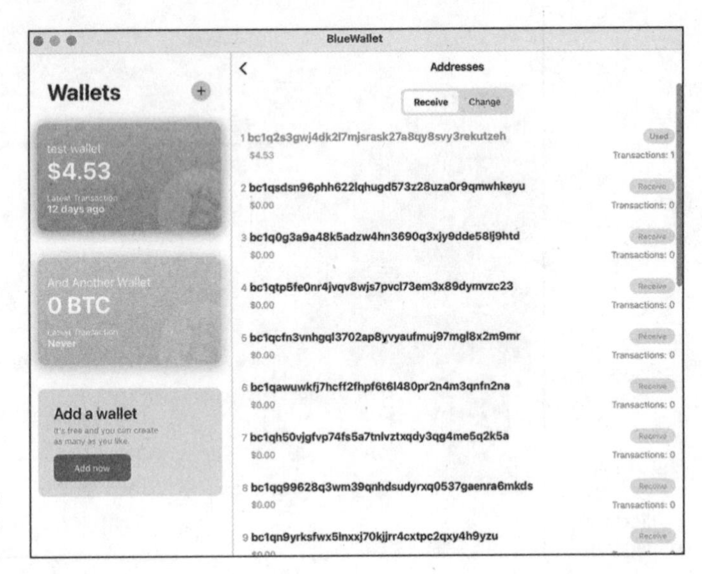

FIGURE 4-10: Your wallet's addresses.

Sending Bitcoin

Once you have Bitcoin in your wallet, you can experiment with the flip side: sending Bitcoin from the BlueWallet address to another wallet's address. Here are the steps:

1. **With the wallet open, click the Send button (refer to Figure 4-7) to see the Send screen (see Figure 4-11).**

   By now, you're probably getting comfortable with this.

2. **Enter a value into the number field at the top.**
3. **(Optional) Click the little vertical arrows button on the right side to change between Bitcoin, Satoshi, and dollars.**
4. **Paste a wallet address into the Address box, or click the little Scan button to use your smartphone's camera or laptop's webcam to scan it.**
5. **(Optional) Add a note to yourself — a reminder of the purpose of the transaction — that will appear in your transactions list.**

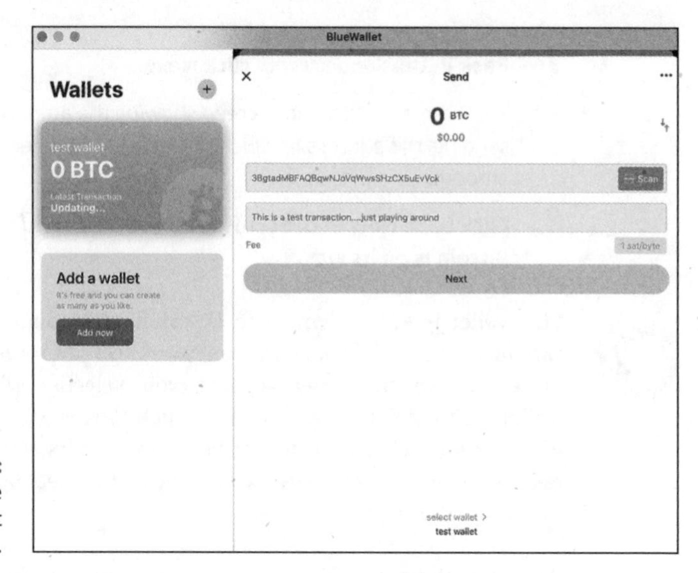

FIGURE 4-11: The BlueWallet Send screen.

6. **Click the little green button on the right side of the Fee line.**

   A box like that shown in Figure 4-12 appears (this time, shown in the Android app). You can determine the network or miner's fee you want to pay and choose how quickly the transaction should process: Fast, Medium, or Slow, from around 10 minutes to as much as a day.

TECHNICAL STUFF

The system shows you the cost in sats (Satoshis) per byte, which isn't terribly helpful. However, had we already entered a transaction value, in the left side of this box, you would see the fee translated into dollars. Fees can vary dramatically from moment to moment. You may pay 10 cents for fast processing now, and a couple of dollars in a few hours.

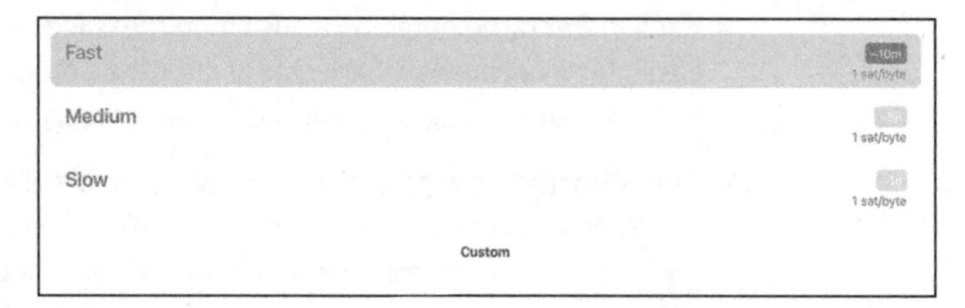

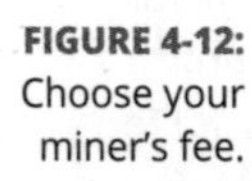

FIGURE 4-12: Choose your miner's fee.

7. **Back in the Send screen, click Next.**

   You'll see a confirmation screen showing the amount you're sending, the address to which it's going, and the fee amount.

8. **Click Send Now in the confirmation screen and the Bitcoin is on its way.**

TIP

The wallet is set to work with U.S. dollars by default, but you can pick whatever currency you want. Go into the Settings/ Preferences for the wallet software (your selection will affect all wallets managed by the software), click Currency, and click on your currency choice in the list box that appears. The exchange rate used by the software is currently provided by CoinDesk (`https://www.coindesk.com/`).

Regarding the network's or miner's fee, by default, *fee bumping* is turned on. If network conditions change, and the fee required for your selected speed of transaction goes up, the system can automatically bump up the fee you're willing to pay, to get the same service. If you don't like this, you can turn Allow Fee Bump off in the menu that appears if you click the little menu icon in the top right of the Send screen (see Figure 4-11).

A variety of other options are available to you in this menu.

- **Use Full Balance:** Send all the Bitcoin managed by this wallet.
- **Sign a Transaction:** This is used for signing multi-sig transactions, a subject we discuss in the later section, "Exploring multiple signature wallets."
- **Add/Remove a Recipient:** You can send multiple transactions in the same outgoing transaction message; doing so saves fees, because you are charged for the amount of data in your message, not the actual transaction value.
- **Coin Control:** You will eventually have Bitcoin assigned to different addresses managed by your wallet. Coin Control gives you some control over which address will be used for the transaction; you can *freeze* an address, so the Bitcoin

WARNING

associated with that address is not used, or select the Use Coin option to specify that a particular address should be used.

Be careful, though. If you find you can no longer send transactions, you may discover that you've frozen an address (coins are not frozen merely for the transaction you're working on, but for all transactions until you unfreeze the address).

TIP

If you have multiple wallets in the smartphone app, swipe right and left to switch between them. In the Mac app, it's a little more difficult. On the MacBook, a two-finger swipe on the trackpad with the mouse pointer above the Address box seems to do it.

Following the money

Don't be shocked, after sending Bitcoin somewhere, that all your Bitcoin seems to have disappeared when you check the Addresses screen (see Figure 4-12). Let's say you had an address with $100 worth of Bitcoin associated with it, you sent $5 worth to someone, and now the address has nothing! What gives?

Well, let's find out a little bit more about the idiosyncrasies of the Bitcoin blockchain. You need to understand UTXOs: *unspent transaction outputs,* which represent the amount of Bitcoin (or any cryptocurrency) that's left over after a transaction has fully completed.

When you send the transaction to the blockchain, the network takes *all* the Bitcoin from the output address, the address from which the Bitcoin is coming. It then sends the transaction amount to the recipient's address, takes out the miner's fee, and sends the rest of the Bitcoin — the unspent Bitcoin — back to an associated address, what is known as the *change address.* Refer to Figure 4-10, which is showing the Receive addresses for this transaction. Click on the Change button to see the change addresses. Figure 4-13 shows two change addresses. The first one has already been used; $1.34 is assigned to this address. The second one has not yet been used; it's been set up and is ready for the next send transaction.

FIGURE 4-13: Your change addresses.

Backing up your wallet

Keeping a backup of your wallet (or your wallets, if you have multiple wallets managed by Blue) helps you protect your Bitcoin (a subject we discuss further in Chapter 5). You may have already backed up your wallet; we suggest you do so when you first create the wallet. Similarly, Peter suggests that you save your seed (or mnemonic phrase or backup phrase, as Blue calls it) in a password-management program; Tyler recommends a metal wallet. One way or another, you should save this information, even if you write it on a piece of paper. That's not a great idea, but it's better than nothing.

If you didn't save the seed when you created the wallet, Blue provides a menu option so you can get back to it:

1. **Open the wallet, then click the ellipsis ( ) menu in the top right of the screen, which opens the screen shown on the left in Figure 4-14.**

   This screen shows you basic information about the wallet: the name and type of wallet, and so on.

2. **Click the Export/Backup button to see the box on right in Figure 4-14.**

   The seed is at the bottom of the box (you may have to scroll down), with the words appearing in a tiny row.

3. **If you haven't done so already, save this in a password program or write it down.**

   You can't copy it to the clipboard, so whether you write it on paper or type it into a password program, *do it very carefully and check then check again*. One small typo — type *kit* instead of *kite*, for instance — and the seed is useless. How can the seed be a "backup" of the wallet? Don't worry about that; we'll explain in a moment.

FIGURE 4-14: Checking out basic wallet info and the export info with a seed.

TIP

You could also take a screenshot of the screen shown on right in Figure 4-14 and print it or save it. (Note that this is a bad long-term security practice, although perhaps okay temporarily.) Of course, Figure 4-14 also shows a QR code; this encodes the seed, allowing you to import the wallet on another device, which we discuss in the next section. You'll be able to snap the QR code during the Import process.

Importing (or recovering) a wallet

Blue also provides a way to import a wallet from another program, which is the same process you can use to recover a lost wallet (which you can do because you saved your seed, right?).

For instance, perhaps you want to manage your Bitcoin on both your smartphone *and* your MacBook. You could create the wallet on one device, and import it into Blue on the other device. At that point, you would have two wallet programs, each capable of sending transactions to the network, and each tracking transactions on the same addresses.

If your BlueWallet is on your iPhone, and it's stolen, you can recover the wallet on your *new* iPhone, or any other device on which Blue runs: Mac, Windows, Android, or Linux. You can even recover your wallet on some other wallet programs, too, such as the Electrum wallet. Here's how:

1. **In the main BlueWallet screen, click the Add Now button (refer to Figure 4-3).**
2. **Click the Import Wallet link, at the bottom of the screen in Figure 4-4.**

   An Import screen appears, as shown in Figure 4-15.

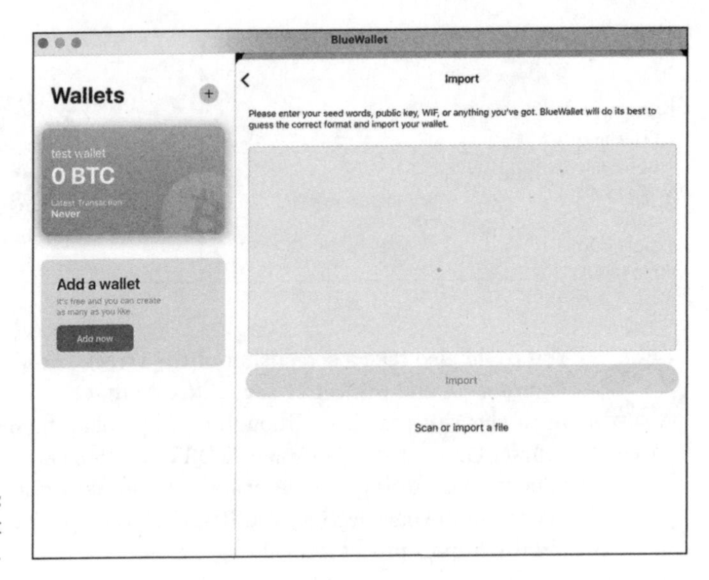

FIGURE 4-15: The wallet import box.

3. **Type the seed into this box.**

   You have a few alternative ways of completing this step:

   a. Click the Scan or Import a File link to open up your camera or webcam, and scan the QR code (from Figure 4-11) directly from the other wallet.

   b. Upload a picture of the QR code if you saved that. (Which we recommend not doing.)

   c. Paste a private key into the box, if you have that.

4. **Click the Import button.**

   Blue passes the seed words through its mathemagical functions and creates the private key and addresses. It also connects to the Bitcoin network, finds your transactions, and loads them into the wallet. Depending on where the wallet comes from, you may be prompted for a passphrase, with which some wallets may be protected.

   That's it; you now have the wallet imported on the new device — or recovered if you're importing from a backup of a wallet that you lost or was destroyed.

TECHNICAL STUFF

What's a WIF, in the list of import options in Figure 4-15? WIF means *Wallet Import Format*, a way to encode a private key to make it easier to transfer — in theory, anyway. It really doesn't make much difference, and you're not likely to run into it.

TIP

You could try this for yourself. Create a wallet on one device — your laptop or desktop PC, for instance — then load BlueWallet onto another device, such as your smartphone. Then import the seed into your second device and watch BlueWallet set up the wallet and grab the existing transactions from the blockchain.

Creating a watch-only wallet

You can also use the Import function to create a *watch-only wallet*, a wallet that cannot send transactions to the blockchain, but that can keep an eye on an address in the blockchain so you can always check the balance. Instead of providing a seed or private key, you enter a public key or an address, and the wallet watches the associated address.

For instance, you could use the watch-only wallet to receive incoming Bitcoin transactions — the wallet will provide you with the address and QR code you can give to the sender — and the most recent balance. However, to *spend* the Bitcoin, you would have to use another wallet, presumably a *cold wallet* that is usually disconnected from the Internet.

You can play with this setup if you like, to see how it all works. Assuming you have a wallet already set up but want to create a watch-only wallet on your mobile device, based on a wallet on your laptop, here's what you would do:

1. **Find the address that contains Bitcoin by opening the wallet and clicking the small menu icon in the top-right corner.**

   The Wallet information screen appears (refer to Figure 4-10).

2. **Click the little "Show Addresses" link immediately above the Export/Backup button.**

   The screen shown on the left in Figure 4-16 appears.

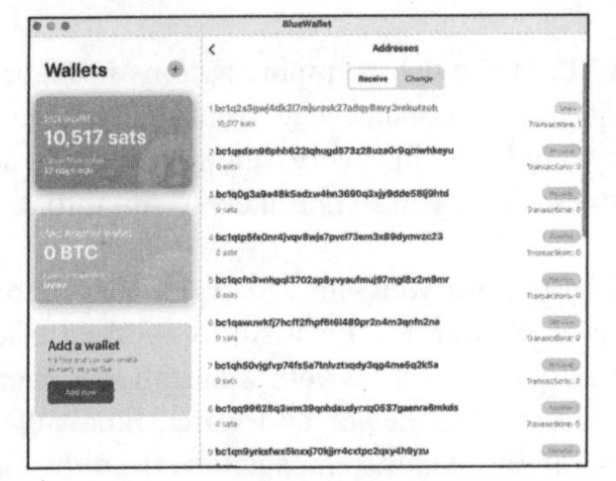

FIGURE 4-16: Choose an address to access its QR code.

Your wallet can create multiple addresses, one for each transaction. You can see which of your addresses contain balances in this list.

3. **Click the address you want to track to open the box shown on the right in Figure 4-16.**
4. **Scan the QR code from the BlueWallet software on the other device.**

   Alternatively, click on the address under the QR code and email or text it to the other device. (Remember, this is an address, not a private key, so it's perfectly safe to send it "insecurely.")
5. **On the device on which you want to create the watch-only wallet, go through the import process: Click the Add Now button and then select Import Wallet.**
6. **In the screen, scan or paste the address from the *other device's* wallet.**

   Your new wallet is created. Even if you gave the wallet a name, it will likely be named *Imported Watch-only* (though this seems like a bug, so maybe it won't by the time you read this).

Notice that in the wallet's main screen, there's a Receive button, but no Send button. The wallet will monitor the address, and also can be used to send the address to someone who needs to send Bitcoin to you. But you can't use it to send Bitcoin to someone.

Exploring multiple-signature wallets

This section dives into the multi-sig feature, the ability to create wallets that require two or more wallets to work together to sign a transaction that will be sent to the Bitcoin network.

Originally multi-sig wallets were a way for joint owners of Bitcoin to work together to manage their joint ownership. For instance, a married couple or a group of business partners may use multi-sig transactions, or a business may use multiple employees to provide signatures for corporate transactions. Transactions cannot be completed by one person; two or more are needed to sign transactions.

Multi-sig wallets also provide an individual with more security. Even if someone manages to gain access to one wallet — they find your password to the program, for instance — they still can't send a transaction without the other wallet (or several other wallets). Ideally, each wallet is stored on a different device in a different location. Some owners of sizeable Bitcoin holdings (hodlings?) use this method to make it harder to send transactions. One wallet may be stored in a bank safe-deposit box and another at home, for instance. Thus, Blue calls this type of wallet a *vault* rather than a multi-sig wallet.

Understanding multi-sig wallets

In the next section, we show you how to set up a very simple multi-sig wallet. If you want to do a more complex wallet, with three or more wallet holders and, perhaps, a smaller number required for signing, you need to read the documentation and review some videos to see how it's done, and then experiment with it to figure out how it all works. We recommend that you don't save large sums using a multi-sig wallet until you're absolutely sure you understand how it works, and have tested a few small transactions.

REMEMBER

Be careful with multi-sig wallets. Everyone managing one of the group's wallets must follow good security processes. Hacking or unauthorized access is perhaps less of an issue in a group, of course. If you need, say, three signatures out of a five-wallet group, an attacker has to hack three of the five wallets to be able to process a transaction. Thus, if one wallet holder is a little sloppy in the security arena, it's not a total disaster.

However, what happens if you don't have backups? If, for instance, you have a group of three, and you require all three wallets to process a transaction, it only takes one wallet holder to lose their password, and the Bitcoin associated with the multi-sig wallets' address is now useless!

It's tempting for one person to save the seeds for all the group's wallets, especially if some of the group's wallet holders are likely to lose access to their wallets. That defeats the purpose of the multi-sig wallet. Multi-sig wallets require that all members save their wallet passwords and backup seeds carefully, so that they cannot be lost or stolen.

Creating multi-sig wallets

You can set up multi-sig wallets (or vaults) in BlueWallet in various configurations, from "2 of 2" (meaning a group of two wallets of which both are required to sign a transaction) to "7 of 7" (a group of seven wallets, all of which must sign). You could, for instance, have a group of five wallets of which three must sign ("3 of 5").

You can do this with BlueWallet on several different devices. But you can also do it using various wallet types on different kinds of devices: BlueWallet on a smartphone, for instance, along with some kind of hardware wallet.

To demonstrate how this works, we assume you're using BlueWallet on two different devices. For more complex configurations, we recommend you do more research and experiment.

TIP

By default, Blue creates "2 of 3" wallets, with no option to change the settings, *unless* you have Advanced Mode selected in the General area of the program Settings or Preferences. If you want to follow along, make sure you have Advanced Mode selected, and follow these steps:

1. **Click the Add Now button or + button on the BlueWallet main screen.**

2. **In the Add Wallet box (refer to Figure 4-4), click Vault, then click the Create button.**

   The box shown on the left in Figure 4-17 appears. The box says, "A vault is a 2-of-3 multisig wallet it needs 2 vault keys to spend and a third one you can use as a backup." In other words, you need to set up two other wallets, on other devices, and in order to process a transaction, you need at least two of the devices to sign.

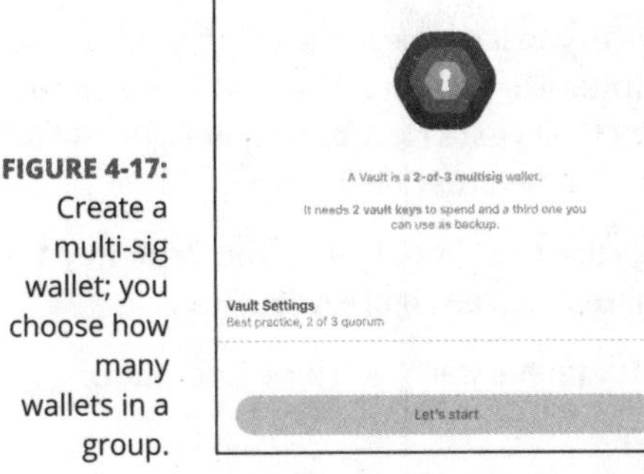

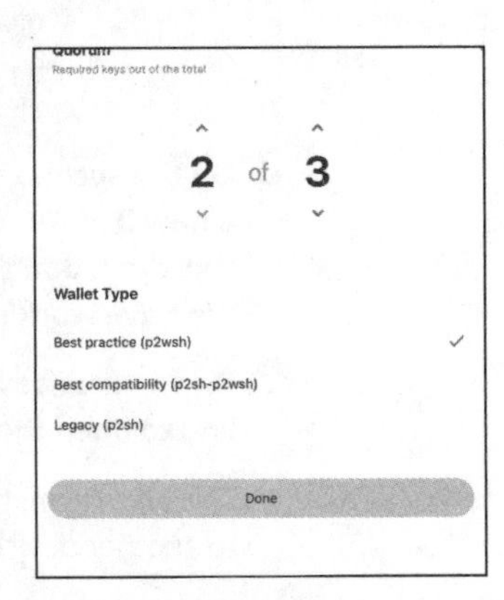

FIGURE 4-17: Create a multi-sig wallet; you choose how many wallets in a group.

3. **Change these settings by clicking on Vault Settings, above the Let's Start button; you see the box on the right in Figure 4-17.**

4. **Use the little up and down arrows to choose how many wallets you want in your group.**

   For instance, 4 of 6 means the entire group is six separate wallets, of which only four are required to process a transaction. (The maximum is 7 of 7.) For this demonstration, we're using 2 of 2.

5. **Click the Done button and then click Let's Start.**

   The box in which you set up your wallets appears (on the right in Figure 4-18).

6. **To create the first wallet in the group of two on this device, click the Create New button on the first line.**

7. **Save the new seed carefully (see on the left in Figure 4-18).**

   You've created a wallet, and that wallet is the Vault Key 1 in your group of two keys.

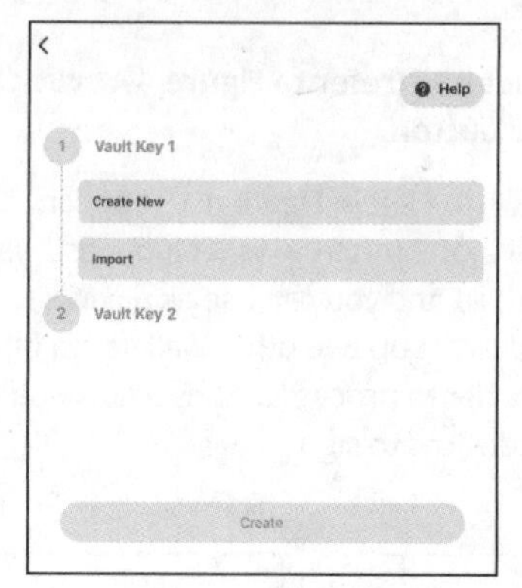

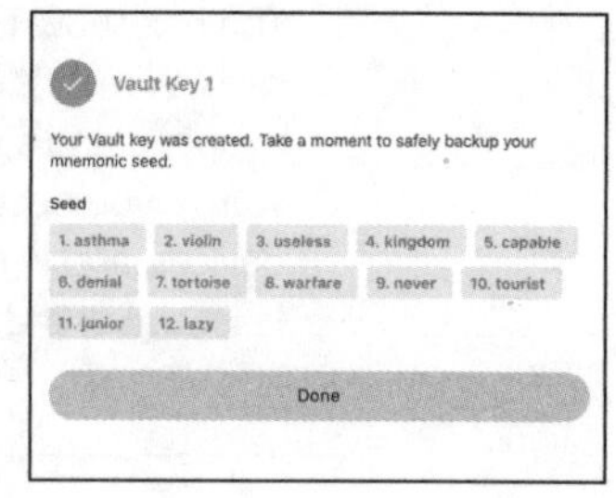

FIGURE 4-18: Setting up your vault wallet and getting your first wallet seed.

8. **On the second device, you'll do the same thing; you'll create a new 2 of 2 Vault (multi-sig) wallet (Figure 4-17). However, this time, don't click the Create New button in Figure 4-18. We have work to do on the other device first.**

9. **On the first device, click the Share link on the Vault Key 1 line to open the Share box (see Figure 4-19).**

   This allows you to transfer the wallet you have just created to another device.

10. **Use the QR code or click the Share button under the QR code to save a file that can be transferred to the other device.**

    This is actually transferring what is known as an XPUB, an extended public key.

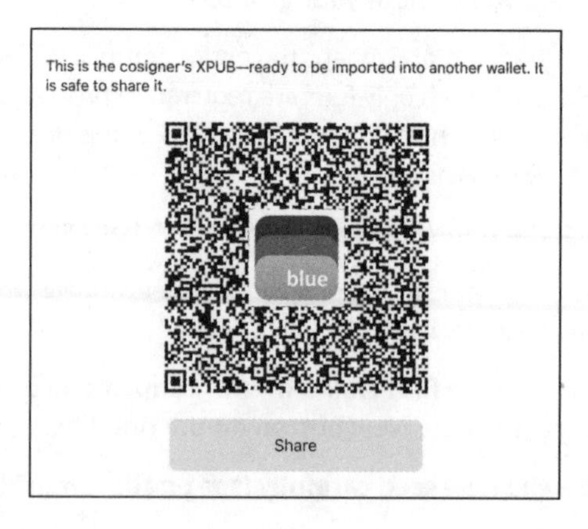

FIGURE 4-19: Your XPUB QR code.

11. **On the second device, click the Import button (located below Create New, on the Vault Key 1 line) to see a screen like that shown in Figure 4-20 (shown on a smartphone).**

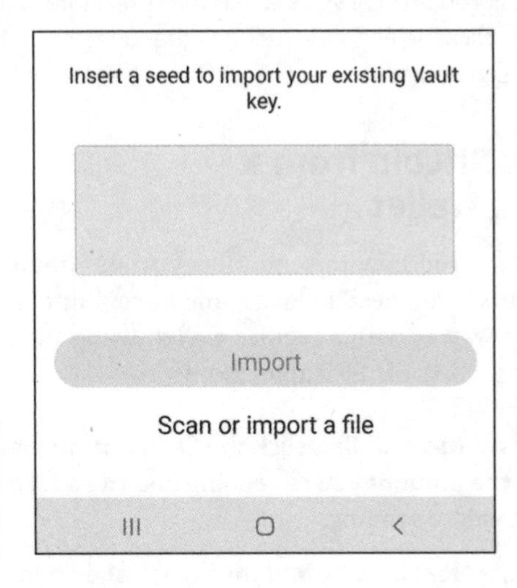

FIGURE 4-20: The Import screen (on an Android device).

12. **Click the "Scan or import a file" link and point the device's camera at the first device's XPUB QR code; your device scans in the code and creates your Vault Key 1.**

    If you can't scan a QR code, you can use the file-save function and transfer the file, which can then be opened via the Import box.

    You are now ready to set up Vault Key 2.

13. **Now we'll set up Vault Key 2.** We're essentially going to repeat what we just did, for Vault Key 2, starting on the second device. On the second device, on the Vault Key 2 line, click the Create New button to create a wallet and see the seed.

14. **Save the seed, then click the Share link to open the XPUB QR code.**

15. **On the first device, click the Import button to see the Import box, the "Scan or import a file" link, and scan the QR code into the first device.**

16. **On both devices, click the Create button on the Vault Key lines.**

    On both devices, Blue creates a wallet called Multisig Vault. (You can rename it if you want in the Wallet information screen; click the ellipsis ( ) menu at the top right of the main wallet screen.)

Sending Bitcoin from a multi-sig wallet

Here we show you how to send money from a multi-sig wallet. First, of course, you need to load some Bitcoin into it; that's done in the same way as with a regular wallet, using the Receive button. Sending starts off the same, too:

1. **In the multi-sig wallet, click the Send button, and then enter the amount you're sending and the address to which you're sending.**
2. **Click the Next button, and the screen shown in Figure 4-21 appears.**
3. **Click the Provide Signature button, and a QR code appears.**

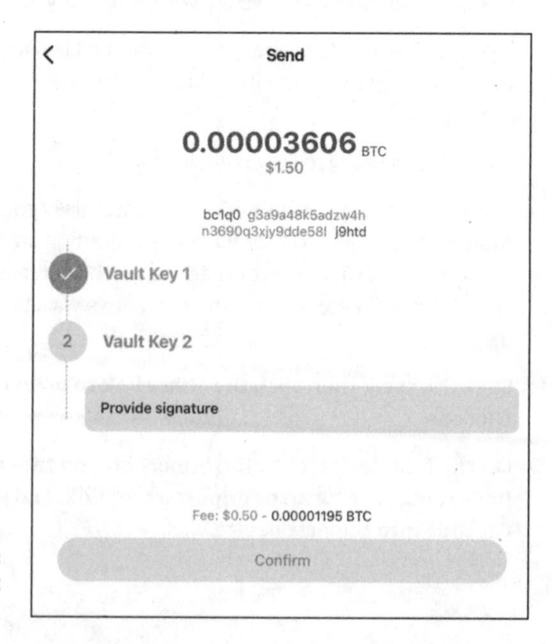

FIGURE 4-21: The Import screen.

4. **On the other device, click the Send button; then click the ellipsis ( ) menu in the top right of the Send screen and select Sign a Transaction.**

   You see the device's camera screen.

5. **Scan the QR code from the other device.**
6. **After the camera has grabbed the QR code, a message box appears, asking you to co-sign the transaction. Click YES.**

   You see a screen like that shown in Figure 4-22. As you can see, you now have two vault keys that have signed.

7. **Click the Confirm button.**

   A summary screen appears, showing the amount of the transaction, the address it's going to, and the fee being paid.

8. **Click the Send Now button, and the transaction is on its way!**

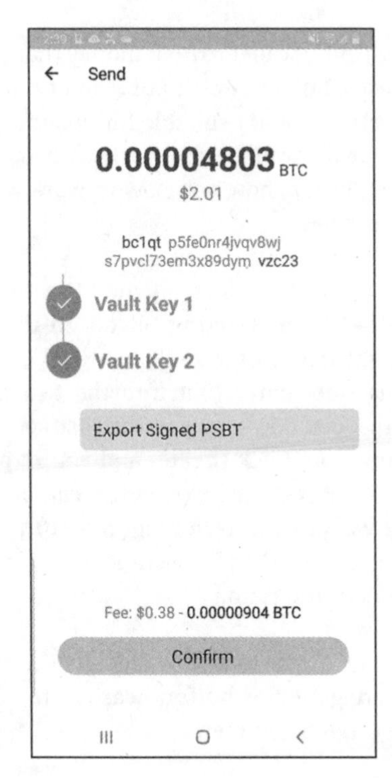

FIGURE 4-22: The Import screen (on an Android device).

Using the Lightning Network

Bitcoin transactions have two significant problems: they're slow and expensive. This doesn't matter too much for purely investing purposes, but it's a real nuisance for making purchases.

An ancillary network known as the Lightning Network is an attempt to fix these problems. This network is a payment protocol that sits "on top" of the Bitcoin network; when you use Lightning, your transactions are sent to the Lightning Network, bundled together, and sent on to the Bitcoin network. The transactions occur very quickly and with very low transaction fees, a fraction of what you would pay for a direct-to-blockchain transaction. The Lightning Network makes "microtransactions" possible, something that content publishers have long been hoping for. A publisher can charge just a few cents for an article or a podcast, for instance. (With credit cards and regular Bitcoin payments, this simply isn't possible, as the fees exceed the transaction.)

You can create a Lightning wallet to hold money that you can then use to make purchases, but you won't put a lot of Bitcoin into the wallet. Lightning wallets are not suitable for hodling your Bitcoin investments. And not all wallets can work with Lightning, but BlueWallet can. We quickly show you how to work with the network using the BlueWallet.

In the steps to set up a BlueWallet, in the "Creating your first wallet" section, rather than selecting Bitcoin in the Add Wallet box, you select Lightning (refer to Figure 4-4). If you have your own Lightning hub, enter that into the text box labelled LNDHub — of course, you don't, so you can just keep the default BlueWallet Lightning hub. Click Create, and you're prompted to back up the wallet. A QR code appears, which can be scanned, as well as a Lightning wallet ID (refer to Figure 4-19); click to copy the ID to your clipboard, and then paste it into, for instance, a password-management program.

You now have to add funds to the wallet. In the wallet main screen, click the Manage Funds button near the top, and choose an option from the drop-down menu.

- **Refill:** This choice lets you transfer Bitcoin from your other wallets, within the BlueWallet program, into your Lightning wallet.
- **Refill from External Wallet:** This lets you send Bitcoin from another wallet to your BlueWallet Lightning wallet.
- **Refill with Bank Card:** This lets you buy Bitcoin from an exchange.
- **Exchange:** This lets you use ZigZag.io to exchange other cryptocurrencies into Bitcoin and deposit into the Lightning wallet.

After you fund your wallet, you can send and receive Bitcoin via the network in a similar way to how you would with regular Bitcoin wallets, though with one significant difference. To receive money, you create an invoice rather than a Bitcoin address, and send the invoice to the person sending you Bitcoin; when you send Bitcoin to someone else, they send you an invoice that you pay.

» Understanding two ways you can lose control of your Bitcoin

» Making a choice: custodial or private wallets

» Finding out the password rules

» Protecting your computer

» Avoiding phishing attacks

» Passing Bitcoin on to your heirs

Chapter 5
Keeping Your Bitcoin Safe

You've probably heard stories of people "losing" their Bitcoin; thousands of people have done so. In fact, in 2017 researchers estimated that somewhere between 2.8 million and 3.8 million Bitcoin had been lost for good. . . perhaps more than 150 billion dollars' worth at current value. But many millions of dollars' worth have also been *stolen* from owners.

This chapter helps you to understand how these losses can happen and what to do so they don't happen to you!

Understanding How You Can Lose Control of Your Bitcoin

Bitcoin actually can't be literally "lost." In Chapter 2, we explain that there really isn't any actual Bitcoin; instead, there's a record of Bitcoin transactions in the blockchain ledger. So Bitcoin can't be lost; it's still where it's always been, sitting in the blockchain ledger.

What can happen, though, is that you can *lose control* of your Bitcoin. Sure, the Bitcoin is still recorded as a series of transactions in the blockchain, but you can no longer get to it, and you can no longer control it. And that can happen in a couple of ways:

1. You *lose* your private key, and thus the ability to control your Bitcoin.
2. Someone else *steals* your private key — thus gaining the ability to control your Bitcoin — and transfers it away from the address controlled by that private key.

REMEMBER

Your Bitcoin is associated with a particular address in the Bitcoin blockchain. That address is under the control of the associated private key, which you are, hopefully, keeping safe. The private key allows you to control that address. The only person who can send a message to the blockchain to transfer some or all of the Bitcoin associated with the address is the person who controls the private key; that's the *mathemagics* we talk about in Chapter 2.

Let's look at the first way you could lose your Bitcoin. Imagine what would happen if you lost your private key. You'd lose the ability to send transaction messages to the blockchain. You'd lose control of the Bitcoin associated with the address associated with the lost private key! No private key, no Bitcoin.

Now consider the second way you could lose control. What happens if someone else gains access to the private key? They now have control over your Bitcoin. Of course, if you still also have the private key, you both have control, and it becomes a game of who gets to it first. If you ever suspect that someone else may have found your private key — or the seed used to create it (see Chapter 4) — you should *immediately* transfer your Bitcoin to an address controlled by *another* private key. Create a new wallet if necessary. And then never use the old wallet again.

If someone who knows what they're doing steals your private key (or, again, the seed used to create the private key), then you probably won't have a chance. The Bitcoin will be gone before you ever discover the key has been lost — in fact, that's probably how you'll discover the key has gone; your wallet will have no Bitcoin left.

There's a popular phrase in the Bitcoin community: *not your keys, not your coins.* In other words, if someone else has access to your private key, they have control over your Bitcoin; it's as if you don't really own the Bitcoin, because someone else can take it from you at any moment. Sure, legally, you own it. But laws haven't helped the thousands of people who have had their Bitcoin stolen.

But it's not just theft you have to worry about. It's the proverbial screw-up, a mistake you make that leads to the loss. This happens a lot. It's easy to find horror stories of people who lost their wallets, and thus their keys and thus control over their Bitcoin. Co-author Peter Kent has a friend who owns millions of dollars' worth of Bitcoin — sitting somewhere in the blockchain — which he'll never be able to access because he sold a computer that had the wallet holding the associated keys.

Well, no, that's not really why he's millions of dollars poorer than he could be; he's millions of dollars poorer *because he didn't have a backup of the seed used to create the wallet on the sold computer!* It's as simple as that. With a little knowledge and a few minutes' work, you can protect your Bitcoin so that you can't just lose it. With a little foresight, Peter's friend would still have access to his Bitcoin, *even though* he sold the computer on which the wallet sat.

HOW 7,500 BITCOINS WERE LOST

A bigger risk these days than having your Bitcoin stolen from a custodial wallet in an exchange hack is the risk of simply losing the hardware where your wallet lives. We're always reminded of the famous case of James Howells, in the United Kingdom. In 2013, he owned 7,500 Bitcoins, at that point worth around $975,000. But that year, he lost a hard drive containing his wallet file; he's not even sure how he lost it, but he thinks it was thrown out during a house cleaning, and that it ended up in the local landfill.

If Mr. Howells had read and understood this chapter, and put into action what we teach here, his Bitcoin would be worth — as we write these very words — $361,893,000, more or less. Actually, even though he hasn't read this chapter, the Bitcoin *is still* worth that sum; it's just that he'll never be able to touch it. Unless, that is, he can convince the local council to allow him to dig up the landfill (he offered them $70 million early in 2021), is lucky enough to find the drive, and can retrieve his seed or private key from a piece of hardware that has been rotting away in the dampness of a Welsh trash heap for eight years (and counting).

Grasping the Goal: Private Key and Seed Protection

To sum it up in a nutshell, your two risks to losing control of your Bitcoin are as follows:

1. You can lose your private keys.
2. Your private keys can be stolen.

Thus, your two goals in keeping your Bitcoin safe and accessible only by you are as follows:

1. Safeguard your keys, so they can't be stolen.
2. Back up your keys so that you cannot lose them.

Here's the problem, though: These two requirements are at odds with each other. The harder you make it to *steal* your keys, the easier you may make it to *lose* your keys. And the harder you make it to *lose* your keys, the easier it becomes to *steal* them.

For instance, you can easily ensure that you don't lose your private key by writing down your seed on Post-it notes and giving them to, say, half a dozen friends and family. (Recall from Chapter 4 that if you have your seed, you can re-create your private key, and in any case, some wallet software hides the private key from you and only provides you with the seed.) You'd better really trust them, though! And not simply trust that they won't rip you off, but trust that they will keep the notes safe from theft by others. The more people who have the keys, the easier it is to steal them.

Or you can make it really hard for someone to steal your private key or seed by keeping a single copy, in a location known only to you. But the fewer backups you have of your seed or private key, the easier it is to lose it, through flood or fire, for instance. (We recall the Bitcoin owner who had his seed backed up on a piece of paper *and* a thumb drive; his computer burned up in a freak malfunction. As the paper and the thumb drive were right next to the computer, the small fire burned them, too, and with them, any hope of getting to his Bitcoin.)

TIP

Here are a couple more goals you may consider:

- **Ensure that you have access to your Bitcoin wherever you happen to be in the world, whenever you need it.** If you have a wallet on your home computer, with a seed saved in a local bank's safe deposit box, well, the only way you can get to your Bitcoin is by being in your hometown. This is an *electronic* currency, so surely it should be available anywhere in the world with Internet access, no? The methods in this chapter teach you how to have access to your Bitcoin anywhere, anytime.
- **How to pass Bitcoin on to your heirs.** Many Bitcoin owners have shuffled off this mortal coil (as Hamlet put it), *and taken their Bitcoin with them!* (Well, not literally we did mention the Bitcoin never leaves the blockchain, right?) In this chapter, you find out how to leave it with your family once you're pushing up daisies, even if they don't have access to it while you're alive.

REMEMBER

Chapter 4 covers wallets, both hot and cold. A hot wallet is connected to the Internet and, at least in theory, is at a potential risk for being accessed by a nefarious third party. A cold wallet, on the other hand, is not connected to the Internet, and cannot be hacked. It may still be at risk of theft, though. Here are a couple points to keep in mind as you read the rest of this chapter.

- **Combine the techniques in this chapter with your wallet strategy for maximum effect:** Whether your wallet is a hot wallet, a cold wallet, or one that's cold most of the time and hot just when you need to send transactions, you still need backups. If you have a single cold wallet, totally immune from being hacked across the Internet but still vulnerable to a fire, you're still taking a huge risk!
- **Backups — such as storing a wallet seed in a password-management program — are a form of wallet themselves:** So this chapter is about keeping your wallets, hot or cold, safe from theft, and duplicated so you can't lose control over your Bitcoin.

Making a Choice: Custodial or Private Wallet?

The first choice you have to make is who is going to manage your Bitcoin wallet (or wallets). Are you going to manage it yourself (a private wallet), or will you allow someone else to manage it (a custodial wallet, which we introduce in Chapter 4)?

Bitcoin purists hate the idea of letting someone else manage their wallets; remember the phrase *not your keys, not your coins?* Whoever controls the private keys has access to your Bitcoin.

The problem has been, historically, that a number of exchanges have been hacked over the years, with the hackers accessing the clients' private keys and stealing their Bitcoin. Some exchanges have been run by scammers, who stole their customers' Bitcoin and disappeared (known in the Bitcoin field as an "exit scam").

WARNING

As we caution you throughout this book, managing Bitcoin can be complicated. Today, the bigger risk for the Bitcoin neophyte is losing access to their Bitcoin rather than having it stolen from them. There are benefits to doing it yourself, but there are dangers, too. If you screw up managing your own Bitcoin, you can lose it, after all. The risks notwithstanding, you may find it easier to allow a large, reputable exchange to manage it for you.

This is a choice you have to make, and many people will choose the option of allowing professionals to look after their Bitcoin. As the market develops, this option will probably become less and less of a danger. As these large companies become better insured, for instance, and their defenses against theft become better, the risk will decline. (Many would say that it's already pretty low for some of the big institutions, at least.)

Still, in the following sections, we discuss how to protect your Bitcoin for yourself. And people who own very large amounts of Bitcoin almost always manage this process themselves, and develop a sophisticated system to do so.

TIP

If you decide to keep your Bitcoin in a custodial wallet, you still need to protect the login information for the account. So the rest of this chapter can still be useful to you; after all, whether you are protecting a login password or a wallet seed, the goal is to ensure that a piece of text is not stolen or lost.

Devising Your Cryptocurrency Safety Plan

Understanding how to protect all your Bitcoin-related information (and other important information, too, such as bank-account logins) begins with the basics: a plan to create strong, safe passwords.

Producing powerful passwords

Whatever you do — whether you use an exchange's custodial wallet, or one or more wallet apps on your various devices — you'll have passwords you need to protect. These should be passwords that can't be guessed, and also that you never lose or forget. Again, we're back at that situation in which the harder it is to forget a password, the easier it is to steal (or guess), and conversely, the harder it is to steal (or guess), the easier it is to forget. For instance, here's a bad password (let's assume that the password owner has a daughter and a son; see if you can guess their names):

JaneAndJoe

Okay, here's a pretty good password; see if you can memorize it:

iu$kG7pNnbs3z^RYe$yiBh

And here, according to a study, is the world's most commonly used password:

123456

That's closely followed by 123456789, by the way; and let's not forget the word *password* itself, which millions of people use as a password! Incidentally, these last three passwords can be guessed by a password-cracking program in less than a second.

TIP

This list highlights a few good (and common) rules for passwords:

- **Use unique passwords for every login you have; *do not reuse passwords*.** Yes, you'll end up with hundreds, but we're going to explain how to deal with that problem.
- **Don't use simple passwords such as the ones suggested here.** When hackers attack systems, they often use programs with dictionaries of common passwords; they already know the passwords used by many people!
- **Don't use easily guessed passwords.** These include your spouse's date of birth, the names of your pets, your kids' names, and so on. These passwords make it easy for someone who knows you, and has time to experiment, to get into your system.

» **Create passwords using multiple unrelated words connected with special characters and digits.** dog!!sure13%blurt, for instance. This is strong, but relatively easy to remember.

» **Use long, random strings of characters.** RkTWGQd9Xy%4#hbcY4t!6J or iW28LQKnJm%Aw8i9Ku4wHYFofZ^vho, for instance.

This last type of password is essentially impossible to guess, for either a password-cracking program or someone who knows you. Of course, they are also impossible for a normal human being to remember, which is why you need a password-management program. In the next section, we show you how to create and use passwords such as iu$kG7pNnbs3z^RYe$yiBh, without having to remember them.

REMEMBER

We're not talking about using strong passwords only for your Bitcoin-related logins, but for *all* your logins, in particular your email login. Hacking into an email system is often the first step a thief uses to access your other systems, such as bank and Bitcoin accounts.

Protecting passwords with password programs

Everybody these days should be using password-management software. It's just not possible, in the modern world, to remember all the passwords you need, unless you re-use passwords between systems and use simple passwords, both of which you should not be doing!

We know what a lot of you are doing, of course. You're writing your passwords down on paper, sometimes leaving the paper right next to your computer as an invitation to anyone who breaks in, or to a tech-savvy house cleaner — an invitation to, um, take you to the cleaners!

The more sophisticated among you are typing the passwords into a word-processing document or spreadsheet — probably named something like *passwords.docx* — and saving the file on your computer's hard drive, very thoughtfully providing the guy who steals your computer with the software preinstalled and the appropriate access passwords all in one place!

When your house burns down, you lose the passwords you wrote on paper. Or when your computer hard drive dies, you lose the passwords in the Word file. There's a better way! Use a *password-management program,* which stores your passwords — along with login URLs and IDs, various notes, and perhaps things like credit-card numbers and PINs, passport and drivers-license numbers, and so on — in encrypted files. You can log into the program to access your passwords, but without the master password, the data is not accessible. It's stored in a scrambled format that cannot be cracked, even by the FBI, CIA, or KGB (okay, *FSB* now, but that doesn't trip off the tongue like *KGB*). Sure, you can encrypt word-processing and spreadsheet files, too, but don't think that's safe; in most cases, these systems' form of encryption is very weak and easily cracked.

Password-management programs allow you to store hundreds — thousands even — of complex passwords, without you needing to remember any of them. All you need to remember is the *master password* that lets you get into the program.

Lots of these programs are available: Dashlane, Roboform, LastPass, TrueKey, NordPass, and many others. Pick something that is well known and widely recommended. Check a few comparative reviews. You'll find these programs have a lot of nifty features that make life so much easier for the password-laden citizens of the modern world. One of the most important is *centralized backup:* You can get to your passwords on your smartphone or laptop, but also through a web browser. The data is synchronized across devices and also stored — in an encrypted format — on the program publisher's servers. So if your house burns down and you lose all your devices, you haven't lost your passwords.

And those complicated passwords? They look this one:

```
woVib%8fQa67#EL8jQ5YgVq4n^9$rk
```

You don't even have to create them; the program creates them — and saves them — for you.

Of course, you can use the password-management program to store all sorts of things: login information, seeds, actual private keys if your software provides access to those, and notes explaining where all your assets are (bank accounts, types of cryptocurrency, brokerage accounts, the name of this book, and so on).

You should also consider using a program that has a *digital inheritance* or *digital legacy* feature, something we explain in the aptly named section, "Using a digital inheritance feature," later in this chapter. This feature helps you pass on your passwords to your family if you suddenly find yourself in a pine box.

You need a good password to get into your password program, the *master* password. This has to be something you can remember, so those long, complicated passwords are out (forget the master password and you won't be able to get into the system, and no, the program publisher won't be able to help you get in either). But it can't be something easily guessed. So, string a few words together with special characters and digits. You may take a line from a book, poem, or song (as long as it's not a short poem that you recite to people every day!), and replace the spaces with those special characters. You may end up with, for instance, something like this:

```
shuffle@OFF&this*mortal
```

If you're still concerned about forgetting it, combine this with the digital legacy feature, so if your memory *does* fail you, you still have a way back into your passwords, with the help of a friend or family member.

This master password is the password program's Achilles heel. Lose that, and you can't get in. Have it stolen or guessed, and someone else can. So protect it carefully!

Protecting your computer

Protecting your computer is also important because, if your computer becomes "infected" in some way, it can compromise everything you do on the computer. You want to keep your master password safe, but there are programs that can spy on your computer and see what you're up to, such as programs that can see every character you type when you log into your password-management program.

A program called Cryptoshuffler, for instance, tracks computer clipboards, in particular, looking for strings of text that look like Bitcoin addresses. It then replaces the address — likely copied out of the Receive box of a Bitcoin wallet (see Chapter 4) — with an address belonging to the Cryptoshuffler programmer. When the address is then pasted into another program — likely the Send box of a Bitcoin wallet — the computer user then unknowingly sends Bitcoin to the publisher. Hundreds of thousands of dollars (millions?) of Bitcoin have been stolen by this program.

Then there's *keyloggers* or *keystroke loggers*, programs that watch everything that's being typed on the infected computer, and report back across the Internet to the attacker. Such programs can steal seeds and passwords. They can be installed on your computer by viruses that infect your computer, or by someone with access to your computer. (Parents sometimes install keystroke loggers on their kids' computers, jealous people on their spouses' computers.)

Even without these threats, lots of bad things (viruses, Trojan Horses, malware, adware, and so on) can happen to your computer if you don't protect it from infection, so you need to do this anyway. *Ransomware* has been in the news a lot recently; it's malicious software that encrypts all your computer's data, locking you out of the data and only unlocking it once you've paid a ransom.

REMEMBER

Keep your computer clean and do these two things:

- **Protect your computer with anti-virus software.** Search for terms such as *best windows antivirus software* or *best mac virus protection*. Find something well-known, reputable, and highly rated. Understand it and run it.
- **Set up your computer to require a password to access it — and never leave it in a public place unlocked.** Don't even leave it unlocked in a *private* space if you have reason to believe someone close to you may be interested in spying on your computer activities (that definitely includes your employer's office). Before you walk away to get that coffee, lock it!

TIP

Requiring a password to access all your devices, including smartphones, is smart. If you have a password program or wallet on your smartphone, you must also protect that device with a secure login — a password, PIN, or fingerprint, for instance. The wallet software itself should have its own password, too. (All password programs require a password to log in.)

Watching out for sophisticated phishing

Take a look at the text message in Figure 5-1, something coauthor Peter received not too long ago. It seems pretty clear; it's a message from Coinbase saying someone had logged into Peter's account. Peter knew he hadn't done so recently, so his initial reaction was one of concern. Someone had logged into his account! How?

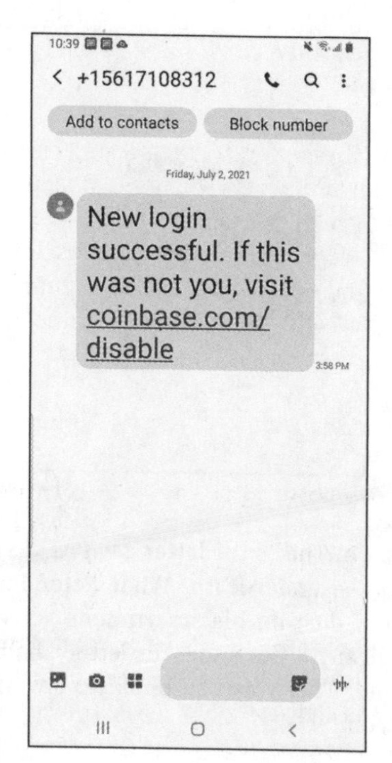

FIGURE 5-1: A warning from Coinbase.com?

Peter's second reaction was, "This doesn't sound real. I've never had a login notification before." His third reaction: "But wait, there's a URL here, pointing to Coinbase.com" He felt this must be a faked message from Coinbase, but how can you fake a URL in an SMS message? That can't be done, can it? SMS messages are plain text; unlike links in an email message, for instance, the link is what it says it is! (In an email message, you may see link text, but the real, underlying link could be different.)

Peter didn't click the link. Instead, he went to his browser on his laptop and typed the URL, coinbase.com/disable into his browser, which loaded a 404 (page not found) message. Hmmm. He went back to his SMS message, positive that it was a fake (*phishing*) message, still wondering how it was possible to type a link into an SMS message, but have the link go to a different URL. Then he noticed something. Take a look at Figure 5-2, where we've enlarged the message to show more detail.

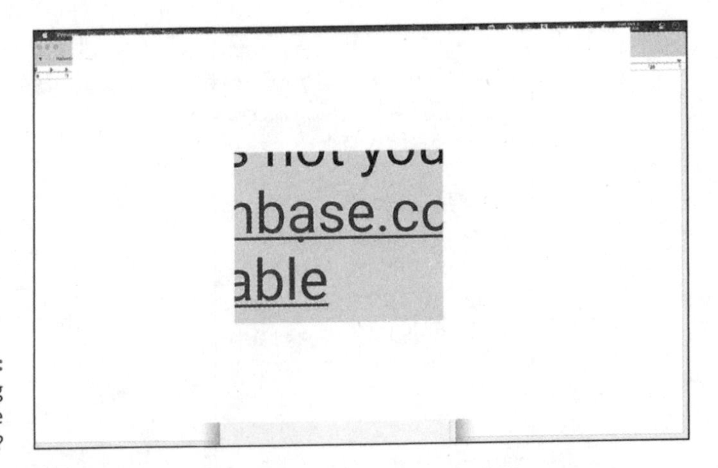

FIGURE 5-2: What's going on with the letter a?

That's not the letter a! That's the letter ạ *with a diacritic*, a small symbol — the dot — underneath. What Peter had originally thought was a bit of dust on his smartphone screen, was part of the letter (specifically, a dot under the letter), half-covered by the link's underline. This wasn't Coinbase.com at all, it was actually Coinbạse.com!

The Internet's domain name system only accepts ASCII characters, which don't include these symbols with diacritics. However, it's still possible to register domain names using these symbols. When you use a URL that includes a diacritic in the domain name, the *Punycode* system converts the letter with the diacritic to an ASCII representation; Coinbạse.com, for instance, is really the domain xn--coinbse-en4c.com.

When Peter went to the referenced page (we do not recommend you click on links in phishing emails), he went to a login page that *looked* like it was on Coinbase.com, but was on a completely different website (at xn--coinbse-en4c.com). Had he logged in, the "phisher" would have received Peter's login ID and password and, most likely within minutes — or even seconds — would have attempted to log into Peter's Coinbase account and transfer all his Bitcoin! (This is an example of why you should use two-factor authentication, which we discuss in the next section.)

Phishing is a form of *social engineering*, in which scammers try to convince you to provide them with information they can then use to get into your online accounts. It's getting pretty sophisticated these days. In Peter's case, the message masqueraded as a message from Coinbase. It really did look like a Coinbase URL.

PHISHING?

The word *phishing* is a form of "leetspeak," a system in which familiar words are intentionally misspelled. *Leet* itself comes from the word *elite*, and refers to the "elite" membership status in some electronic bulletin board systems in the 1980s. Leetspeak may have been a way to get around the use of text filters these systems used to block discussions of unauthorized subjects, such as hacking and cracking (*cracking* is actually the more correct word for what most of society calls hacking these days). But leetspeak is almost certainly a form of community language used to exclude those outside the community. Anyway, the term *phishing*, perhaps not surprisingly, is leetspeak for *fishing*. The scammers are fishing for your login information.

Watch out for these kinds of phishing scams. If you get an email or text that you find suspicious, or that you don't expect, don't blindly click the link. One way to identify such a scam in an email is to point your mouse pointer over the link; the actual underlying URL should pop up so you can see where the link actually goes. And in text messages, carefully read the URL! If you're still unsure, contact the service, not through the text or email, but by going to the website directly and checking with customer service.

Employing two-factor authentication

You've almost certainly run into two-factor authentication by now (often known as 2FA). You're familiar with basic logins, of course; you provide an ID (often an email address) and a password. With 2FA, you have to provide something more. The three most common additional authentication factors are as follows:

- A code sent to you via text message by the system you are logging into (some systems can deliver the code by speech to a voice-only phone number)
- A code sent to you via email
- A code created by an authenticator app

For those of you who have just emerged from the proverbial cave into this new online world, here's how it typically works:

1. You go to the website you want to log into.
2. You enter your ID and password and press Enter or click Login.
3. The system sends a 2FA code to your email address or in a text message to your phone; or it requests a code from your authenticator app.
4. You enter the code you've received, or taken from the authenticator, and the system lets you in.

And what, you may be asking, is this about some kind of *authenticator*? Well, these are apps — typically running on smartphones but also available for Windows and the Mac — that provide a code you can use to log in. Figure 5-3 shows an example of one — the Google Authenticator, which runs on the iPhone and iPad, as well as Android phones. These tools don't need to be connected to the Internet. Even if your phone's service is down, they still provide you with a usable code.

FIGURE 5-3: The Google Authenticator app.

When you set up an account that offers the 2FA feature, you're given the option of setting it up — or you may be told you *must* set it up. Just follow the instructions.

TIP

You may want to set up two or more 2FA methods. For instance, if you lose your smartphone, you can't get SMS texts or use your authenticator, and you are therefore locked out of your systems (such as your Bitcoin exchange accounts). Thus, many systems provide backup codes, half a dozen or so one-time 2FA codes you can save for future use. These should be stored safely somewhere, such as in your password-management program.

HOW'S THAT AUTHENTICATOR THING WORK?

Have you ever wondered how those authenticator apps magically work? How can an app on your smartphone possibly know what code a web server thousands of miles away wants to see? Well, it's magic. Mathemagic!

When you first set up your account for 2FA using an authenticator, you are given a special code to enter into the authenticator. This is a secret key that the app saves for future use. Later, when you need a login code, both systems use this secret key, in combination with the time and date, to both mathemagically calculate the same code; because both the server and the authenticator have the same secret key, and both know the time, they both come up with the same code.

There are various 2FA mechanisms, such as codes provided via voice calls, and even hardware devices that you plug into your computer. You may have come across *push notifications*, too. Each time you try to log into your account, a message (the push notification) is sent to your phone, alerting you that someone is trying to log in. You're not provided with a code; you simply respond Yes or No to show whether or not that current login attempt is coming from you.

With these 2FA methods, though, always ask yourself the question, "What happens if I can't get to my 2FA code?" Figure out a fallback position.

The dangers of 2FA

We believe you should use 2FA, which provides an additional, significant layer of protection. However, as with everything else, 2FA has weaknesses. If someone has access to the 2FA code, they have access to your account. For instance, they know your email address, which means they likely know your login to various systems, such as your Bitcoin-exchange accounts. Now, even without knowing your password, they can gain access to your account by doing a password reset, *if* they have access to the system that will receive or create your 2FA code.

In some cases, it could be that they have access to your email account (if you're receiving the code via email); perhaps they have hacked into your Gmail account, for instance. Or perhaps they have gained access to your smartphone. In many cases, if they have access to your smartphone, they likely have access to all three of the normal 2FA code systems: your text messages, your emails, and your authenticator app. So, how do you protect yourself?

- **You *must* have smartphone login protection, with a secure login that can't easily be guessed.**
- **Never leave your smartphone unattended and unlocked.** In fact, you should always know where your smartphone is. Keep it on your person or close by.
- **Protect your email account.** Use a good password that can't be guessed or easily cracked, don't leave your computer unlocked when unattended, and so on.
- **Protect yourself from SIM swaps!** SIM stands for *subscriber identity module*. The SIM card is a chip that holds information about the user and the mobile network — unique information that nefarious people can use to get control of your stuff.

The danger of SIM swaps

This really isn't a huge risk for most people, but it is a risk for people who are known to have large Bitcoin holdings, and who then become a juicy target for thieves. The idea is that the thief directs your phone line to their phone, using a process known as a *port-out scam*, *SIM swapping*, *simjacking*, and so on. Here's how it works:

1. The thief — let's call him Jesse James — discovers that Ritchie Rich owns a huge amount of Bitcoin. (***Bonus security tip:*** Don't boast about owning a huge amount of Bitcoin!)
2. Jesse discovers that Ritchie has stored much of his Bitcoin with a large exchange. Jesse also finds out Ritchie's email address and phone number, something that's pretty easy to discover.

   Jesse has spent days, weeks maybe, investigating Ritchie, and now knows everything about Mr. Rich, from his social security number to the names of his family members. He may have even tricked Ritchie Rich into giving him some of the information directly, but plenty is available online anyway.

3. Jesse hacks into Ritchie's email account. Now, if Jesse can just get hold of Ritchie's phone line, he can go to the exchange, use Ritchie's email address to do a password reset, get the 2FA code sent to the phone, use the code to authenticate, get a password-reset link, and get his filthy hands on Ritchie's riches.
4. Jesse calls the mobile-phone service Ritchie uses, and tells them that he has a new phone, and needs to switch SIMs — that is, point the phone number to the SIM card on the new phone.
5. Jesse provides them with enough information to convince them that he's Ritchie, and they switch the phone line to Jesse's phone!
6. And away Jesse goes, into Ritchie's account and, with Ritchie's Bitcoin in hand, off to a tropical paradise.

Yes, this has actually happened. The phone companies can be pretty bad with security at times. You may want to call your mobile-phone company and ask how to protect against SIM swaps. Some companies, for instance, issue a PIN number without which your SIM cannot be swapped (you would save the PIN in your password-management program, of course).

In the U.S., the Federal Communications Commission has gotten involved in this issue, and is in the process of issuing new rules that the phone companies will have to follow to reduce the risk of SIM swaps.

Exploring More Ways to Protect Your Bitcoin (and Everything Else)

Security really is a big subject. There's plenty you can do to protect yourself, and the more you have at risk, the more time and energy you'll want to spend doing so. But remember, we're not just talking about your Bitcoin. We're also talking about your bank accounts, investment accounts, retirement accounts, and so on. Sensible security measures are important for everyone, Bitcoin owner or not.

So, here are a few more things to consider:

- **Use a separate email for your Bitcoin.** Some people use special email accounts to access their various Bitcoin accounts, email accounts that they use for nothing else. This makes it hard for a potential hacker to figure out their login IDs.

  TIP

  You can simply set up another freebie email account — Yahoo! mail, Gmail, or whatever — or perhaps set up an account with a secure email provider such as ProtonMail.com. This particular service is set up in Switzerland, making it hard for even law enforcement in other countries to access information about your email. You can use a system such as Tor to access your Proton emails through a web browser in a totally untraceable way.

- **Be very careful about using public Wi-Fi.** Whenever you connect to Wi-Fi, you should use VPN software to protect the connection between your computer and the websites you access. (Search for VPN; you'll find plenty of information.)
- **Be extremely careful with public computers, such as those in libraries and Internet cafes.** It's not unheard of for such computers to have keylogging software installed, watching every keystroke made on the computer; if you log in to a site, the text you type into the ID and password fields is recorded.
- **Install wallets only on your own devices, not a device owned by an employer.** You never know how much control over the device the employer has, or when you may lose it at a moment's notice.

TIP

There's a simple trick to confuse (some) keyloggers. You type a character of your password, then click outside the password box and type a jumble of random characters. Then click back in the password box and type the next character . . . then outside the box and hammer away at the keyboard again. This protects your password as the keylogger records all the text and doesn't know which characters are part of the password and which are not — *unless* the keyword logger is also recording mouse clicks!

Yet another problem is that some browser plugins can actually read text as it is being typed into a password field. So, keylogger software or not, mouse-click tracking or not, your password can be stolen that way.

How can you use a public computer if you really need to? Well, it's possible, if you plan ahead. You can use an "OS on a stick," a simple operating system on a USB stick. You plug the USB stick (thumb drive) into a USB port, then reboot the computer and have it boot from the thumb drive, which has a clean, simple operating system installed. Now you have a computer running *your* operating system, not the Internet café's, so no keylogger software or password-reading browser plugin. Here are a few sites to check out if you're interested in an OS on a stick:

- `https://www.makeuseof.com/tag/5-best-linux-distros-installation-usb-stick/`
- `https://tails.boum.org/install/mac/usb-overview/`
- `https://elementary.io/`

There's still one problem: It's possible to install keyloggers on keyboards! So even though the computer is not recording what's going on, the keyboard itself may be recording what you type, such as the domain name of a Bitcoin exchange followed by login information.

How do you get around that? As much as possible, use the operating system; use the mouse to select bookmarks to load Web sites; use a password-management program to automatically log in, or use an on-screen keyboard. Or you can also use the trick we explain earlier, typing a character of the password, clicking outside the password box, typing a jumble of characters, and so on.

This is not the end. People with very large holdings create very complex and sophisticated protection methods. Consider the Winklevoss twins, for instance, Tyler and Cameron. They sued Facebook for breach of contract, and won a settlement variously reported as between $65 million and $120 million. They took most of this money and put it into Bitcoin. That makes them billionaires now!

How do they protect their billions of bucks of Bitcoin? Well, you can believe they're not managing it all from an old Android phone. One system they use is a combination of paper wallets, in which they printed just part of a private key on each piece of paper, then deposited these papers in various safe-deposit boxes stored around the country. This makes it very hard for someone to put a gun to one of the twin's heads and say, "Send someone to the safe deposit box to bring back the private key."

Knowing What Happens When You Kick the Bucket

So you've invested in Bitcoin. You made some money, perhaps a lot, and your family's future is assured. Then you get hit by a bus. What's next? Maybe you're in a coma, perhaps your family is making funeral plans what happens to your Bitcoin?

Well, it's still where it has always been: in the blockchain. The question now is, if you've hidden your information — the seed and the private key — will they be able to find the information and thus access the Bitcoin?

You actually need to pass two things on to your heirs:

- Your wallet seed phrase
- Information about how to use it

As for the latter, maybe a copy of this book would be helpful. Or the name and phone number of someone you trust to guide them through the process of rebuilding a wallet and gaining access to your Bitcoin. Or maybe teach your family about Bitcoin *before* you move on from this planet. As for saving the seed in a manner in which it can be passed on when you've gone well, read on.

The challenge is to keep your Bitcoin's seed, and thus the private key, safe while at the same time providing a way for your family to get it when you're no longer here.

What you definitely shouldn't do is to simply give everyone in your family a printout of your seed. That's asking for trouble. Five years from now, how many of the printouts will be lost? And there's always the risk of careless talk among friends leading to a theft.

A better option is to simply put the information into a safe deposit box (or better still, two), and make sure your family knows where the box is and where the key is. In most cases, this scenario is fine, but it still carries risks. Sad to say, sometimes couples divorce, and sometimes children are "out of control," so your safe deposit box can become not so safe.

Choosing the multi-sig solution

We're mentioning the multi-sig option because it's often cited as a way to solve the inheritance problem (not because we believe it's a great solution). We cover multi-sig wallets in Chapter 4. Let's say you have a spouse and three children. You could set up a multi-sig wallet group with five wallets, and three required to sign (five, because you need to have one of the wallets, right?). If you pop your clogs, your family can get to the Bitcoin as long as three of them still have access to their wallets.

However, this really isn't a great option. First, to access your Bitcoin when you're alive, you need the assistance of two of your family members. There's a way around that problem, though. You set up a *four*-wallet group for your spouse and kids, with an address that has no Bitcoin. Then you manage your Bitcoin using wallet software that allows you to schedule transactions in the future. You schedule a transaction that moves all your Bitcoin from your address to the family wallet group six months in the future. Then, you cancel the transaction a few days before the event, and reschedule *another* six months in the future. If you ever become incapacitated — or die — when the time comes around, the Bitcoin automatically transfers.

However, there are other problems with the multi-sig solution. What happens if multiple family members are hit by the same bus at the same time, or if some family members lose access to their wallets? You could end up in a situation in which the Bitcoin is inaccessible.

Scheduling future transactions

The scheduled transaction system could also be used in another way. You set up a single wallet with an empty address, then set up a scheduled (periodically cancelled) transaction from your wallet to that address, and then provide the seed for that wallet to each family member. In this case, you still have the problem of the seed being found by someone else or lost by someone, or of a family race to see who can get a wallet set up first after you've gone.

WARNING

There's another problem, though; you'll need a wallet app that can schedule transactions, and few can right now, even though there are functions built into the Bitcoin code that can accomplish this. This may become a more viable option in the future. (Some wallet software will help you set up transactions prior to sending them, but the software needs to be online to actually send the transaction when the scheduled date comes around. If you're in line at the Pearly Gates, you may find it hard to accomplish this.)

Using a digital inheritance feature

But here's a nifty way to do what you need to do, to ensure that you, and only you, have access to your essential Bitcoin information while you're alive and *compos mentis* and yet ensure that your loved ones have access when you're counting worms.

You can use a password-management program's *digital inheritance* or *digital legacy* feature. We talk about password-management programs earlier in this chapter. Here we quickly describe how this particular feature works. Not all such programs have this feature, but most of the more popular, sophisticated ones do.

Here's essentially how they work:

1. You decide who you want to pass on the information to in the event of your death or incapacity; that person installs a copy of this software.

Most of these programs duplicate and distribute the data, so there is a copy online, on the user's smartphone, and on the user's laptop, for instance, which helps assure a hardware error on one device (or even both) won't lead to a loss. In some cases, a free version of the software may be enough for this feature to function.

2. On your version of the software, you designate that person as your heir, or emergency contact, and you also enter a *timeout period,* an amount of time that must pass before your heir gets access.

3. You become incapacitated or die. Using their version of the software, your heir requests access to your passwords.

   They don't get access right away because you set a timeout period, and they won't get in until it's over. For instance, perhaps you set it to three weeks.

4. The company that publishes the password-management software emails you a message, saying your heir has requested access. You can't respond because you're in hospital in a coma, or you're taking the proverbial carriage ride.

5. After three weeks, your heir is granted access. However, if, by some miracle, you revive and read your email *before* the timeout ends, you can deny access to your heir.

TIP

To be really safe, you'll probably want to provide emergency access to two or more people. Redundancy is always a good thing in computing. If two of you are hit by the same bus, the third can still get to the information. If one of your heirs forgets the password, the other heir can still get in. You could even set up accounts for all of your heirs, along with *cascading timeouts*, in order of who you want to have access to the information first. Your spouse gets the shortest timeout, for instance, your oldest child (or perhaps a sibling if your children are young) gets the next shortest, and so on.

» Deciding whether Bitcoin is a viable asset or a bubble

» Understanding stock-to-flow

» Is Bitcoin digital gold?

» Deciding what investment strategies make sense for you

» Considering another option: non-Bitcoin cryptocurrencies

» Learning why *NFTmania* is so risky

Chapter 6
Investing in Bitcoin

Why do people own Bitcoin? For the great majority, the answer is simple: *to make money!* But, as we explain elsewhere, Bitcoin — for the moment, at least — is not a true currency. Sure, you *can* buy things with it, if you go out of your way to do so, but *why?* There are far more convenient ways to buy your groceries or pay for a night at the movies. If you think Bitcoin will go up in value, it makes sense to own some; but if you think Bitcoin will go up in value, then why would you buy coffee with it? If you think Bitcoin will go *down* in value then why would you own it just for the *inconvenience* of buying stuff with it?

No, the vast majority of people who own Bitcoin do so because they believe that it will appreciate in value and multiply their wealth. In fact, Bitcoin is really an *asset*, not a currency. Even the U.S.'s Internal Revenue Service has ruled that it should be treated as an asset for tax purposes, like gold or art.

There are, of course, others — those we call the true believers — who really do *believe* in Bitcoin. People who think it's the future of money, that if it's not a currency now, it will be one day, and who often also believe that Bitcoin is the beginning of a new and better world in which governments do not control money. But let's be frank. Whatever their beliefs, they also want to make money!

Isn't that why *you*, dear reader, are reading these very words right now? Isn't that why you — and certainly most readers of this book — bought, borrowed, or stole it in the first place? Yes, it is, so in this chapter we talk about investing in Bitcoin, and also about investing in other cryptocurrencies (just a little), because to a great degree, that's where a lot of the action is these days.

REMEMBER

A quick word of caution: We don't pretend to be seers. Neither of us is Nostradamus. The following information is based on our observations of the cryptocurrency markets over the last few years. As you'll see as you read through this chapter, we've tried to be cautious. We have explained, for instance, *what other people have done*, which doesn't mean we are saying that *you should do the same!* We strongly recommend that before you invest more than "play money" in Bitcoin or other cryptocurrencies, you further your education in the Bitcoin and cryptocurrency field (Chapters 10 and 11 can direct you to a starting point) and make up your own mind about what investing strategies might make sense for you.

Bitcoin: Valuable Asset or Bubble About to Burst?

The decision on whether to invest in Bitcoin really comes down to one thing: *Do you believe Bitcoin will continue to rise in value?* Of course, that's true for any asset you would buy as an investment. The difference between Bitcoin and other assets is that the other assets have a track record — years, even hundreds or thousands of years of fluctuations in value — while Bitcoin is so new that nobody can say for sure what will happen.

Bitcoin is what is often known as a *store of value.* That is, you can use it to store your wealth, then retrieve that wealth at a later date. There's no question that Bitcoin is a store of value right now, though an unstable one. The questions are, though, will it continue to be a store of value, and will it go up in value?

This debate has smart people on both sides. Some intelligent, educated people believe that Bitcoin will inevitably increase in value; and some intelligent, educated people are just as sure that it will eventually collapse. We're in uncharted territory with no long-term history to point to or learn from; these are all projections.

The following sections lay out reasons for why Bitcoin is bound to continue rising in value. . .and why it's bound to collapse.

Bitcoin's got to rise in value!

We begin with several reasons showing why Bitcoin's value will increase:

- **The Bitcoin market is currently worth almost a trillion dollars.** That represents millions of people who are already believers, who are not likely to cut and run. They want — and expect — the Bitcoin market to continue.
- **More money is flooding into Bitcoin from billionaires.** A few examples are Elon Musk (of Tesla), Jack Dorsey (of Twitter), Michael Saylor (of MicroStrategy), and the Winklevoss twins (of Facebook fame — who admittedly became billionaires because of their Bitcoin investments). A lot of wealthy people believe in Bitcoin.
- **As an asset, Bitcoin has a lot of advantages.** It's highly portable, far more portable than gold, the closest tangible asset to Bitcoin. It's also international, allowing people around the world to easily transfer money between nations.
- **Gold doesn't have much intrinsic value, and yet it has endured as a store of value for thousands of years.** Even crypto-skeptic economist Paul Krugman concedes that Bitcoin may endure, too, for the same reasons that gold has. (See Chapter 12 for more of Krugman's thoughts on Bitcoin.)

- **The Global Chief Economist at Citigroup once called gold a "6,000-year bubble" and even "shiny Bitcoin."** If gold can last, without much intrinsic value, for 6,000 years, can't Bitcoin (let's call it "weightless gold") survive for a while at least? (See Chapter 12 for more on gold as a 6,000-year bubble.)
- **Bitcoin is very attractive to citizens of countries with problem currencies.** For example, citizens of Zimbabwe, Turkey, Venezuela, and other countries can buy into an asset that's far more stable (as volatile as it is) than their nations' currencies.
- **Bitcoin is very attractive to people fleeing their homelands.** It's a refugee's perfect asset, safer and more convenient than cash, jewelry, diamonds, or gold when escaping one's nation. Afghanistan, for instance, has recently become a Bitcoin hotspot.
- **Major financial institutions are getting into Bitcoin.** You can buy Bitcoin from PayPal, the Square Cash App, Robinhood, Venmo, and so on.

In economic terms, *intrinsic value* refers to an asset's value that's not related to its market value. Intrinsic value refers to the objective value an object has due to its intrinsic properties, not the value assigned to it by an investment market. Gold, for instance, is valuable because it's regarded as a store of value. But what if it *wasn't* regarded as a store of value? What if its only value was related to its industrial uses? Then its value — its intrinsic value — would be far less, a fraction of its current market value.

REMEMBER

The fact that Bitcoin has no intrinsic value doesn't really seem particularly relevant to us. After all, many stores of value have little or no intrinsic value: gold, art, baseball cards. A store of value doesn't need to have intrinsic value to be a store of value. It needs to be in short supply relative to demand, with no way for anyone to flood the market with new supply.

Bitcoin's bound to bust!

On the flipside of the Bitcoin, here are several reasons foretelling its doom:

- **Bitcoin has some significant disadvantages.** Either it's easy to use (but also easy to lose — perhaps as many as 20 percent of all Bitcoin has already been lost), or it's very secure but very complicated.
- **Bitcoin has no intrinsic value.** Thus, in the words of economist Paul Krugman, it isn't tethered to the real economy.
- **Bitcoin is used for illicit transactions.** Examples include funding terrorism, the drug trade, gun sales, money laundering, and so on. It follows that such transactions will lead to Bitcoin coming under more government scrutiny.
- **Bitcoin uses obscene amounts of electricity.** It takes a lot to keep the network running and the miners mining.
- **Bitcoin processes transactions too slowly.** It can take minutes to process a transaction, whereas the Visa network, for example, processes tens of thousands of transactions *per second.*
- **Bitcoin is simply too volatile to last.** Its volatility is an indicator that it isn't fully trusted.
- **Bitcoin is not backed by anything.** It's not backed by governments, not by gold, not by anything.
- **Scarcity itself is not a source of value.** Bitcoiners often point to its scarcity as being important, and in response critics say, in effect, "Scarcity isn't enough. There has to be something more!"
- **Bitcoin is a "fraud" and "worse than tulips."** At least, according to Jamie Dimon, CEO of J.P. Morgan, it is. We explain the tulips reference later in this chapter.

Many of the complaints about Bitcoin are actually due to a misunderstanding about the nature of the beast. Illicit transactions? Isn't cash used for those, too? It's not backed by anything? It's backed by the millions of people who believe in it, just as gold is. It processes transactions too slowly? It processes transactions plenty fast enough to act as a tradeable asset, and developments are under way to make it fast enough to work as a currency (if anyone really cares about that). Too volatile? Have you looked at the gold market recently? And so what if it's volatile; it has performed better than gold over the past few years, even *with* its volatility.

Oh, and about Jamie Dimon. He may not have changed his personal views, but J.P. Morgan actually created its own cryptocurrency, JPM Coin, and recently provided access for its investors to six cryptocurrency funds.

And about the idea that scarcity is not a source of value. Consider the comments made by Professor Eswar Prasad, the author of a book about the future of money (titled *The Future of Money*) in *The New York Times* (June 14, 2021). He points out that Bitcoin has no intrinsic value, and then responds to "Bitcoin devotees" claim that its value comes from scarcity, by saying

> scarcity by itself can hardly be a source of value. Bitcoin investors seem to be relying on the greater fool theory — all you need to profit from an investment is to find someone willing to buy the asset at an even higher price.

But can't the same be said about gold? It has very little intrinsic value. It has only been valuable for the last 6,000 years because there's always been someone (another fool?) willing to buy the otherwise worthless metal, often at a higher price.

Speaking of gold, let's talk a little about the *stock-to-flow* concept.

Understanding stock-to-flow

We believe that the stock-to-flow model is a useful concept to know, to help you understand *how* Bitcoin can be a valuable asset. The *stock-to-flow model* is a measure of the *scarcity* of an asset.

The basic idea is that if the ratio between stock (the stockpile, how much of an asset already exists) and flow (the amount of the asset being created each year) is very low, the asset won't have much value. For instance, the stock-to-flow for potatoes is essentially 1:1, with most potatoes produced each year being used each year; current stock is being replenished by new flow. Gold, on the other hand, has a very high stock-to-flow ratio. The amount of new gold created every year is a very small proportion of the world's current stocks.

This is why gold has stood as a valuable asset for thousands of years. It's relatively scarce, something required by valuable assets. But in addition, it has a high stock-to-flow ratio. That is, not only is there much not of it, in relation to the demand, but there's also not much more coming on the market. Gold production each year is pretty inflexible and low. Even if it were possible to double the annual output to 6,000 tonnes, it would still be a small proportion compared to the stockpile.

By some measures, 180,000 tonnes of gold are already in peoples' hands, but generally less than 3,000 new tonnes come out of mines each year. (A *tonne* is a metric ton, which is a unit of mass equal to 1,000 kilograms.) Thus its stock-to-flow ratio is around 1:60.

Plenty of other metals could be used as a store of value, but most have much lower ratios. Gold does have the additional value of being pretty, of course. So does silver, but silver has a lower ratio. Around 550,000 tonnes of silver are already out of the ground, but 25,000 tonnes are mined each year, representing a stock-to-flow ratio of 1:22.

Now let's consider Bitcoin. At the time of writing, 18,907,156 Bitcoins are in the blockchain. Over the next 12 months, somewhere around 328,500 more Bitcoins will be mined (6.25 every ten minutes or so, 900 a day; see Chapter 7). That's a ratio of 1:57.6, very close to that of gold.

Of course, this ratio is always increasing. The following year, there will be another 328,500 or so Bitcoins mined, but the stock will be around 19,235,656 (it now includes new Bitcoin that will be added to the stock next year), so the ratio will be closer to 1:59. And sometime in mid-2024, the number of Bitcoins mined every year will drop to around 164,250, at which point the ratio will soar to around 1:120. Four years later, the mined Bitcoin will halve again — again doubling the ratio — and so on.

LOST BITCOIN?

The actual ratio for Bitcoin is actually a bit less than we show here, because millions of Bitcoin have been "lost" and can never again be used; they might as well not exist, because they can't be bought and sold. (Estimates of how many have been lost go as high as 20 percent.) Still, we don't know the exact number of lost Bitcoin so we're going to ignore this issue for the purposes of this explanation, and in the *long term*, it doesn't make much difference to the ratio. See Chapter 5 to make sure you don't lose your Bitcoin.

In Chapter 1, we talk about rai stones, the unwieldly stone currency of the Yap islands. For many years they held value. Only a few new rai stones were mined and went into circulation each year. We don't know what the ratio was, but it was high enough for rai stones to remain valuable.

But in 1871, an Irish-American ship's captain, David O'Keefe, found out about the rai stones (legend has it that he was shipwrecked on the islands, though that may not be true) and started mass producing the stones. This — combined with the fact that after contact with Europeans, the Yapese themselves started to use metal tools to speed up production — led to an overproduction; in effect, the stock-to-flow ratio dropped, with the new annual production representing a large portion of the existing stock. (But not before O'Keefe made enough money to buy his own island and declare himself king. About 80 years later, Burt Lancaster played him in a movie, *His Majesty O'Keefe.* You can watch it on at least a couple of different streaming services.)

Anyway, that's what happens to an asset that has a declining stock-to-flow ratio: it drops in value, collapses even. But that's something that can't happen to Bitcoin. In 2024, the ratio will be twice that of gold, and it will keep going up from there. Bitcoin will end up in the not-so-distant future with a stock-to-flow ratio four times, then eight times, then sixteen times that of gold — and then more — until eventually the ratio becomes infinite, as the mining of new Bitcoin grinds to a halt.

So Bitcoin *is* like gold. It's a scarce commodity, with very little new Bitcoin coming on the market every year, and no way to increase flow (it's always going to be dropping). Gold supply, on the other hand, despite having a large stock-to-flow ratio, can actually increase a little; as the price goes up, gold mining becomes more profitable.

But Bitcoin is also digital, and thus easily shippable. Satoshi Nakamoto, the founder of Bitcoin, described it like this in a BitcoinTalk.org forum posting:

> *As a thought experiment, imagine there was a base metal as scarce as gold but with the following properties:*
>
> *- boring grey in colour*
>
> *- not a good conductor of electricity*
>
> *- not particularly strong, but not ductile or easily malleable either*
>
> *- not useful for any practical or ornamental purpose*
>
> *and one special, magical property:*
>
> *- can be transported over a communications channel*
>
> *If it somehow acquired any value at all for whatever reason, then anyone wanting to transfer wealth over a long distance could buy some, transmit it, and have the recipient sell it.*

Bitcoin doesn't have some of the characteristics of gold that we really don't care about. But like gold, Bitcoin is scarce, unforgeable, and unhackable, and its stock-to-flow ratio is high (soon to be higher than gold's and going higher still). It's also digital — it's more valuable gold that can be emailed!

Bitcoin: digital gold

There's a good case to be made that Bitcoin is a form of digital gold. Gold has a long history; small amounts have been found in caves inhabited by humans 40,000 years ago, and humankind has been creating gold artifacts for at least 6,000 years. So gold, with relatively little inherent value, has lasted as a store of value for at least 6,000 years. If something else came along with some of the same characteristics — and additional advantages — shouldn't that also be able to serve as a store of value? So, let's take a look: gold versus Bitcoin, as shown in Table 6-1.

TABLE 6-1 Gold versus Bitcoin

Characteristic	Gold	Bitcoin
Limited supply?	Yes. There's only around 180,000 tonnes out of the ground, and 57,000 tonnes left to mine. Compare that with the 30 billion–tonnes reserves of aluminum.	Yes, currently only 19 million coins.
Pretty gold color?	Yes. That's what drew human attention in the first place.	No; but for the purpose of storing value, that really doesn't matter!
High stock-to-flow ratio?	Yes, around 1:60.	Yes; it will be close to 1:60 soon, and a year or so later, it will reach 1:120 and beyond.
Easily transportable?	No, at least not in large quantities. A million dollars' worth weighs about 35 lbs.	Yes! A million dollars' worth weighs nothing.
Can be transported quickly?	Only as quickly as it can be carried.	Can be sent to the other side of the planet in seconds.
Intrinsic value?	A little, but not much compared to its asset value.	None. Not even adornment.
Fungible	Yes, more or less. One gold bar of the same purity is the same value as another gold bar of the same purity.	Yes, absolutely.
Excellent conductor of heat and electricity?	Yes!	Um no. But we don't care.
Resistant to most acids?	Yes!	Um, well actually yes, it is!
Usable as a currency?	Not really, not in today's economy.	The Bitcoin "cryptocurrency" is not a currency, at least not at present.

Characteristic	Gold	Bitcoin
Long-term belief?	Yep, 6,000 years.	No, we're just getting started.
Easily sold?	Well, you might have to take it to a coin dealer or one of those mail-your-gold-to-us companies.	Yes, quickly and easily.

It really looks like Bitcoin is digital gold. It's like gold in a number of ways, and the ways in which it *differs* from gold either really don't matter (no, it's not pretty and doesn't conduct electricity), or offer a dramatic advantage (the ease of transportation). Perhaps the only significant difference is that gold is ancient, while Bitcoin is new.

So You Want to Buy Bitcoin. . .

Let's say you come down on the side of Bitcoin continuing its rise; you want to join the crowd and buy in. You have a few basic questions to consider before you begin:

- Are you buying at a reasonable price?
- Can you keep your Bitcoin safe?
- Are you *over*-investing?

WARNING

First, make sure you read Chapter 3 and understand how to buy Bitcoin at the best price, though you should balance this with security. Sometimes Bitcoin is "cheap" for a reason (you're being scammed, for instance!). You also need to really understand how to keep your Bitcoin safe. You don't want to be one of the thousands of people who have had their Bitcoin stolen or who have simply lost access to it. See Chapter 5 for that information.

And then you have to ask the perennial investing question: Are you risking too much? What if you're wrong, and Bitcoin doesn't survive?

WARNING

Don't invest more than you can afford to lose (or that you can stomach losing).

Be very careful you don't get caught up in *FOMO* — Fear of Missing Out. Yes, if you'd taken all your savings early in 2016 and put them *all* into Bitcoin, you would have multiplied your money 40 times (at the time of writing; maybe *more* by the time you read this). But that was then; there's no going back. Millions of people in the history of the world have ruined themselves financially by taking the big bet and losing.

REMEMBER

Investing in Bitcoin is definitely a bet. Don't get too greedy. Invest a sum that won't ruin you if the naysayers prove to be right, a sum that you can shrug off if necessary. Perhaps you shrug it off after a period of anguish, but you shrug it off at least eventually!

The basic strategy — buy and hodl

Here's the primary strategy for investing in Bitcoin:

1. **Buy Bitcoin.**
2. **Hold it.**
3. **Wait for it to go up in price.**
4. **Keep holding it because it will probably go up more.**

TIP

This might be termed a *hodling strategy* (we explain hodl in Chapter 4). And perhaps this sounds very simplistic, but it really is the primary investment strategy, and many people have become very rich using this strategy.

Let's take a look at the price of Bitcoin over time. We'll use CoinMarketCap.com, a great site for checking the pricing of a huge selection of cryptocurrencies. Figure 6-1 shows the rise and fall of Bitcoin between the beginning of 2016 and December 2021. The first price shown on this chart is $433 per Bitcoin; the last is $46,727, and the peak was almost $67,000.

Yes, Bitcoin pricing has a lot of volatility; it's a wild ride. But a hodl strategy from 2016 would have worked extremely well. You'd be entering 2022 having increased your investment around 50 to 60 times. Even if you had bought at the peak in 2017 (when Bitcoin really came to the attention of the masses) and then continued hodling during the precipitous decline in early 2018, you'd still be way ahead. You'd have more than doubled your money.

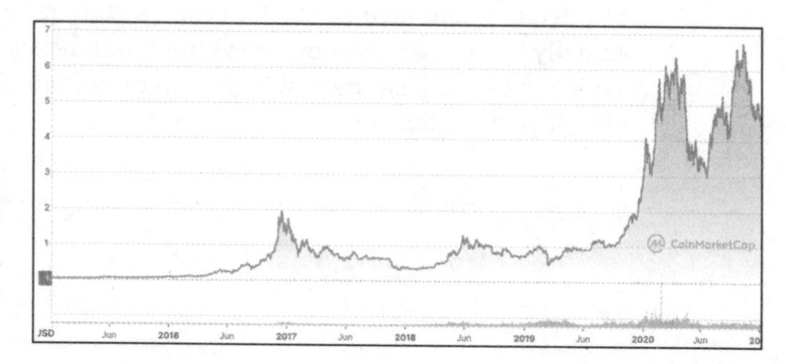

FIGURE 6-1: We're betting you're wishing you bought Bitcoin early in 2016 (or even earlier).

Dollar cost averaging

Dollar cost averaging (DCA) is a popular strategy in the Bitcoin field and is an investing concept that's been around for a long time. It's related to investing in traditional investment vehicles or assets such as mutual funds.

The idea is that you invest a set sum on a regular basis — every week or month, for instance. You don't pay much attention to the price at any point; you simply invest that sum every period. When the price is high, you'll be buying less of the asset; when the price is low, you'll be buying more.

The purpose of dollar cost averaging is to keep you investing in an asset that has a history of rising in value over time, without the risk of trying to time the market with a large lump sum and getting it wrong. You don't think about the investment, you just do it each time it's scheduled.

So, many people DCA into Bitcoin. For instance, you might decide you want to invest $1,000 in Bitcoin this year. (Let's call it $1,040 to make the math easy.) You set up an auto-purchase at an exchange to invest $20 every Friday, so you spread your $1,040 over 52 weeks.

You can see this at work using a dollar cost averaging calculator such as dcaBTC (`https://dcabtc.com/`) or the one at `https://www.bitcoindollarcostaverage.com/`. Figure 6-2 shows what would have happened if you'd invested $20 a week starting three years ago, as shown in the dcaBTC calculator. According to this calculator, you would have invested $3,140; at the current value of Bitcoin, you'd own $17,829 worth. ($3,140 at $20 a week is actually three years and one week for some reason. We're not saying these calculators are highly accurate, but they give an idea of what's going on.)

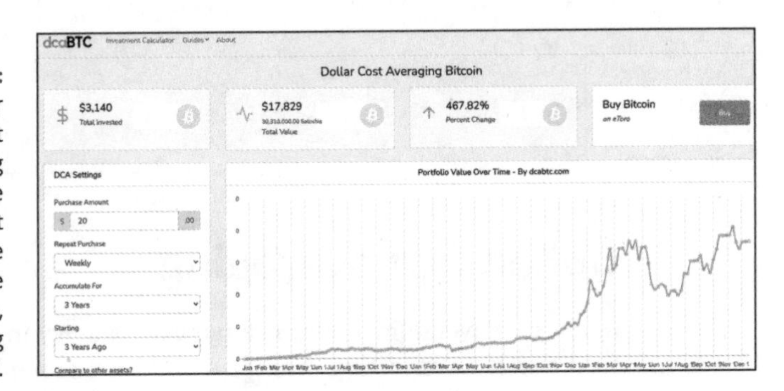

FIGURE 6-2: How dollar cost averaging would have worked out over the last three years, according to dcaBTC.

TIP

Here are a couple of things to understand about dollar cost averaging:

- **It doesn't protect you from losses when you invest in a highly speculative asset that collapses in value.** It's an investment strategy that works well to give people the discipline to invest in an asset that's known to rise over time, despite periodic drops in value. Bitcoin definitely has periodic drops in value, and definitely has, to date, risen over time. Will it continue to do so? That's a decision you have to make, whether you believe it will or not.
- **If you're sure the asset will rise over the long term, then a lump sum invested early might drop in value over the short term — but over the long term provide much higher returns than DCA.** Had you invested three years' worth of weekly $20 periodic investments ($3,120) at the *beginning* of the three-year period, the value would now be over $20,000. But again, market timing is very difficult, and we don't know what's going to happen over the *next* three years.

Timing the market

If you can figure out how to time the market, you can make much more money. Let's say you invested $1,000 into Bitcoin in February 2017 when it was $1,000 a coin, and then:

1. You held it until late in 2017 and sold it when it peaked. Your $1,000 is now about $19,000.
2. You cleverly held it until the price bottomed out and bought again at around $3,400 at the end of 2018. Your 1 Bitcoin is now around 5.5 Bitcoins.
3. You knew there would be another peak, so you watched carefully. In April of 2021, you sold your 5.5 Bitcoins for $349,000. In four years, you increased your investment 349 times.

Simple! *That's* the way to get rich: Time the market! Keep in mind, though, if you screw up your timing, it won't work so well. Is timing the market possible? Plenty of people will tell you it is, all sorts of Bitcoin prognosticators, who have all sorts of theories.

Consider, for instance, Über Holger's Bitcoin Rainbow. The idea is that Bitcoin is on a long-term upward curve, but with fluctuations. It's like a rainbow curving up into the sky, but sometimes the price of Bitcoin is at the bottom edge of the rainbow, sometimes near the top. See what we mean in Figure 6-3.

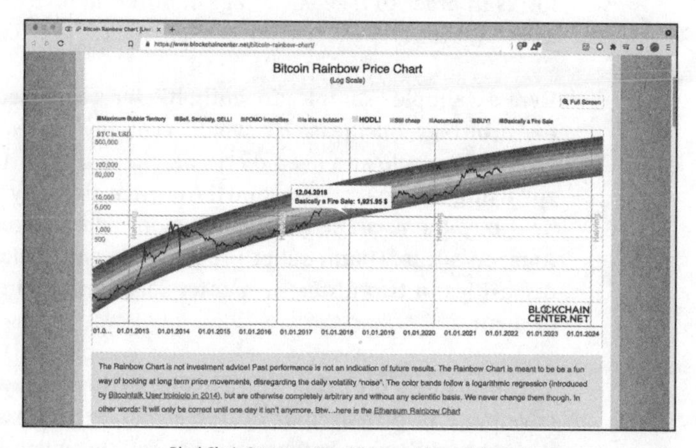

FIGURE 6-3: The Bitcoin Rainbow.

BlockChainCenter.net (see `https://www.blockchaincenter.net/bitcoin-rainbow-chart/`*)*

The closer the price is to the upper edge of the rainbow, the stronger the signal to sell; the closer it is to the lower edge, the stronger the signal to buy.

There are a couple of things to consider with this model. If you just hodl, you'll make money anyway. The rainbow is on an upward curve, remember! Plus, well, we'll let Mr. Holger tell you. The Rainbow curve is not intended as investment advice, and as you've no doubt heard many times, past performance is not an indication of future results. As he explains:

> *The Rainbow Chart is meant to be a fun way of looking at long term price movements, disregarding the daily volatility "noise." The color bands follow a logarithmic regression (introduced by Bitcointalk User trolololo in 2014), but are otherwise completely arbitrary and without any scientific basis It will only be correct until one day it isn't anymore.*

You can find plenty of market-timing advice if that's what you want; we'll let you seek it out. Just be aware that timing markets is very difficult to get right, and quite easy to get wrong.

Arbitrage

Another investment technique some people use is *arbitrage*. The term means "the simultaneous buying and selling of securities, currency, or commodities in different markets or in derivative forms in order to take advantage of differing prices for the same asset" (`https://www.lexico.com/en/definition/arbitrage`).

Here's a simple example. Co-author Peter's son used to be in the toy arbitrage business. He would visit toy stores looking for products on sale at a deep discount, check their prices at Amazon using his smartphone, and if the price disparity was enough, he'd buy them, ship them to Amazon, and sell them through Amazon's third-party seller program. He was looking for price disparities in two different marketplaces and taking advantage of them.

The principle's the same with Bitcoin. In this case, you're taking advantage of pricing that differs across exchanges. (However, it's probably closer between exchanges these days than in the past.) The goal is to find a big enough difference between two exchanges to make it worthwhile to buy on one, then sell on the other.

There are, of course, problems with this. Often the differences are very slim on the more reputable exchanges. In the U.S. there's often a fraction-of-a-percent difference — a 1 percent difference is often a big deal — so you'll need to trade a lot of Bitcoin to make much money. You have to consider exchange fees and transaction fees, and you should also beware of rapid price fluctuations that can ruin your move within seconds.

Still, some people play these games and are even involved in "triangular" arbitrage. This is when you start with Bitcoin, trade it for another, undervalued, cryptocurrency, and then trade that for something else. Then you trade the last cryptocurrency to get back to Bitcoin, with a little more than you started with. Arbitrage "bots" can automate the process. But we're not going into any more detail. If you really want to play this game, first do some serious research and get all your ducks in a row.

Other Bitcoin-related investment vehicles

You have other ways to invest in the Bitcoin revolution, some without even buying Bitcoin itself. You might want to invest in the picks and shovels.

The concept of *picks-and-shovels investing* is the idea of investing not directly into a new industry, but in the companies that support that industry. The name refers to the North American gold rushes of the 19th century. While most people rushed to the gold fields to mine for gold, many people decided instead to support the miners by, for instance, operating bars, restaurants, and hotels, and selling supplies (the picks and shovels). Many got rich doing so (with far less effort and risk than mining gold).

You'll find numerous investing opportunities in the picks and shovels of the Bitcoin revolution:

- Bitcoin exchanges, such as Coinbase (COIN), which is already public, and Kraken, which probably will be soon.

- Cryptocurrency mining companies, some of which have gone public, such as Riot Blockchain (RIOT), Hive Blockchain Technologies (HIVE), and Marathon Digital Holdings (MARA).
- Companies making mining equipment, such as Canaan (CAN).
- Exchange traded funds (ETFs), which are funds traded on a stock exchange like an actual company stock but are funds that invest in particular types of investments or a particular market. Some ETFs now invest in Bitcoin and other cryptocurrencies. Grayscale, for instance (`www.Grayscale.com`), has a variety of cryptocurrency funds, including the Bitcoin Trust.

Don't forget your retirement

How about using some of your retirement savings to invest in cryptocurrency? How can that be done?

Well, before we explain, don't forget what we said earlier: Do not invest more than you can afford to lose. You may be projecting vast gains to make you comfortable in your retirement, but if things go sideways in the crypto markets, you don't want to end up unable to retire!

So, investing with your retirement funds. The first thing to consider is, of course, that picks-and-shovels investing is available to you through regular investment accounts. Coinbase, for instance, is a publicly traded company (COIN, on NASDAQ). Kraken is likely to be public soon, and numerous other crypto picks-and-shovels companies are publicly traded.

Then, of course, there are the ETFs we mention in the previous section. As we explain, ETF stands for *exchange traded funds*, so they're also available through regular investment accounts.

But there are a couple more options. First, there are the crypto-focused retirement account IRAs and 401(k)s such as those provided by Bitcoin IRA (`www.BitcoinIRA.com`), iTrustCapital (`www.iTrustCapital.com`), and IRA Financial (`www.irafinancialgroup.com`). These are linked to exchanges, such as Coinbase, and allow you to trade your retirement funds in cryptocurrency. But be careful, these plans are sometimes very expensive to set up and manage; they often have high transaction fees, for instance.

These companies are actually providing what are known as *solo* or *self-directed* retirement accounts, which have been around for decades. Solo IRAs and 401(k)s allow you to invest in various different forms of assets: real estate, private companies, land, mortgages, private loans, gold and coins, foreign currency — and cryptocurrency.

If you're already working with a brokerage company — perhaps you already have an IRA or 401(k) — they can quite likely set up a solo account for you, but here are a couple caveats:

- **It's quite rare for these companies to do this.** You may have trouble getting through to the right people who understand what you are trying to do and how to do it.
- **You must follow complex rules with a Solo retirement account.** In fact, you need special, complicated paperwork to set up one of these accounts. You may have to go to a company such as IRA Financial to do the paperwork first, and then go to your brokerage to set up the actual account to which you submit funds.

  You could go to one of the directed-account custodians that don't focus on cryptocurrency, companies such as Equity Trust (`www.trustetc.com/`) or The Entrust Group (`www.theentrustgroup.com/`), that will handle the paperwork and provide an account from which you can manage your investments.

If you set up a Solo account through a brokerage company, then take all the money out and trade it through, say, Coinbase, the brokerage company may see an empty account and close it. This is a real problem because you have to maintain an open account to comply with regulations.

So, it may be easier to simply work with one of the dedicated solo-account companies rather than working with your old, familiar brokerage company. Do some research and figure out what's best for you; this is not a simple area to work in, but you may find it well worthwhile to do the homework.

Hodling II — An Even Better Strategy

The big hodling gains in the Bitcoin market, of course, went to people who bought well before the big appreciation of 2017. These people were well ahead of the game, buying, mining, and hodling Bitcoin in 2015, 2014, or earlier.

Consider Satashi Nakamoto, who created around a million Bitcoin starting in 2009. Multiply one million by $50,522.20, the price as we write these words. (We'll save you time: It's more than 50 billion dollars). And then consider that he created this Bitcoin *out of thin air* at a time when it had essentially *no value*. It cost essentially nothing more than a little electricity to run a personal computer. (Don't get excited; mining no longer takes "nothing more than a little electricity." It now takes a major investment in electricity.)

This is an important concept, so bear with us a moment. Here's an even better hodling strategy than the one we described earlier:

1. Build a time machine.
2. Go back to 2009.
3. Buy or mine Bitcoin (in vast quantities).
4. Hold it.
5. Wait for it to go up in price.
6. Sell it. (Just how much money do you need?)

REMEMBER

This may sound trite, but it is a really important concept because you must understand that the really big Bitcoin gains are over!

Stories of huge profits have, to a great degree, generated the interest in Bitcoin that led you to this book. There are people who bought or mined Bitcoin at a price of, say, $1. Those Bitcoins have multiplied in value over *fifty thousand times!* (We're using a starting price of $1 because we don't know how to divide $0 into $50,522.) That simply cannot happen again. $50,000 multiplied by 50,000 is $2.5 billion. Dramatic stories like these have generated such a huge interest, but it's simply not realistic to believe the entire stock of Bitcoin will one day be worth $48,000,000,000,000,000 or so (somewhere around 500 times the world's Gross National Product).

Consider the value of gold. Currently, the entire worldwide store of gold is worth around 9 to 13.5 trillion U.S. dollars, depending on how you measure it. Let's assume, then, firstly that the larger number is the correct one, and that Bitcoin takes over from gold entirely, and the value stored in gold shifts over to Bitcoin. (This isn't likely to happen, by the way, as perhaps half of all gold is stored in the form of jewelry, and whatever praise you might have for Bitcoin, it's never been described as an attractive adornment.)

The value of Bitcoin is currently around 900 million U.S. dollars. In our scenario, with Bitcoin going from 900 million to 13.5 trillion dollars, it would increase in value 15 times. Very significant, but not exactly 50,000 times.

That's not to say that Bitcoin can't still double, triple, quintuple in price, or even much more. But it does mean that if you are looking for greater profits, if you are looking for 20x or 50x in the short term, you have to look elsewhere.

The New Frontier — Other Cryptocurrencies

The really big gains are currently being made in cryptocurrencies other than Bitcoin. Look at the most recent one-year gain for Bitcoin compared with a bunch of other cryptocurrencies:

Bitcoin (BTC):	2.1x
AAVE (AAVE):	2.6x
XRP (XRP):	3.4x
Safe Haven (SHA):	4.3x

Basic Attention Token (BAT):	5.5x
Horizen (ZEN):	6x
Ethereum (ETH):	6.9x
Solana (SOL):	149x
Polygon (MATIC):	151x
Gala (GALA):	1,563x
SHIBA INU (SHIB):	35,000,000x (no, really!)

We don't talk much about other cryptocurrencies in this book, which is, after all, *Bitcoin For Dummies*. But much of what you can learn here is the same or similar for other cryptocurrencies:

- They all use blockchains.
- They all have networks and nodes.
- You can buy them on exchanges — often the same exchanges (Coinbase, for instance, trades around 130 cryptocurrencies).
- They all use wallets, and those wallets are protected in the same ways.

So this book should provide a solid introduction not just to Bitcoin, but to the world of cryptocurrency.

What we're not going to do, though, is tell you which cryptocurrencies to buy. That's a really big question, and the answer changes all the time. The Internet has plenty of blogs and investment services that will tell you. (Whether they are right or not is a different question.)

For instance, the popular Internet-based investment advice service, Motley Fool, which has been in business for more than a quarter of a century, now has a cryptocurrency track called *Digital Explorers*. The team (Motley Fool has around 300 employees; this is no one-man blog) looks for cryptocurrencies that are already established to some degree — not brand-new cryptocurrencies with no track record at all — and that seem to solve real problems using "distributed ledger technologies." The cryptocurrency arena is doing far more than just creating the equivalent of gold and currency; it's revolutionizing the financial arena. You've probably heard the terms *defi* (decentralized finance) and *fintech* (financial technology) by now; we're seeing a revolution in money and the management of financial transactions, and so Motley Fool is looking for cryptocurrencies that will survive and be part of this future.

Motley Fool is not alone. You'll find plenty of advice. Get onto your favorite search engine and look for *cryptocurrency investing*, then settle in for a few weeks of research!

Don't skimp on the research. There's a lot to learn, partly because there are a lot of scams. Here are a couple of things to be aware of:

- *Pump and dump schemes,* where groups of people jump into a cryptocurrency and buy a lot, then start touting the stock in social media, pointing out the high volume of sales. Investors who are not in on the scam jump in and start buying, pushing the price up. Eventually, the original group coordinates a sell-off, leaving the unsuspecting buyers holding worthless crypto!
- Another game often played is for people trying to promote a new cryptocurrency to start trading it *between their own wallets* at high prices. This makes it appear as though the cryptocurrency is worth a lot and a lot of trades are happening.

So, if you do decide to get into this arena, you still have more to learn beyond what you learn in this book. Don't skimp on your research!

NFTs — What's It All About?

Another area in which people are currently making huge profits is non-fungible tokens (NFTs). You might think of these as the digital equivalent of collectibles, or investing in art. You should understand, however, that the NFT market, despite all the hype, is most likely to collapse at some point in the not-too-distant future. Let us explain.

First, what is a non-fungible token? Well, we'll begin with the term *token*, which we haven't used much in this book because it applies more to other cryptocurrencies than to Bitcoin. A token is a digital representation of something. A coin, such as a Bitcoin, is a form of token. Typically, however, when we refer to a token that is stored on its own blockchain — as Bitcoin tokens are stored on the Bitcoin blockchain — we call it a *coin*.

However, there are blockchains — notably the Ethereum blockchain — that allow the creation of different kinds of tokens. Ethereum has its own coin (Ether), but it's also possible to create and store other things on the blockchain, which we call tokens. So these tokens — sometimes called *cryptoassets* — are essentially digital records of ownership of something. They can actually work just like coins, or they can represent something else, such as a physical object or a piece of digital art.

Okay, that's a *token*. But what's a *non-fungible token*, or NFT? The term *fungible* refers (according to Google and the Oxford Languages dictionary) to something that can "replace or be replaced by another identical item; mutually interchangeable." A dollar bill is fungible; one dollar bill is worth the same as another. A Bitcoin is fungible; all Bitcoins have the same value. A bottle of Coca Cola is fungible; one bottle of Coca Cola is the same as another.

So non-fungible means that something is not fungible; it's unique. The *Mona Lisa* is non-fungible; there are no other *Mona Lisas* with which the painting can be switched out. Thus a non-fungible token is a *unique* token; it's not the same as *any* other token, and thus its value is unrelated to the value of any other token (again, unlike Bitcoin in which the market sets the value of all Bitcoins the same).

Tokens can be used to prove ownership of things. So, for instance, a token could be associated with, say, a house, and the person who controlled the token would be able to prove ownership of the house by proving ownership of the token. (Sure, this isn't common, but look for these kinds of uses to become common in the future.) So there are genuine and useful purposes for

NFTs, but what we're talking about here is the recent digital-art NFT insanity.

The NFT digital-art market took off. NFTs can be used to prove ownership of any kind of digital file: a photograph, drawing, animation, video, audio, video games, video game virtual real estate, NBA virtual trading cards, anything you can store digitally can be "NFT'd" (or "minted" as they say in the NFT business).

Effectively, a token in the blockchain is related to the digital file, perhaps links to the file that's stored elsewhere, and the owner of the token can then prove ownership of that digital file. Tokens can also be the equivalent of limited editions. Visit an art gallery or art fair, and you'll see that printed art is often sold as part of a limited edition; the artist may print and sign, say, 100 copies, and mark each one ("1 of 100," "2 of 100," and so on). The same can be done with NFTs: 10 or 100 tokens "own" the digital rights to a piece of art. (If this seems crazy to you, you're not alone; read on.)

In 2021, digital art was tokenized and began selling for ridiculous sums. Take a look at the page from Rarible.com in Figure 6-4, for instance. The art shown on this page is priced in ETH — the Ether currency of the Ethereum blockchain. (Most NFTs, though not all, are stored in the Ethereum blockchain.) The prices, on the day we snapped this screenshot, ranged from 8 ETH to 31,337 ETH. What's that in real money, you ask? $4,000 to $125,140,862.

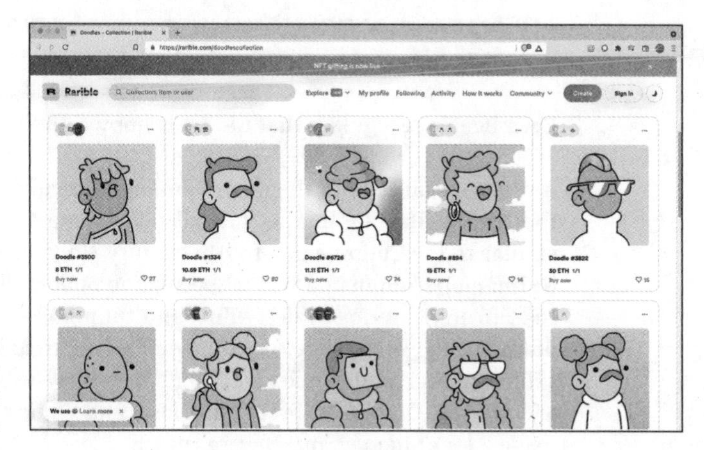

FIGURE 6-4: NFT'd art for sale, on Rarible.com.

We've no idea if they will really sell at this price, but certainly many NFTs have gone for crazy sums, like Beeple's NFT-backed collage, put up for auction by esteemed auction house Christie's. It had a starting price of $100 but sold for more than $69 million! Take a look at the collage in Figure 6-5, or go to `https://onlineonly.christies.com/s/first-open-beeple/beeple-b-1981-1/112924` and zoom in to get a close look. We personally think this guy is a pretty good artist, but $69,000,000 good?

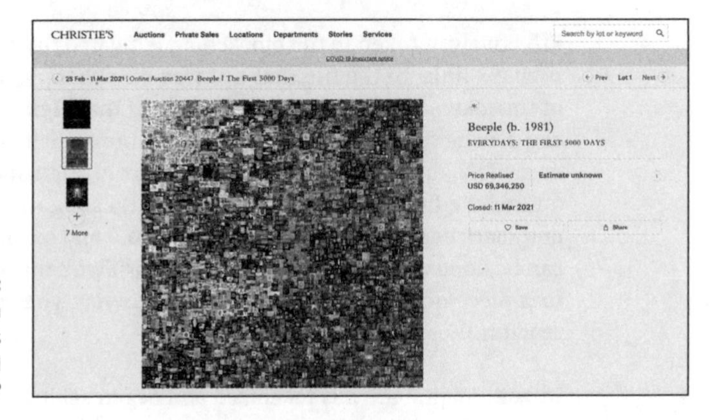

FIGURE 6-5: $69 million for this NFT-linked collage?

So why is the current NFT art market likely to crash at some point? *Because it's crazy!* It really makes no sense. First, let's hear what Beeple has to say on his website about his own art:

> *BEEPLE is mike winkelmann he makes a variety of art crap across a variety of media. some of it is ok, but a lot of it kind of blows a$$. he's working on making it suck less everyday though so bear with him. . . :)*

Even Beeple recognizes that his art is not worth $69 million!

Anyway, regardless of the quality of any particular piece of art, the NFT digital-art market has all the hallmarks of a bubble, similar to the Tulipmania of 17th-century Holland. (Let's call it *NFTmania.*) Tulipmania was a speculative bubble that ran from 1634 to 1637, during which tulips and tulip bulbs rose in price dramatically; some were the equivalent of an annual wage for a skilled laborer, and in one case, a bulb had the value of five average houses. Of course, it couldn't last, and while some people made a lot of money, many were ruined.

Now, don't think we can't see the irony. Here we are writing a book about a digital asset that many believe is a bubble with nothing behind it — that has at times been compared to tulips! — accusing the NFT market of being a bubble with nothing behind it and similar to Tulipmania. But the two are completely different things.

First, the fact that NFTs are non-fungible actually hurts the market. Non-fungibility is something that NFT proponents tout as an important characteristic — *every NFT is different, woohoo!* But actually, it's a huge problem, for two reasons. First, why should *this* NFT be valuable, but not *that* NFT? What is it that makes any particular NFT valuable, in fact? There is no real answer to that question, and thus it's hard to see how any particular NFT can be valuable.

But also, it means there's an unlimited supply of NFTs; anyone can create a new one at any time. Pricing is clearly *not* based on the value of the art, after all; the NFT market is clearly a speculative market.

During Tulipmania, a problem soon appeared; it turned out *you could grow tulips!* At some point soldiers were employed to trample tulip fields into the ground, in order to limit the supply. Well, there will be no trampling of NFTs; unlike Bitcoin with its slow coin issuance and eventual 21-million-coin limit, there will be no limit to the supply of NFTs.

If Bitcoin is the equivalent of gold — and many Bitcoiners believe it is, just a better form of gold — then what are NFTs? Well, imagine that alongside the gold market there was a market for different stones; we'll call it the NFR market. Anyone could go out into the country and find interesting-looking stones (and let's face it, some of the NFT art hasn't taken a lot more effort to create), and sell those individual stones on the Non-Fungible Rocks market. Would that make any sense? *No, of course not!* And the NFT market doesn't make sense, either.

Look, we're not saying that the entire concept of NFTs makes no sense. Certainly, there will be a value to proving ownership of genuinely valuable digital goods — such as movies or the Rolling Stones' music — but the ability to prove ownership of some piece of rubbish that someone just created. . .what's the value there!?

Investors in the NFT market seem to be confusing proof of ownership with proof of value. Okay, so an NFT proves that you own something. But it doesn't prove that item has any value! And yet, NFTs linked to digital goods that a year ago would not have been regarded as particularly valuable are now selling for ridiculous sums, as if somehow the fact that the good has a related NFT means that the good must be valuable. THIS DOES NOT MAKE SENSE!

Still, there are people making a lot of money in the market; co-author Peter recently heard about one person who had invested a couple of thousand dollars and is now holding a hundred thousand dollars' worth of NFTs. The problem is, this investor doesn't understand that the NFT market is clearly an asset bubble, and one day those NFTs will be worthless.

Just like some people during Tulipmania made a lot of money by selling their tulips before the price crashed, and many others lost their investments, the same thing is likely to happen with NFTs. The "smart money" will get out before the crash. The true NFT believers — those who believe there is a real value in NFTs and plan to "hodl" them — are likely to lose their investments. Maybe a few NFT artworks will keep their value; the great majority won't.

WARNING

We're not saying you shouldn't dabble in the NFT market; just that you'd better really understand it, and also understand that it won't last. The market is a little complicated, beyond the scope of this book, so you'll need to do research before you can safely invest if there even is such a thing as safely investing in NFRs (oops, we mean NFTs!).

3 Getting Geeky

IN THIS PART . . .

Understanding how transactions get added to the Bitcoin ledger

Finding out about transaction fees and change addresses

Learning about Bitcoin mining

Reviewing Bitcoin acceptance around the world

Discovering a few Bitcoin problems

» Defining types of nodes on the network

» Learning about transaction fees and change addresses

» Requesting that the blockchain add your transaction

» Understanding the basics of Bitcoin mining

Chapter 7
Understanding the Bitcoin Network and Bitcoin Mining

Chapter 2 covers the basics of how the Bitcoin blockchain functions — public and private keys, the peer-to-peer network, and so on — and Chapters 3 and 4 show you how to use it in practice: working with exchanges and wallets, sending and receiving, and buying and selling Bitcoin.

In this chapter, we delve back into the technology. This isn't stuff you absolutely must know in order to work with Bitcoin, but for those Bitcoin inquiring minds out there, it explains in a bit more detail how the network functions — in particular, what happens when a transaction message leaves your wallet software and arrives at a node in the network. How does that transaction message end up being incorporated into the blockchain?

In fact, this chapter answers the question, "Where does Bitcoin come from?" As you learn in Chapter 1, every ten minutes, 6.25 new Bitcoins are created and enter into circulation. How does that happen? Yep, we're going to look at the *mining* process, too.

The Bitcoin Network

In Chapter 2, we explain that Bitcoin has its own network of nodes, operating across the Internet, and this network has both peer-to-peer and client-server aspects, depending on how you choose to interface with it and which software you use.

The Bitcoin network is a peer-to-peer network of *full nodes,* computers that receive and validate transactions and blocks to make sure they abide by the rules of the network and are all valid; this is the network that is doing the work of maintaining the blockchain. These nodes are peers because they're all equal and work together. (And some of these full nodes, though not all of them, are also miners.) These nodes communicate with each other across the Internet using a particular protocol (a computer language) called the *Bitcoin peer-to-peer protocol*, just like email servers communicate across the Internet using a protocol designed for that purpose.

Client programs — the software wallets we cover in Chapter 4 — are what people use to send transactions to the full nodes to be added to the blockchain. When you install wallet software on your computer or smartphone, or when you set up a custodial wallet by creating an account at an exchange, you're working with a client program that can communicate on your behalf with the peer-to-peer network of full nodes. (These full nodes are servers to your wallet client.)

Instead of merely using basic wallet software to communicate with the network, some Bitcoin true believers like to run their own nodes, to eliminate any unnecessary intermediaries and be directly connected to the network. These nodes receive and verify their own transactions and act as a peer in the peer-to-peer network.

A typical personal computer can function as a node with the correct software. In fact, some of those software programs make running a Bitcoin node on a PC pretty simple.

- **Bitcoin Core:** https://Bitcoin.org/
- **Umbrel:** https://getumbrel.com/
- **Samourai Dojo:** https://Bitcoin-on-raspberry-pi-4.gitbook.io/
- **OpenNode:** https://www.opennode.com/
- **BTCPay Server:** https://btcpayserver.org/

Certain specialized hardware devices are designed to only run a Bitcoin node. These dedicated hardware nodes often consume less electricity compared to a typical PC and can be much smaller in size. If you're interested in doing this (the average Bitcoin owner really doesn't need to), here's a short list of providers that specialize in dedicated Bitcoin node hardware.

- **Lightning In A Box:** https://lightninginabox.co
- **Nodl:** https://www.nodl.it
- **Samourai Dojo:** https://samouraiwallet.com/dojo
- **myNode:** http://mynodebtc.com/products/one
- **Raspiblitz:** https://raspiblitz.com/
- **The Bitcoin Machine:** https://theBitcoinmachines.com/
- **Start9 Labs Embassy:** https://start9labs.com/

There are actually various kinds of nodes. Nodes on the Bitcoin network have around 150 configuration settings, so there's really an almost infinite number of different types of nodes. What follows is a bit of a simplification; understand that the following types of nodes have a lot of overlap.

The nature of the network allows nodes to connect and disconnect, to come and go as they please, and the network and nodes function just fine. Any computer connected to the network is a node, but different nodes do different things:

- **Full nodes** — more correctly known as *fully validating nodes* — are systems that fully validate blocks and transactions. Full nodes check that the blocks and transactions being passed around the network follow the network rules. The nodes then pass the blocks and transactions on, across the network to other full nodes, and those nodes will also validate the blocks and transactions. A full node may contain a copy of the entire blockchain, but not all do; nodes may opt to *prune,* or remove, redundant data to save space. (Currently the Bitcoin blockchain is about 390 GB, so pruning can be worthwhile!)

  Most full nodes also accept, verify, and relay valid incoming transaction messages from wallets. Full nodes may be *listening nodes* (often known as *super nodes*) or *nonlistening nodes*. Some full nodes are connected to *mining rigs,* specialized computer equipment that can mine Bitcoin.

- A **listening node** or *super node* is a publicly connectable full node that allows large numbers of connections with other nodes. The node "listens" for connections from other nodes on particular ports, is generally running all the time, and is not blocked by a firewall. The Bitcoin network has around 10,000 to 15,000 of these super nodes.

- A full **nonlistening** node is one with the *listen* configuration parameter turned off. Having a full listening node can require a lot of bandwith, so most nodes have listening disabled to reduce communications with other nodes. They do not broadcast their presence to the network, and so are not publicly connectable; rather, they have a small number of outgoing connections. Nonlistening nodes are often used by people who want to have wallets that also validate transactions and blocks, but do not want to use the resources required by a listening node.

  By some counts, there are around 80,000 to 100,000 nonlistening nodes on the Bitcoin network, though during Bitcoin's December 2018 peak, there were likely around 200,000.

» A **lightweight node** is one that does not receive and verify every transaction. Most lightweight nodes are wallets; the simple wallet software on your laptop or smartphone is a form of lightweight node. Lightweight nodes communicate with full nodes to transmit transactions and receive information about transaction validation. They're at the mercy of the full nodes — that is, lightweight nodes perform only the transactions or block validations needed for their own transactions.

  Lightweight nodes use a method called *Simple Payment Verification* (SPV) that can verify just the transactions they care about by communicating with other nodes and retrieving a copy of the block headers.

Full nodes connect to each other and pass transactions and blocks between each other, but they don't trust each other. Suppose a node receives a transaction from a wallet, and the node confirms the transaction is invalid; it won't pass that transaction to another node. This doesn't mean a node automatically assumes that a transaction passed to it by another node must be valid. Rather, the node will validate the transaction for itself.

In fact, if a node gets a transaction that it discovers is invalid — for example, if the transaction is spending more money than is available on the address from which the money is coming — the node throws away the transaction, and it also blocks the node that sent the bad transaction. In this way, the network polices itself; valid transactions and blocks are verified by thousands of different nodes, bad data is disposed of quickly, and bad actors are quickly isolated from the network.

TIP

It's this lack of trust that builds trust. Nodes are blocked by other nodes, and thus the system is self-regulating. For example, depending on the infraction, nodes may be blocked for a few hours, or permanently blocked for repeated, obviously intentional misbehavior. Because nodes don't trust other nodes, the overall system can be trusted.

If you'd like to get an idea of the extent and distribution of the Bitcoin full node network (as it appeared at the time of writing), take a look at `https://bitnodes.io`, shown in Figure 7-1. This chart shows just the full listening nodes; there are likely eight or ten times this number of full nonlistening nodes.

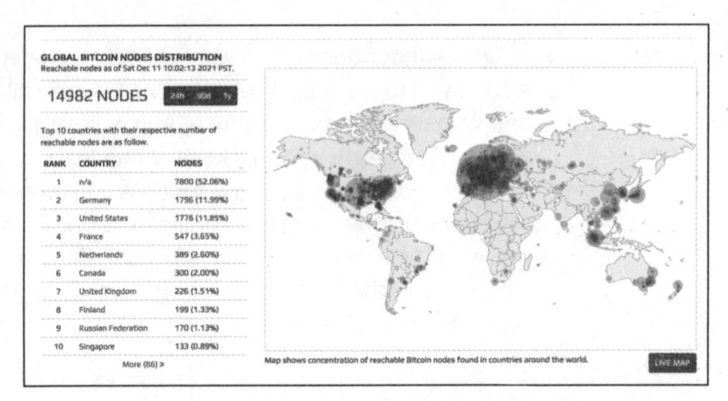

FIGURE 7-1: A live view of the full listening node count on the Bitcoin network plus the distribution of these nodes across the world.

From Bitnodes, `https://bitnodes.io/`

Submitting Transactions

In this section, we follow a transaction from your wallet, out onto the network, and into the blockchain. Let's say that you want to send someone some money, some of your Bitcoin. Perhaps you're making a purchase, donating to a charity, or selling some of your Bitcoin. For whatever reason, you're transferring Bitcoin from one of your addresses to someone else's.

And let's say that you have a single Bitcoin associated with an address in the Bitcoin blockchain, and you want to send one tenth of that money (0.1BTC) to Joe.

So, using your wallet software, you enter Joe's address, the Bitcoin address he gave you to use for the transaction. You designate how much Bitcoin you're going to send him (0.1BTC). You also designate how much of a fee you're willing to pay for the transaction. You saw all this in action in Chapters 3 and 4.

Looking at transaction fees

Fees are often measured in Satoshi/byte and can range between 1 to over 2,000 Satoshi/byte (that is, the fee is based on the size of the transaction message your wallet sends to the blockchain, not the value of the transaction). The busier the network, the higher the fee required to incentivize miners to include your transaction in a block quickly.

A Satoshi is the smallest unit of Bitcoin — one hundred millionth of a Bitcoin. If your wallet balance is 1.00000001BTC, the last digit denotes one Satoshi. Your wallet software will probably suggest a fee, estimated on current rates and network congestion; some wallet software will pick the fee for you, while other software lets you set that fee manually for more precision and to avoid overspending. Pay too little, and the transaction may not go through or may take a long time; pay too much, and, well, you paid too much. Transactions with higher fees will get picked up by mining software more quickly than those with lower fees, of course; the more high-fee transactions in a block, the more the winning miner will earn.

For our example, say that you decide to pay a 0.0004BTC fee. Now, say this is your address:

```
1x6YnuBVeeE65dQRZztRWgUPwyBjHCA5g
```

Remember, it has a balance of 1BTC. That's what's known as the *input* for the transaction.

And here's Joe's address:

```
38DcfF4zWPi7bSPkoNxxk3hx3mCSEvDhLp
```

That's one of the *outputs* in the transaction. So far, the transaction looks like this:

```
Input
1x6YnuBVeeE65dQRZztRWgUPwyBjHCA5g - 1BTC
Output
38DcfF4zWPi7bSPkoNxxk3hx3mCSEvDhLp - 0.1BTC
```

But wait, we need another output. We're putting 1BTC into the transaction, giving 0.1BTC to Joe, so we have to decide what happens to the other 0.9BTC (actually, the other 0.8996BTC, as 0.0004BTC is being paid to the miner as a fee). So, where does the 0.8996BTC go? It goes back to you, of course, as your change, to a "change address." So the transaction might now look like this:

```
Input
1x6YnuBVeeE65dQRZztRWgUPwyBjHCA5g - 1BTC
```

```
Outputs
38DcfF4zWPi7bSPkoNxxk3hx3mCSEvDhLp - 0.1BTC
1x6YnuBVeeE65dQRZztRWgUPwyBjHCA5g - 0.8996BTC
```

We've shown 0.8996BTC going back to the original address. It's like going into a store with a ten-dollar bill, and paying $1 for something. You take $10 out of your pocket, hand it to the clerk, the clerk gives you $9 back, and you put the $9 into your pocket.

Change address

We've shown the change coming back to the same address used for the Input, and that's certainly possible. However, most wallet software will use a different address, or a *change address*, for the second of these outputs. Either way, you get the change back to an address owned by you, managed by your wallet software. We show you in Chapter 4 how to see the change address in the example wallet software we used.

Note that nothing is stated in the outputs regarding the fee. That's because the transaction sent by your wallet doesn't explicitly state the fee. Rather, it says, "Send 0.1BTC to the first address, send 0.89996BTC to the second address, and keep the change!" And that's just what the miner who wins the right to add this transaction to the blockchain will do: The mining rig will keep the change as a transaction fee.

TECHNICAL STUFF

This transaction information is put into a *script*, a text message that will be sent over the crypto network. Your wallet software uses your private key to sign the transaction — that is, it encrypts the transaction information using the private key. It then adds the associated public key to the message and sends the transaction out onto the Bitcoin network. (See Chapter 2 for a primer on private and public keys.) Within seconds, a node will receive the transaction just as when you send an email, and within seconds your email will be received by a mail server. (You can think of your wallet program as a special form of messaging software.)

PUBLIC KEY ENCRYPTION

Cryptography is the crypto in cryptocurrency; it uses what's known as *public key encryption*. It's how you prove that you own the money associated with an address. The person spending the cryptocurrency uses a private key to encrypt the message and then bundles the associated public key with the message. The miner can determine that the address from which the cryptocurrency is coming is associated with the public key, and thus if the public key can decrypt the message, the message must have been created by the person controlling the associated private key. (All three — private key, public key, and address — are mathematically and uniquely associated.) See Chapter 2 for more details.

Verifying the transaction

The first thing the node does when receiving the transaction is to use the public key to decrypt the message so that it can read it. It must then *verify* the transaction. This process ensures that the transaction is valid, based on a number of different criteria. We won't go into all the details, but essentially, the node asks itself (and answers) questions like these:

- Is the message properly structured and not exceeding the maximum message size?
- Does the message contain valid information — for example, does it contain valid input and output addresses and sums, within valid ranges, assigned to the addresses?
- Does the input address exist in the blockchain with a valid balance?
- Is a sufficient transaction fee associated with the transaction?
- Does the wallet sending the transaction have a right to send the transaction — that is, is the public key sent with the message associated with the address from which the cryptocurrency is being sent?

What happens if the message is not valid in some way? The node throws it away because there's no point sending it on to the next node. But if it's valid, the node adds it to a pool of valid transactions (a *memory pool* or *mempool*), and sends it to other nodes on the network. These other nodes will do the same: decrypt and verify the transaction and add it to their mempool if they find it valid. (That's part of the *consensus* process, ensuring that everyone agrees.) Thus the message, in a matter of seconds, *propagates* (spreads) across the crypto network, being picked up by node after node.

TECHNICAL STUFF

The mempool is a collection of transactions waiting to be confirmed, solidified, and included into a block. The size of the mempool ebbs and flows depending on the current number of transactions hitting the network; as the network congestion goes up, transaction fees go up. (Check out this very useful site for inspecting the current backlog of transactions in the mempool and current transaction fees: `https://jochen-hoenicke.de/queue/#0,all`.)

Now, *some* nodes are mining nodes. These nodes add blocks to the blockchain, in a competition to earn Bitcoin. These nodes are also creating mempools, collections of transactions to add to the blockchain.

Mining for Bitcoin — the 10-minute contest

Here's how the mining competition works. We'll begin at the point at which one contest has just ended, and a new one is about to begin. (Each contest lasts approximately ten minutes and is immediately followed by the next one.) The miner that won the just-ended contest has won the right to add a block to the blockchain (and in return earns the transaction fees and the 6.25-Bitcoin block subsidy).

When this happens, the winner sends the winning block out across the network, and it gets picked up by the other nodes and added to their versions of the blockchain. That's when the next competition begins.

Each round of this game is designed to last around ten minutes. One purpose of mining is to dribble new Bitcoin into the blockchain at a set rate: currently 6.25 Bitcoins every ten minutes, halving every four years. On average, a miner succeeds at the game every ten minutes, is rewarded in cryptocurrency, and the game restarts.

A miner receiving the new block first compares the block to the miner's mempool and removes transactions from the mempool that have been added to the latest block, leaving only transactions that have not yet been added to the blockchain.

The miner then gathers transactions from the mempool into a new block, which is known as a *candidate block*. This block can be added to the blockchain, *if* the miner wins the competition.

The miner creates a block header for the block, which includes a timestamp, a software version number, the hash of the previous block, and a few other things we don't need to cover. One thing we do care about, though, is the *nonce*, a number that's going to be used in the competition. We'll come back to that in a moment.

Thousands of mining computers around the world have created *candidate blocks* of data — records of transactions — and are eager to add their own blocks to the blockchain. So the system has a choice to make: Which block, from which miner, will be added to the blockchain? That decision is based on a combination of chance and computing power. The Bitcoin network uses something called a *proof of work (PoW)* task. All the miners are given the same task to undertake, and the first one to accomplish it wins, adds their block to the blockchain, and takes home the block reward: the combined transaction fees and block subsidy.

HASHING?

A hash is a long number that is a kind of fingerprint for a set of data. That data, when passed through the same hashing algorithm, will always produce the same hash, and that hash cannot match any other set of data. The hash identifies the data uniquely. For more on hashing, see Chapter 2.

The various cryptocurrencies that use proof of work tasks use different methods. A PoW task can be almost anything, as long as it is a complex task that takes a more or less predictable amount of work and results in an answer that's quickly and easily verifiable.

Primecoin, for example, has a proof of work task that involves finding chains of prime numbers that are then stored in the blockchain and available for use by mathematicians for, well, whatever it is they do with prime numbers. However, in the case of Bitcoin, the PoW task has no practical use beyond securing transactions in the blockchain. Here's how Bitcoin's PoW task functions. (In this chapter, by the way, when we refer to the *miner,* we mean the mining software, of course. The actual *human* miner sets everything up to run, but it's the mining computer — the *rig* — and the mining software actually doing the work.)

The miner is looking for a number that matches a particular criterion; it must be a number that is below a certain target (that target is an additional item stored in the block header).

The number is created by hashing the block header, creating, in effect, a digital fingerprint. The hash is a 256-digit binary number, expressed as a 64-digit hexadecimal number. (For more on hashing, see Chapter 2.) Here's an example:

```
000000000000000000074f788dcd5082178c6559e0c1dcbe115d57b64
    ef9309d
```

The task for the miners is to find a hash number that is *equal to or less than* the target number. Look at the preceding hash. It starts with 19 zeros and is actually a winning hash from a moment ago. The more zeros at the start of the target number, the smaller the target number, and therefore — as you'll see when we explain how the contest is carried out — the harder it is to find a number that is equal to or less than the target (because there are quite simply fewer possible numbers equal to or less than the target).

By the way, over time, the difficulty of the contest typically goes up; this is because, over time, the target number is becoming smaller and smaller. Our example has 19 leading zeros, but over time, the number of leading zeros will increase (in effect, the number will get smaller).

The smaller the target number, the harder the task, right? This is because fewer numbers are below a small number than a large number, and we need a hash that is less than the target. The miner does not have to find a particular hash, simply a hash that is equal to or less than the target number. Thus, the larger the target number, the more possible matches there are, and the smaller the target number, the fewer possible matches there are.

So, the miner hashes the block header. But every time you hash a piece of data, you're going to get the same result, right? (That's the whole point of a hash: it uniquely identifies a particular piece of data.) So if the miner hashes the block header and finds that it's *not* less than the target, it can't simply try again, or it'll get the same result. It has to change the block header first, and *then* hash it again.

Remember that the block contains a nonce? Well, the *nonce* is simply a number. The miner changes the nonce and hashes again. This time, the result of the hash will be different. Chances are, it's still not less than the target number, so the miner changes the nonce, hashes again, and checks the number, and so on.

Now, the magic of the hashing algorithm is that you can't predict which nonce will get you the result you want. The only way to find the result you want is to try, and try, and try again — thousands of times — until you get a hash that is less than the target. And if you do this before anyone else, you win!

This task is hugely difficult. A 64-digit hexadecimal number has this many possible variations (whatever this number is called!):

39,400,000,000,000,000,000,000,000,000,000,000,000,000,000,000,0
00,000,000,000,000,000,000,000,000,000,000,000,000,000,000,000,0
00,000,000,000,000,000,000,000,000

REMEMBER

The vast majority of hashes, purely based on chance, are going to exceed the target number. And again, the lower the target number, the fewer chances of picking a number below the target. Still, at some point a miner *will* find a nonce that, when added to the block header, results in a hash below the target number — the miner wins!

Winning the Bitcoin

So, the miner announces to the network that it's won. It then creates a block header for the block, which includes a timestamp, a software version number, the hash of the previous block, and the hash of the block's transaction's Merkle tree root (never mind, we don't have to know about Merkle trees). The miner then sends its *candidate block*, with its block header and the header's hash, to the network, so other nodes can check it. And check it they do.

REMEMBER

A block doesn't get added to the blockchain unless it's been verified. To make sure the miner has actually won, the nodes hash the block header and check the result against the existing block header's hash. The proof of work task is very difficult to perform but easily verified; with the right nonce in the header, hashing the header will result in a winning hash number, so it can be quickly seen that the miner actually did win the contest. The nodes then add the miner's block to the blockchain, and the contest resets and begins again. Oh, and the winner gets the block reward — the transaction fees and the 6.25-Bitcoin block subsidy — assigned to their address in the new block.

That's mining!

Who typically wins these contests? It's a combination of both chance and computing power. Each time a miner changes the nonce and hashes the block header, there's a mathematically defined chance of winning. It's low, but possible. Hey, the miner might just win on the very first try! (You might, but it's just not very likely.)

How does a miner increase its chances of winning? By adding a nonce and rehashing over and over and over, millions of times — as many times as possible. Each time a miner hashes, it's like buying a lottery ticket. So more lottery tickets means better odds. More powerful mining rigs can carry out more calculations, as quickly as possible — and thus increase their chances of winning.

The more equipment a (human) miner has, and the more powerful that equipment, the more chances that miner has of winning. There are around 144 of these contests every day, 4,320 every month. That's 27,000 new Bitcoins being created every month (and thousands more earned by miners in transaction fees), so the stakes are huge. (27,000 Bitcoins are currently worth over $1.3B.)

Bitcoin Presets

All of these preset rules and system guidelines are baked into the software that runs the Bitcoin blockchain. A block contains around 2,000 transactions (it varies slightly, depending on how much information is in each transaction). One block is added every ten minutes, more or less. In order to maintain this block emission rate, the software has to adjust its difficulty rules every now and then — every 2,016 blocks (more or less every two weeks).

If it's taking less than ten minutes for each block, on average — because more computing power is being used for mining, as more miners and mining rigs come online — then the target number will be proportionally reduced, to increase the difficulty. If it's taking more than ten minutes, though (as the price of Bitcoin drops, fewer people mine), then the target number is increased, reducing the difficulty.

Another preset baked into the underlying mathematics is the "halvening." Every 210,000 blocks — around every four years — the block subsidy is halved. At the time of writing, the subsidy is 6.25BTC, but sometime in 2024 it will drop to 3.125BTC, in 2028 it will go to 1.5625BTC, and so on.

This process may all sound very complicated, but the hard work is carried out by the mining rig and the node software. Miners are not sitting down every ten minutes with paper and pencil hashing the block header! They set up the appropriate hardware and software and let it run.

WARNING

However, before you think, "Wow, I should get into mining," we recommend that you read *Cryptocurrency Mining For Dummies* because mining is a complicated subject. You can't simply hook up your computer to the Internet and run mining software. Well, you *can*, but you're highly unlikely to be successful. These days, mining Bitcoin requires specialized equipment and a lot of knowledge about how the entire process works. It also requires a lot of electricity! Mining is really not for everyone, so check out our mining book before you get too far down that road.

» Exploring why El Salvador *isn't* good for Bitcoin!

» Understanding why troubled nations seek out Bitcoin

» Delving into why emerging nations love crypto

Chapter 8

Bitcoin Adoption in the Real World

In Chapter 6, you learn about investing in Bitcoin, and that chapter, we believe, gives a reasonably balanced view. In it, we explain why Bitcoin is bound to survive and also why it's bound to collapse. We leave the choice of what you'll believe up to you.

But we do think there's something else worth taking into consideration while you're making that choice: just how much the use of Bitcoin (and other cryptocurrencies) is being adopted around the world. The use of Bitcoin and other cryptocurrencies is growing, and growing fast. Chainalysis (a blockchain analysis company we discuss in this chapter) noted that adoption has skyrocketed recently, in particular starting at the end of 2019. Adoption around the world, they discovered, grew 23 times over the next 18 months or so.

Cryptocurrency is no longer the virtually invisible domain of crypto geeks, libertarians, and hackers. It's entering the mainstream in a way that, many would argue, guarantees it's here to stay. So in this chapter, we take a look at how Bitcoin is being accepted and picked up around the world.

Bitcoin in the Boardroom

The depth of involvement in Bitcoin of large corporations is important in various ways. It legitimizes what otherwise would be seen as little more than a cult. It also boosts the price, of course, as more money — big money — chases a relatively fixed asset. And it surely helps improve the likelihood of Bitcoin's survival. If large corporations see Bitcoin as a worthwhile asset, with a genuine purpose in the world's economy — and are willing to accept that it's a very volatile asset — that definitely improves Bitcoin's chance of a long and fruitful future.

And large corporations are most definitely involved. Early in 2021, Tesla bought $1.5 billion worth of Bitcoin, and the markets saw a sudden boost in price. MicroStrategy currently hodls around $4 billion worth. Block.one owns more than $6 billion worth.

Then there are the investment firms getting into the space; in fact, the largest holder of Bitcoin is the Grayscale Bitcoin Trust, with around $26 billion worth. Dozens of funds and ETFs (exchange traded funds) dabble in cryptocurrencies, including Bitcoin, such as the ProShares Bitcoin Strategy ETF, which trades in Bitcoin futures (and has around $1.4 billion in assets).

If you'd like to get an idea of who is holding Bitcoin, check out `https://bitcointreasuries.net/` and `https://www.kevinrooke.com/bitcoin`.

Bitcoin in Nations

Bitcoin is now being accepted and even adopted by nation states. Before we get to the details of that, though, consider that Bitcoin already rivals most of the world's currencies in terms of total value.

You can find a fascinating comparison on the BitcoinMoneySupply website (at `https://bitcoinmoneysupply.xyz/`; the chart is updated only periodically). This table compares the M2 money supplies of 132 nations, measured in U.S. dollar value. M2 includes cash, traveler's checks (does anyone use traveler's checks anymore?), bank checking, savings, and other demand deposits, money-market account deposits, and other time deposits (such as CDs) under $100,000.

Where does the total value of Bitcoin sit? At the time of writing, it was at number 16, just after the Netherlands and just before Russia. The value of Bitcoin is greater than the value of the Indian rupee, Brazilian real, or Swedish krona, countries with a combined population of around 1.6 billion people. Perhaps that puts it in perspective.

So, what are countries doing about Bitcoin? China is trying to kill it — or at least stop its citizens from using it — perhaps not surprising considering the government's obsession with control. Egypt, too, has banned the use of Bitcoin, for the same reason. In total, nine nations have completely banned its use, including Algeria, Bangladesh, Iraq, Morocco, Nepal, Qatar, and Tunisia.

Another 42 (or so) nations have *implicit bans*, which means there's no outright ban on owning Bitcoin, but certain Bitcoin-related functions are banned, such as running an exchange or the trading of Bitcoin by banks. (The U.S. Library of Congress publishes a periodic report regarding the status of Bitcoin. Do a search at `https://blogs.loc.gov/law/`.)

That's approximately 50 countries, more than double the number the Library of Congress reported in 2018. The number of countries *regulating* Bitcoin has increased to 103; this may sound bad, but paradoxically it's a good thing. A libertarian strain running through the Bitcoin community certainly wants government to have no role whatsoever, but that's not terribly realistic; without regulation of some sort, Bitcoin cannot gain wide acceptance. If you want the price of Bitcoin to continue rising, you should applaud (sensible) regulation.

Thus these 103 countries allow the use of Bitcoin, but have regulations regarding, for instance, the tax treatment and reporting of Bitcoin transactions. This represents 103 countries that accept Bitcoin and recognize that cryptocurrencies are here to stay.

These nations typically regard Bitcoin as an *asset*, not a currency. The crypto "press" occasionally gets excited about countries that, the press claims, are using Bitcoin as "legal tender." But only one country in the world regards Bitcoin as a currency that can be used to satisfy any debt or in any commercial transaction (El Salvador; more about that in a moment). A country that wouldn't consider banning its citizens from owning gold or silver probably wouldn't ban them from owning Bitcoin either, if that's what they want to do. Why would it? Countries with that kind of freedom and regard for personal rights aren't likely to ban cryptocurrencies.

Thus, at present, in effect, one third of the world's nations ban Bitcoin, while two thirds accept it. It does appear, however, that India may soon ban it in some form, which would mean that the world's two largest countries — India and China, representing more than a third of the world's population — have outlawed it. However, within most of the countries explicitly or implicitly banning Bitcoin, tech-savvy citizens are still able to buy and sell cryptocurrencies, which are very hard to ban if your country has an open Internet! Are the reported 100 million Indians who own Bitcoin going to get out of the market? It's not very likely.

When governments love Bitcoin

Some nations are not merely accepting Bitcoin, but actually *embracing* it. The best-known nation to do so — and the one with the firmest embrace — is El Salvador. This corrupt little Central American semi-democracy has *fully* embraced Bitcoin. The country now has two currencies: the U.S. dollar and Bitcoin.

Now, this isn't actually a good thing for Bitcoin, despite what many Bitcoiners believe, as we'll explain. But we want to be clear that the Salvadoran Bitcoin debacle says nothing about the use of Bitcoin *as an asset* and says little about Bitcoin's potential use as a currency in the future. It merely shows that tin-pot dictators sometimes do stupid things.

In the summer of 2021, El Salvador enacted the Bitcoin Law, rammed through in one day by El Salvador's dictator (that's what the president actually calls himself). Nobody had even seen the law before it was issued, but the nation was given just 90 days to get ready. The law declares Bitcoin to be legal tender; all businesses have to accept Bitcoin transactions, and citizens can pay their taxes using Bitcoin, too. We should perhaps say Bitcoin is *partially* legal tender because it's not fully regarded as legal tender. Merchants don't have to accept Bitcoin if they're technically unable to do so, and many smaller and poorer merchants don't accept it.

It's popular among Bitcoiners to point to El Salvador with glee, but this isn't actually a moment of triumph for Bitcoin; it's not going smoothly and could even turn into a total disaster (it's already raised the interest rates on the country's national debt). How could one expect to convert a technically sophisticated nation — let alone one in which most citizens have little or no Internet access — to Bitcoin in 13 weeks?

This situation is ironic for Bitcoiners, who point to governments "printing money" as a reason to use Bitcoin as a currency. It seems that Dictator Nayib Bukele — who has maintained his popularity by increasing spending without increasing taxes — is trying to fix his economic problems by using various economic shenanigans to use Bitcoin to, in effect, pump more money into the Salvadoran economy! Yep, to *print money*. This is a fascinating story we don't have space to go into here. If you want to learn more, search the interwebs for *el salvador bitcoin printing money*.

The country has its own wallet software — the Chivo — that was provided free to everybody, along with $30 worth of Bitcoin. Using a government-issued wallet — especially one named *goat*, with private source code that can't be independently reviewed — sounds like a terrible idea to us. For any Bitcoin true believer who wants to get government *out* of the money business, it just makes no sense at all!

Still, many Salvadorans signed up, took their $30 worth of Bitcoin, spent it or converted it to U.S. dollars, and never went back to their Chivo. There are reportedly now more Chivo accounts in

El Salvador than traditional bank accounts. (The $30 bonus led to an epidemic of identity theft, by the way.)

Salvadorans can use other wallet software if they want, though, and many will probably want to switch after reports from hundreds of people claiming their transactions are sometimes not completed (the money leaves their Chivo wallets, but never arrives at the other end), and that Bitcoin appears to be disappearing from their wallets. (A one-time inspector general of the El Salvador National Civil Police has put together a group of almost a thousand complainants.)

However, another problem with adoption has been that many people aren't using Bitcoin because they simply don't understand it or trust it. It's unclear how many Chivo users will be able to switch to another wallet. Yet another problem, of course, is the current volatility of Bitcoin, which makes it totally unsuitable as a national currency.

There's more to this story, much more, and none of it is pretty. Unfortunately, El Salvador's experiment is a terrible advertisement for Bitcoin. But then, it was a poorly thought-out and implemented plan, based on a crackpot idea from El Salvador's emperor (as he also likes to be known). Apart from a way to increase the money supply, it's unclear what benefit using Bitcoin was intended to provide; in any case, El Salvador's inflation rate has been low since they dumped the colón for the U.S. dollar in 2001.

El Salvador's experiment, while it suggests that Bitcoin isn't easily useable as a currency (as we've said elsewhere in this book!), says nothing directly about Bitcoin's viability as an *asset*. Other countries are embracing Bitcoin in a less controversial way. It's been reported, for instance, that Bulgaria is holding 200,000BTC. They originally seized the Bitcoin in operations against organized crime, and if they are *still* holding it, they've done very well indeed. It was worth about $3 billion back then and around $10 billion at the time of writing.

Seizing Bitcoin from criminals is a common way for Bitcoin to get into the hands of governments. The U.S. government has seized —and auctioned off — billions of dollars' worth. Had they held onto it, rather than getting rid of it, the national debt would be a bit lower! For instance, in 2014 they sold 30,000 Bitcoins to venture capitalist Tim Draper. That would be worth more than $15 billion now, but the prescient Mr. Draper paid just $19 million at the time.

The government of Ukraine has been reported to be carrying over 46,000 Bitcoin on its balance sheet (over $23 billion), and in September of 2021 passed regulations that were intended to turn the nation — which already had a thriving cryptocurrency sector — into a world hub for Bitcoin and other cryptocurrencies.

Nations promoting crypto

A number of countries are actively promoting Bitcoin and cryptocurrency endeavors in a move to create friendly environments for the companies of the crypto-future to thrive in:

- **Malta has passed several laws intended to create a crypto-friendly base in which companies can operate.** The large exchange, Binance, actually moved operations from Japan to Malta for this reason.
- **Portugal has a Digital Transitional Action Plan designed to make the country a crypto hotspot.** The plan includes making certain Bitcoin and cryptocurrency transactions tax-free in many cases. Portugal also has various visa programs that may make it easier for crypto traders and others working in the Bitcoin and cryptocurrency space to live there.
- **The Baltic nations of Latvia, Lithuania, and Estonia are all known to be crypto-friendly.** Numerous cryptocurrency startup companies operate in the region, and national companies, such as AirBaltic and the Bank of Lithuania, are involved.

» **Gibraltar, a self-governing British Overseas Territory, is on its way to be a cryptocurrency hub.** The government of Gibraltar is in the process of reviewing a proposal under which Valereum, a blockchain company, will buy the Gibraltar Stock Exchange (GSX). If it goes through, GSX (only operating since 2015) will be the world's first stock exchange in which cryptocurrencies can be traded. The territory has also issued crypto regulations, and has licensed 14 cryptocurrencies and blockchain firms.

The goal is to turn Gibraltar into a world cryptocurrency hub: *Blockchain Rock*, as some are calling it. If they can pull it off, it will be a huge win for a "nation" of only 33,000, with only three stock-exchange employees!

Additionally, a number of countries are considering, or actively developing, their own digital currencies. Sometimes called *Central Bank Digital Currencies* (CBDC), these countries have been watching the cryptocurrency world and have seen that these transactions can be cheaper and faster. Essentially, the idea is that nations would create their own electronic money, denominated in the same currency as the nation's legal tender. Rather than running transactions through the banks or credit-card networks, this electronic money would allow consumers to make payments directly to vendors through the digital-currency network.

China is already introducing a digital currency, the *e-Renmimbi*; billions of dollars' worth of transactions have already been processed. Mobile transactions have been big in China for some time, with more than $40 trillion worth of such transactions taking place over the last few years, so moving to an actual digital currency will be a relatively easy step.

In the U.S., the Federal Reserve has been researching the issue, but won't yet say whether it believes such a currency should be introduced. In the UK, the Bank of England is taking a similar stand: actively researching the implications of introducing a CBDC, but not yet saying whether or not it should do so.

According to PricewaterhouseCoopers (PwC), more than 60 central banks are investigating digital currencies (some have been doing so since 2014), and a number of nations, in addition to China, have already begun a rollout. The Bahamas and Cambodia have already launched digital currencies that citizens can use, with pilot systems operating in Ukraine, Uruguay, Ecuador, the Eastern Caribbean, Sweden, and South Korea. Even more nations are already running advanced pilot digital-currency systems for use by financial institutions.

REMEMBER

These national digital currencies don't have the characteristics that, according to Bitcoin true believers, are essential for them to be true cryptocurrencies, most notably independence from governments. Governments would still be able to issue more digital currency, for instance. Networks would also be centralized, although most would still use blockchain functionality. Regardless, we believe the move towards digital currencies does one important thing: It legitimizes the cryptocurrency space and shows that Bitcoin and cryptocurrencies can and do have a value.

It's not just the rich

When considering adoption of Bitcoin and other cryptocurrencies around the world, note that it's not just the obvious nations whose citizens are getting involved. Adoption is widely spread around the globe and high among many poorer countries, too. Indeed, poorer nations are often where the use of cryptocurrency is most significant.

Chainalysis, a blockchain analysis company (`https://www.chainalysis.com/`), reviews the use of cryptocurrencies in over 150 nations around the world, and gives each nation a score weighted according to that nation's *purchasing power parity* (a measure of the country's wealth per resident). You might expect to see the United States in the top 20, and it is (currently at number 8). You might expect to find China there, too, and it is (number 13). But how about Vietnam? (number 1), Kenya (number 5), and Nigeria (number 6)?

This list shows the latest top 20 countries that are adopting cryptocurrency (go to `https://blog.chainalysis.com/reports/2021-global-crypto-adoption-index/` to see the 2021 analysis):

1 Vietnam	11 Colombia
2 India	12 Thailand
3 Pakistan	13 China
4 Ukraine	14 Brazil
5 Kenya	15 Philippines
6 Nigeria	16 South Africa
7 Venezuela	17 Ghana
8 United States	18 Russian Federation
9 Togo	19 Tanzania
10 Argentina	20 Afghanistan

Not a single Western European nation is in the top 20. Canada's not there, nor is Australia. But Venezuela and Afghanistan are.

In wealthier nations, growth in the adoption of cryptocurrencies is mainly driven, according to Chainalysis, by "institutional investment." In many poorer countries around the world, however, it's ordinary people who are putting their money into cryptocurrencies. Why? To protect their wealth and savings in countries with weak currencies, and also to send and receive *remittances* (wages sent home by family members working abroad in wealthier countries). Sending money home via a cryptocurrency blockchain is often cheaper than using traditional money-transfer methods (such as Western Union).

In more developed nations, a very large proportion of transactions is going through large exchanges, but in developing nations, much of the business is through peer-to-peer (P2P) networks — trading platforms that let people carry out transactions from one person directly to another person, with no go-between third party (like an exchange or a bank) necessary.

In many countries, a new business has evolved: that of the *crypto-to-cash broker*, who converts cash to crypto and crypto to cash. (Unfortunately, such P2P systems and brokers are often risky.)

Ironically perhaps, some of these poorer nations are actually primed to use cryptocurrency in a way that people in wealthier nations are not. In the West, people use credit and debit cards for a very large portion of transactions, but in sub-Saharan Africa, for instance, people have become accustomed to using mobile phone–based banking and transactions. Mobile payments are also hugely popular in India, where more transactions are mobile-based than credit card–based. They've been using their smartphones to send money to-and-fro for years; the idea of doing the same with cryptocurrencies must seem familiar and comfortable to many people.

Cryptocurrency wallets can, of course, be installed on smartphones (most are), and even in poor countries many people — including not just the middle class but poor people — now have smartphones. We may think of these poor nations as being technically backwards, but in many ways they're on par with wealthier nations. India, for instance, has around 440 million smartphone users; Bangladesh, with a population of 165 million, has 53 million smartphone users. Smartphones are becoming ubiquitous and enable cryptocurrency use for even very poor people.

When the nation collapses

Did you notice Afghanistan on that Chainalysis top 20 list? As one of the world's poorest countries, perhaps you wouldn't imagine that the country would appear high on a list of crypto adoption. But as this war-torn nation descends into financial catastrophe, middle-class Afghans are using cryptocurrencies as a more stable way to move their money around. After the U.S. pulled out and the Taliban took over, the banking system came close to collapse; in many towns, banks closed or ran out of cash, and the companies managing international transfers stopped operations. Many Afghanis turned to cryptocurrencies to protect their finances.

It's sad that the adoption of Bitcoin and other cryptocurrencies is helped along by strife — by economic collapse, hyperinflation, coups and civil disturbances, civil war — but it makes perfect sense that it should be. If you're living in an economy in which the currency is in precipitous decline, or from which you think you may have to flee at any moment, wouldn't it make sense to shift your assets into something that can be easily carried and that, despite its short-term volatility, rises in value over the long term?

If you're in a nation where you can't trust the government or banking system to not freeze or even steal your savings, wouldn't an independent, international form of currency be attractive? It's been reported that countries at the bottom of the "Human Freedom Index" (issued by the Cato Institute) are countries that are near the top of the list of nations where people are likely to search online for information about cryptocurrencies.

The idea is spreading worldwide — Bitcoin and other cryptocurrencies can be a safe place to store your savings:

- **When the Lebanese lira dropped in value by around 80 percent over a couple of years, and the banks put limits on withdrawals and transfers, many Lebanese adopted Bitcoin.** Downloads of the BlueWallet — the wallet software we use as an example in Chapter 4 — in Lebanon grew dramatically, 18 times higher in 2020 than in 2019, and many merchants began accepting payments in Bitcoin.
- **Venezuela, which has the world's worst inflation, saw a huge increase in the use of Bitcoin and other cryptocurrencies.** Venezuela is number 7 on the top 20 list of countries with the highest crypto adoption rate.
- **Argentina's inflation rate has also soared over the last couple of years.** Argentina is number 10 on the same list; see the earlier section, "It's not just the rich," for more info.
- **Turkey's current economic disaster has led to an increase in crypto use in that nation.**

We may think of cryptocurrencies as being a first-world technology, but people in poorer countries have seen the advantages and adopted these currencies quickly, in the same way that they had already adopted the use of smartphones and mobile-based money.

Cryptocurrencies can be attractive to people in troubled nations for a few reasons.

- **Avoiding inflation:** You may think the value of Bitcoin is volatile, but it's nothing compared to damage done by the huge inflation rates of some currencies. And so far, although Bitcoin's value may have dropped, it has always come up again. At the time of writing, Argentina's inflation rate was over 50 percent, and Turkey's over 20 percent. Venezuela's was estimated to be 2,700 percent in 2021. Shifting savings into Bitcoin was a really good move in these countries.
- **Avoiding banking crises:** If there's a risk that your money will be seized by a corrupt regime, or frozen in a banking crisis, moving it into Bitcoin is a great idea. Nations in economic crisis often impose restrictions on the movement of capital; they can't control Bitcoin, though.
- **Bypassing sanctions:** If your nation is the subject of international sanctions, cryptocurrency may be the only way for you to get your money out of the country or to make an international purchase.
- **Remittances:** There are nations that earn 10 percent, 20 percent, or more of their Gross National Product from their citizens who work overseas and send money home. Cryptocurrencies provide a cheap, fast way to shift money across the world. It's almost certain that cryptocurrencies are the mechanism of the future for these kinds of transfers. Within a year or two, estimates show that around 50 percent of all remittances will be sent via cryptocurrencies, though probably not Bitcoin. Even Facebook is targeting this market with its Diem cryptocurrency (though it's not clear when — or even if — it will launch; see `www.Diem.com`).

- **Highly transportable:** If you're forced to flee your nation (hey, it happens, as co-author Peter, the son of a war refugee, is well aware), you may have to convert a lifetime of savings into something you can carry. Refugees become targets of assaults and thefts, and often lose the savings they need to support themselves during their journeys. Drop some money into the blockchain and it's *omnipresent.* It's everywhere. Wherever you end up, there's your money (as long as you follow careful security protocols; see Chapter 5).
- **Rapid, cheap transfers:** Not only do cryptocurrencies allow you to move your savings to anywhere in the world, these transfers are also very fast and cheap. A transfer that might take several days using more traditional methods can take literally ten minutes with Bitcoin, and cost a fraction of the fee.

- Knowing where Bitcoin volatility comes from, and where it will go
- Worrying about government bans (don't!)
- Understanding why Bitcoin is *not* a Ponzi scheme. . .
- . . .and looking at why it *could be* a bubble (a long-lived one)
- Digging into the Bitcoin fee, security, and energy usage problems

Chapter 9
Bitcoin Botheration

You may have noticed that nothing in life is perfect, even your partner or kids (especially your partner and kids?). The same is true with Bitcoin. Like everything else, it's an imperfect system, with a few drawbacks and annoyances, a few *botherations.*

When engineering such a system, physical limitations exist and so design tradeoffs must be made. This means many of the criticisms that have been made of Bitcoin are based on kernels of truth, and indeed may have some validity, even though they may be misunderstood or overblown. In this chapter, we explain some of the more well-known of these problems.

Bitcoin Is Too Volatile

A common complaint regarding Bitcoin is that the price changes too much and too rapidly to make it viable as a good currency, medium of exchange, or store of value. Sometimes large swings are accompanied by overleveraged traders risking big in often illiquid markets, triggering the loss of their positions and huge swings in price. This volatility has proven joyfully profitable for some and terribly catastrophic for others.

Indeed, as we have agreed elsewhere in this book, Bitcoin is currently not suitable as a currency, due to this volatility and various other reasons. But as a store of value or an investment asset? That's a different question.

The massive price swings that Bitcoin experiences are in part due to natural *price discovery* (the process of finding and setting the price for something) as the market begins to understand and learn about the technology and accurately price it. After all, price is a function of supply and demand.

REMEMBER

The Bitcoin supply is programmatic, predefined, and certain, while the demand for Bitcoin is always fluctuating.

The really big cause of this volatility is, of course, that the world is still learning about Bitcoin; more people, companies, and institutions are discovering Bitcoin and trying to decide whether it's "real." Overall, the world seems to be deciding that it is, which is why the demand — and thus the price — is, overall, on the way up. But in a world that has not completely decided how to think about Bitcoin, we'll inevitably have up days and down days (or weeks, or months).

Bitcoin certainly appears volatile when compared to more traditional assets, but all assets have some level of volatility, and vary between each other in their volatility (gold, for instance, is far more volatile than real estate). But the Bitcoin market is much smaller and more immature; it's growing and evolving, so volatility should not be a surprise.

But imagine a world a few decades from now in which Bitcoin is accepted by the world, in the same way gold is. (We've already seen periods, by the way, during which the volatility of gold and Bitcoin has been about the same.) Most likely, Bitcoin's value would stabilize and perhaps be volatile to a similar degree to gold. In other words, as Bitcoin markets mature, they should become less volatile and easier to use as a medium of exchange.

You can find an interesting visualization of Bitcoin volatility, compared to that of gold and several currencies, at `https://charts.woobull.com/bitcoin-volatility/`. Check it out.

If Bitcoin catches on, the price will stabilize over time — which reminds us of a quote about buying Bitcoin, from a famous person:

It might make sense just to get some in case it catches on. If enough people think the same way, that becomes a self fulfilling prophecy.

– SATOSHI NAKAMOTO, 2009

Governments Ban Bitcoin

Many people avoid or denigrate Bitcoin based on their belief that governments will ban it. Indeed, some have. We have seen plenty of governmental interference in certain countries or regions, but we haven't seen any action that has been able to shut down the network, or that comes close to doing so.

Bitcoin founder Satoshi Nakamoto said, "Governments are good at cutting off the heads of a centrally controlled network like Napster, but pure P2P [peer-to-peer] networks like Gnutella and Tor seem to be holding their own." Bitcoin is, of course, an example of a peer-to-peer network. Napster (a file-sharing system accused of enabling copyright infringement of music) had founders to go after, a company to sue and bankrupt, a corporate headquarters, and so on. It took about a year for Napster to get shut down, be bankrupted, and have its name sold. (Today, the Napster name is used by a legitimate music-streaming service.)

With a peer-to-peer network — such as Gnutella, Tor, or Bitcoin — who does the government go after? Some governments have restricted or even outlawed Bitcoin by banning corporations from getting involved in Bitcoin transactions. Draconian decrees in practice, however, have little effect other than keeping law-abiding citizens and businesses from participating.

We hate to compare Bitcoin with booze and drugs, but, well, let's do so. How successful are governments at banning booze and drugs? Prohibition lasted 13 years in the U.S., 2 years in Canada, and merely a few months in Hungary. As for the war on drugs, the U.S. is rushing headlong into marijuana legalization (there's money to be made!). The fact is, governments have difficulty stopping the masses from doing what they want to do.

In any case, there just doesn't seem to be an appetite for banning citizens from owning Bitcoin in most of the world. Most countries regard it as something that people should be allowed to do if they want to — it's their decision, just as investing in gold is their own decision, too.

How effective can countries with a different attitude be at stopping encrypted information on the Internet? China has banned the use of Bitcoin, and yet many Chinese citizens continue to own and trade Bitcoin. Despite a ban on cryptocurrency mining, a recent study published on cnbc.com shows that Bitcoin mining is alive and well in China. "Bitcoin withstood a nation-state attack of China actually banning mining," one observer stated, "and the network shrugged it off."

China's exercise in futility reminds us of the various Chinese bans on overseas trade during the Ming and Qing dynasties of the 14th to 17th centuries (sometimes boats were burned and ports destroyed). The bans were ignored, had little effect, or led to serious harm to China's development. Did China just make a massive 21st-century blunder by banning Bitcoin and setting their digital ships afire?

Bitcoin: A 21st-Century Ponzi Scheme

A *Ponzi scheme* is an investment fraud that takes money from new investors to pay earlier investments. The term is named after Charles Ponzi, who ran a con game based on investing in *international reply coupons* (*IRCs*) in the "roaring 20s." (Not *these* roaring 20s, the last century's roaring 20s.) Here's how IRCs worked: A letter writer from one country (you remember letters, right?) could include an IRC with the letter, allowing the recipient in another country to exchange the IRC for sufficient postage to respond with a letter back to the first country.

Anyway, Mr. Ponzi came up with an idea. He could buy cheap IRCs in Italy, and then exchange them for stamps of a higher value in the U.S. (a kind of *stamp arbitrage!*). He raised money from investors and paid them a high rate of interest, encouraging others to invest. At the same time, he discovered his IRC plan was totally impractical to run at scale; he would have had to transport shiploads of IRCs across the Atlantic. Still, he also realized that he had a very profitable business of taking money from investors! If any investors wanted out, Ponzi would pay them back with money from more recent investors, and everyone was earning interest paid from new investment funds. (Most investors reinvested their money.) Of course, eventually he ran out of new investors.

Today, the term *Ponzi scheme* refers to a fraudulent investment program, in which early investors are paid not from genuine investment gains, but with money from *later* investors. A recent example is Bernie Madoff's famous multi-billion-dollar Ponzi scheme, the biggest in history. (Madoff died in prison while serving a 150-year sentence.)

Bitcoin is sometimes described as a Ponzi scheme. It's clearly not, though. Certainly there have been scams, frauds, and pyramid-type schemes in the Bitcoin and cryptocurrency arena. A great example of this is OneCoin, which *was* a complex cryptocurrency Ponzi scheme that brought in around $4 billion. (*The Times* of London called it "one of the biggest scams in history.")

But Bitcoin itself? Clearly not a Ponzi scheme. The system is open, transparent even. It's run by a community that's open to anyone (anyone can set up a node). No central body oversees Bitcoin and scams people. It's definitely not a Ponzi scheme, but how about a bubble?

The Bitcoin Bubble

Another common criticism of Bitcoin is that it's nothing more than an investment bubble. Skeptics often compare it to other famous historic investment bubbles, such as the Dutch Tulipmania in the early 17th century, the South Sea Company (early 18th century), and the Internet, or Dotcom, bubble (from 1994 to 2000).

Co-author Peter has a personal interest in financial bubbles; he lived through, and intimately experienced, the Dotcom bubble. Around the time the bubble began (1993), he was writing *The Complete Idiot's Guide to the Internet.* (He dates the start of the bubble to the dramatic growth in press coverage, and the millions of Americans jumping online, in the summer of 1994.) Early in 2000, he read *The Internet Bubble* (Harperbusiness), a book predicting the coming crash; he was running a venture capital–funded Dotcom at the time, and circulated the book among his company's executive staff. The bubble burst later that year.

The authors of this book, Anthony Perkins and Michael Perkins, editors at Red Herring (a Dotcom-business print magazine that ironically did not long survive the bubble bursting!), wrote that financial bubbles typically last six to seven years. The South Sea Company's stock price crashed about nine years after the company was founded (though it's hard to say exactly when the bubble began, of course). The Dotcom bubble burst about six years after the Internet craze began.

How about Bitcoin, though? It's now 13 years old and has undergone historic gains, with multiple crashes of more than 80 percent, only to see its price rebound back to and beyond the price it was at when it crashed. So at least the six-year theory doesn't seem to hold. (Unless you date the start to the summer of 2017, when Bitcoin really came to the attention of the public at large, in which case maybe 2023 is the bubble-burst year!)

REMEMBER

The idea that Bitcoin is a bubble is actually more rational than the idea that it's a Ponzi scheme. It is possible. But remember this: Although the Internet investment bubble burst, the Internet is still with us (we wouldn't have Bitcoin if it weren't), and many very profitable endeavors and businesses survived the bubble bursting (even though investors lost billions of dollars in the companies that didn't survive).

Another thing to remember is the words of a one-time Global Chief Economist of Citigroup, who has described gold as a 6,000-year bubble. As we explain elsewhere in this book, gold and Bitcoin share real similarities (he even called gold "shiny Bitcoin"). Perhaps Bitcoin is the next 6,000-year bubble.

In February 2021, the *Financial Times* was quoted as saying that "Bitcoin isn't so much a bubble as the 'last functioning fire alarm' warning us of some very big geopolitical changes ahead." Many Bitcoin purists like to think that no, Bitcoin is not a bubble, but it very well could be the pin that bursts the bubble of misguided monetary and fiscal policy.

Bitcoin Costs Too Much to Use

Another reason Bitcoin doesn't currently function well as a currency is that Bitcoin transactions are simply too expensive. As we write these words, the average transaction fee, for a ten-minute transaction, is around $1.67. If you're buying, say, a book for $10, that's significant. Of course, when you use your credit card to buy a book, the merchant is paying a fee, but $1.67 is still more than three times a typical credit-card merchant fee.

REMEMBER

Sometimes the transaction fees go far higher. At one point in April 2021, the fee was around $34. Occasionally, at times of peak network congestion, when possibly many thousands of transactions are pending and waiting to be confirmed into a block, fees can spike to over $50 per transaction to be included in the next block! Fees are, like the price of Bitcoin itself, very volatile, bouncing around dramatically from day to day and even throughout a day, as shown in Figure 9-1. Here are a couple of places to see what fees are right now, and what they have been in the past:

» `https://privacypros.io/tools/bitcoin-fee-estimator/`

» `https://ycharts.com/indicators/bitcoin_average_transaction_fee`

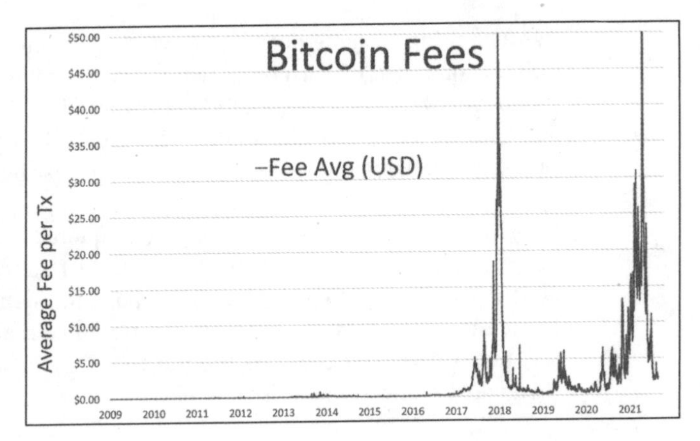

FIGURE 9-1: Average network transaction fees over time, measured in US$ per transaction.

High transaction fees mean Bitcoin can't operate as a currency, but it can still function as an asset. Moving, say, $100,000 worth of Bitcoin for a buck or two is quite reasonable!

Bitcoin's design allows users to select the fees they want to pay for their transaction. Bitcoin users can choose either fast or nearly free. Want your transaction included in the next block no matter the cost? You have to outbid every other Bitcoin user trying to send transactions; sometimes users have paid fees of $50 to $100 for a high-priority transaction. Want your transaction to be as inexpensive as possible and have no time preference for confirmation? You can set your fee low, but it might take a long time for the transaction to complete.

Also, let's not forget the Lightning Network (see Chapter 4). This system sits "on top of" the Bitcoin network, and provides very fast and very cheap transactions. The Bitcoin we have today is not the Bitcoin of tomorrow.

Bitcoin Security Risks

Is Bitcoin secure? Can it be attacked? In fact, we're concerned with two types of security risk:

- Risks to the Bitcoin network
- Risks to our own Bitcoin

We discuss the risks to your own Bitcoin in Chapter 2: the risk that your private keys are discovered by someone else, and your Bitcoin is stolen; that a custodial wallet managing your Bitcoin is hacked, and your Bitcoin is stolen; or that you risk losing your private keys so you can no longer access your Bitcoin. See Chapter 5 for ideas on how to deal with these risks.

But how about the risk to the network itself? Can the Bitcoin network be attacked and subverted? Well, Bitcoin miners, developers, and users spend a lot of time, energy, and computational resources to make sure each Bitcoin block is mined to certain specifications. (If you'd like to get really deep into how this functions, see *Cryptocurrency Mining For Dummies* by us!)

As gold is defined by its physical atomic properties, Bitcoin is defined by its digital and mathematical properties. These properties are underpinned by work performed by miners, work that adds transactions to the blockchain, extending the chain of transaction blocks. Just as fire forges steel, electricity fabricates Bitcoin. However, electricity does more than just mint new coins; it also provides ongoing security to the entire network.

The nodes, miners, and code developers all have unique counterbalancing control of certain aspects of the network that creates a competitive yet surprisingly cooperative environment. Bitcoin nodes carefully create and relay transactions in the hopes that miners will consider them valid and place them in a hashed block; meanwhile, the miners expend energy to hash blocks in the hope that nodes will accept them as valid. Each can reject the work of the other. All the while, the software developers drafting code expend time and effort in the hope that nodes and miners will accept their software as valid and choose to run that code. Each party in the system has a type of veto vote over the others that mathematically motivates the cooperation of other entities to function.

REMEMBER

The point is, the network is being run by tens of thousands of people, all working together, and all actions require consensus. Any attack on the network would need to overwhelm this consensus. That is, anyone wanting to attack the network would need to have more than 50 percent control of the network, thus the term *the 51% attack*. If a group controlled more than 51 percent of the mining capacity — the hash rate or computing power — on the network, that group could control the network. But Bitcoin has many thousands of miners, and no one group comes close to having this kind of power. At the time of writing, the biggest mining group controls around 19 percent of the hash rate. For a breakdown of hash rate by mining group (also known as a *mining pool*), see any of these resources:

- `https://btc.com/stats/pool`
- `https://www.blockchain.com/pools`
- `https://cash.coin.dance/blocks/thisweek`

Much ado has also been made about the future risk to the Bitcoin network from quantum computing. Will quantum computing be able to break Bitcoin's cryptography? Two thoughts. First, this is in the future, so it's not imminent. Second, quantum computing may be a real challenge to current cryptography, but it will most likely bring along with it quantum cryptography, already a subject of study in research centers around the world.

Bitcoin Energy Usage

Bitcoin has been bashed for its high energy use, with some estimates claiming it uses more than a medium-sized nation. Indeed, the Bitcoin network does require a lot of electrical energy to run.

Some Bitcoiners will tell you this amount of energy is clearly necessary to secure a modern monetary system. For example, how much energy is consumed creating paper money, running the various banking and credit-card networks, running banks, and powering armored trucks? And the list goes on.

However, the exact amount of energy used by Bitcoin is in dispute and, in fact, is very difficult to calculate precisely; estimates vary dramatically. Various reputable sources have calculated the energy consumption of the Bitcoin network's proof of work equations, resulting in different estimations of energy consumption. Here are a variety of estimates of Bitcoin's instantaneous power consumption for mining in Gigawatts (GW) and yearly energy equivalents (in Terawatt-hours/year — TWh/Year).

- **CoinShares:** 4.70 GW, 41.17 TWh/Year (June 2019). `https://coinshares.co.uk/research/bitcoin-mining-network-june-2019`
- **University of Cambridge Bitcoin Electricity Consumption Index:** 5.48 to 36.76 GW, 48.8 to 322.21 TWh/Year. `https://cbeci.org/`
- **Coin Center:** 5.00 GW, 44.00 TWh/Year (May 2019). `https://coincenter.org/entry/evaluating-estimates-of-bitcoin-electricity-use`
- **The International Energy Agency (IEA):** 6.62 GW, 58.00 TWh/Year (July 2019). `https://www.iea.org/newsroom/news/2019/july/bitcoin-energy-use-mined-the-gap.html`
- **Electric Power Research Institute (EPRI):** 2.05 GW, 18.00 TWh/Year (April 2018). `https://www.epri.com/pages/product/3002013910/`
- **Marc Bevand:** 2.10 GW, 18.39 TWh/Year (January 2018). `http://blog.zorinaq.com/bitcoin-electricity-consumption`
- **Hass McCook:** 12.08 GW, 105.82 TWh/Year (August 2018); this estimate includes energy used in manufacturing mining equipment. `https://www.academia.edu/37178295/The_Cost_and_Sustainability_of_Bitcoin_August_2018_`

» **Alex de Vries:** 8.34 GW, 73.12 TWh/Year (July 2019). `https://digiconomist.net/bitcoin-energy-consumption`

These various estimates are shown in the chart in Figure 9-2. The chart shows the energy estimates measured in Terawatt-hours per year (TWh/Year) on a timeline, along with the Bitcoin network hash rate, measured in Exahashes per second (EH/s), over recent years. (As the hash rate goes up, power consumption rises.)

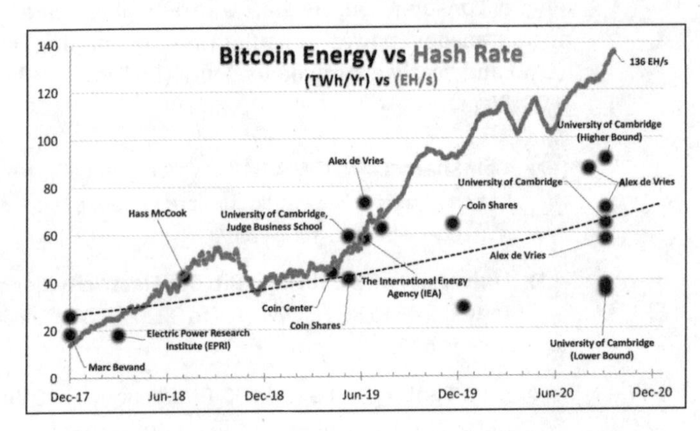

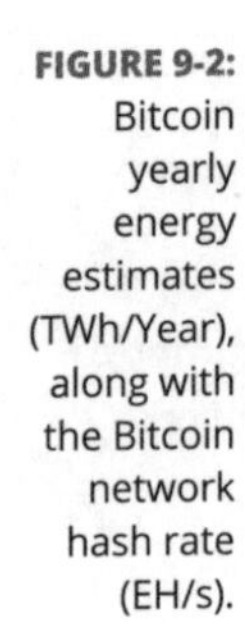

FIGURE 9-2: Bitcoin yearly energy estimates (TWh/Year), along with the Bitcoin network hash rate (EH/s).

As the Bitcoin network has become more powerful in terms of hash rate, it appears to have also increased its efficiency to the point that hash rate is increasing, but energy estimates are beginning to flatten. This trend could continue and energy usage could further decouple from the amount of hash rate and security on the Bitcoin network.

Part 4
The Part of Tens

IN THIS PART . . .

Getting motivation to invest

Understanding price prediction and technical analysis

Discovering numerous learning resources

Finding data visualizations

Thinking about possible Bitcoin futures

IN THIS CHAPTER

» **Understanding that you must expand your understanding**

» **Getting started requires that you. . .start!**

» **Deciding whether to run your own Bitcoin node**

» **Planning for disaster and testing your security**

» **Learning about price prediction and technical analysis**

Chapter 10
Ten Tips to Hodl and Stack Sats

"Stacking sats" is Bitcoinspeak for gradually increasing your Bitcoin ownership over time. In this chapter, we provide you with ten tips to help you get started moving in that direction, tips we believe will motivate you and allow you to become a Bitcoin investor safely and — we hope — profitably!

Invest in Knowledge, Do Your Homework

Bitcoin, the first of the blockchain-based cryptocurrencies, began functioning early in January of 2009. It's young! We don't know for sure what's going to happen as time goes on, so if you want to be involved with Bitcoin — and other cryptocurrencies — you definitely need to keep up with the field, to learn, and to continue your education. Arm yourself with the tools and weapons that information affords you.

TIP

Spending time now to learn is better than later regretting that you didn't make the investment in education. Make sure to study up and do your homework. We provide plenty of resources for continuing education on the topic of Bitcoin in Chapter 11.

Get Off Zero (₿)

A common phrase in the Bitcoin lexicon is "Get off zero," which is in reference to the amount of Bitcoin an individual owns. (Zero, of course, is ₿0.00000000.) In other words, *get started*. Don't sit on the sidelines and wonder if you should be involved, but get in and start investing. Yes, there are risks, and as we explain in Chapter 6, you should never invest more than you can afford (or stomach) to lose (that's true for any kind of investment). But if you read this book, if you continue your education, if you decide that something really revolutionary is happening and Bitcoin *is* here to stay, then get started!

TIP

The cost to get off zero today can be as a low as a single dollar (at the time of writing, ₿0.000024). Read Chapter 3 and buy a little Bitcoin here and there — at an ATM, at Coinbase or some other exchange, or from PayPal.

Have a friend send you a penny on the Lightning Network, today valued at 24 Satoshi. Better still, some Bitcoin exchanges and apps will give users a $10 dollar sign-up bonus to start using their product; there's nothing better than *free* Bitcoin. Getting off zero is more than just passing the threshold itself; it starts the user down the path of learning how everything fits together, including addresses, keys, and the mechanics of wallets.

After zero, the next threshold some Bitcoiners like to suggest is grabbing *fair share* of the world's Bitcoin. There will only ever be 21,000,000.00000000 coins, and there are about 8 billion people on the planet. This equates to just about ₿0.00262512 or 265,512

Satoshi per person according to `http://bitcoinsperperson.com/`. This can be bought today for the cost of US$109.

Lower Your Cost Basis, Buy the Dip

The *cost basis* is the original price you paid for an asset; it's a term most commonly used in a discussion of taxes owed on a sale. (If you owe taxes on the increase in value, then you need to know the original *basis* so you can figure out that increase.)

Of course, it's always a good thing to pay less for something than more! It's always good, when investing, to *buy low and sell high.* (Co-author Peter discovered many years ago that in real-estate investing, for instance, buying high and selling low doesn't seem to work well!)

So you want to pay as little as you can for your Bitcoin. We can think of three ways to do that.

- **Shop around:** You find out about this in Chapter 3; Bitcoin is cheaper at some places than others, so why not buy at the best price you can? (However, sometimes "you get what you pay for." If you find a source of *very* cheap Bitcoin, it could be a scam. Only buy from reputable sources.)
- **Buy the dip:** This is not necessarily easy, of course; it depends on a belief that even if Bitcoin has dropped today, even if the price stays down for a while, over the long term it will go back up.

  Many Bitcoin investors buy more Bitcoin when they see a significant drop in price. If the price of Bitcoin drops 25 percent, which due to its volatility it often does, some people view this as the market having a "Bitcoin Sale" and an opportunity to buy some at a discount.
- **Buy now:** The last way to lower the cost of your Bitcoin — and again, this requires that you believe its price will go up in the long term — is to *buy now!* Why wait until it doubles or triples in price?

Dry Powder, or Get on Zero ($)?

Dry powder is what some people call extra currency set aside to purchase an asset when the price falls. (Dry powder used to refer to stores of gun powder that was kept safe and sound out of the rain or sea, ready to use when needed in battle.) Dry powder would be a stash of local government currency patiently waiting and ready to buy Bitcoin if it "goes on sale."

However, many investors don't like this strategy. Many true Bitcoin believers view Bitcoin as a better bet than fiat currency (and over the last decade, of course, they have been quite correct!). Why leave it in a bank account in dollars, when it can be in Bitcoin and, despite volatility, grow significantly in value?

Run Your Own Bitcoin Node

When you run Bitcoin-node software on your own computer, you're removing trusted third parties from the equation and directly plugging into the Bitcoin network. Bitcoin is a peer-to-peer system that anyone with Internet access can use. If you can operate an Internet browser, download and install a program, or send and receive an email, you can likely handle the simple keystrokes required to become a peer on the Bitcoin network. (Though you also need to be willing to invest time and effort in education.)

Once you're a peer and connected to the network, you have direct and unfettered access to the network to send and receive transactions. To the Bitcoin true believer, the advantage is being able to verify and validate one's Bitcoin transactions by oneself, without trusting or relying on someone else.

If you deposit a check, it might bounce; if you accept cash, the bills might be counterfeit; if you buy gold, it might be a fake tungsten gold bar. But running the Bitcoin software yourself ensures at a basic level that your transaction is your transaction and that your keys are your keys, without you having to trust a third party's software telling you that the transaction has completed.

The exchanges and companies selling Bitcoin regularly suspend accounts and seize funds from folks who do not follow their terms of service. They can do so for political reasons, too. In 2010, when payment processors (such as credit-card processing services) blocked Wikileaks, the organization started taking Bitcoin donations. (This Bitcoin eventually became worth tens of millions of dollars; today, Wikileaks accepts donations using six different cryptocurrencies, among other methods.) Now, we're not sure of the specifics of how Wikileaks set up its technology, but we suspect they set up their own node. In any case, they're a perfect example of why an organization might want to do so.

Had they worked through any other system — through an exchange, or even wallet software — they could have been blocked. Wallet software connects to the network through a particular node, for instance, so the publisher of the wallet software could be forced by authorities to block node access to certain parties.

TIP

Setting up your own node sounds scary, complicated, and difficult. However, it's actually a few clicks and a single software install on any computer or laptop; even smartphones have Bitcoin-node software available now. We're not suggesting there's no learning involved, but you might be surprised at how easy it is to set up your own node.

Secure your Keys, Test Seed Backups

Not your keys, not your coins. One of the most important things a Bitcoin user can do is to secure their own private keys. (In Chapter 2, you discover how important your keys are, and in Chapter 4, you find out all about seeds.) Thousands of Bitcoin users over the years have suffered a loss of funds, often because they trusted someone else to hold their keys for them, or because they took the responsibility of looking after their private keys for themselves, but didn't do it well!

As you find out in Chapter 5, letting others look after your keys is dangerous — numerous attacks on exchanges have led to the loss of billions of dollars' worth of Bitcoin — and doing it yourself is dangerous, too.

The answer, many Bitcoin purists believe, is to never let anyone else look after your keys, so you can't suffer when that party is attacked (or absconds with your Bitcoin). Bitcoin users believe that they should retain ownership of their keys *because they can*. Users can access the network directly and not go through a trusted third party. Why go through a middleman that you must trust, when you do not need to?

WARNING

However, if you're going to do this, you have to be really careful about protecting your seeds and keys. As we explain in Chapter 5, you need to come up with a bulletproof method for protecting seeds and keys.

TIP

But it's a really good thing to test periodically, to "war game" scenarios! What happens, for instance, if your computer and smartphone, the devices on which you keep your wallets, both burn up in a fire, or are both stolen? How do you recover your wallets and retain access to your Bitcoin? What happens if your house burns down, taking your devices and the wallets they contain, and your backup? What then? (Of course, you do have a backup somewhere else, right?)

Bitcoin Price-Prediction Models

Many Bitcoin fanatics try to predict the future performance of the Bitcoin market using past results. Some of these price-prediction models have even been accurate in the past, but only time will tell if they hold true going forward.

These price-prediction models may even become self-fulfilling prophecies because some portion of the market's participants actively trade based on these models, believing them to be true.

Price discovery, a concept in economics, is the idea that the price of a product can be determined through interactions of buyers and sellers in a marketplace. However, a related concept is asymmetrical information, the idea that some participants in the market have better information than others.

Thus, buying and selling based on these models is based on the idea that the market will, over time, set the correct price of Bitcoin through price discovery, but that it's possible for some participants to have a better understanding of what will happen in the market. Thus, when the market is underpricing Bitcoin, those participants can buy, and when it is overpricing Bitcoin, they can sell.

REMEMBER

We're definitely not proposing you use any particular model, nor are we picking "winners" in the market of Bitcoin pricing models. Still, if you really want to discover more, you'll find plenty of information on the web (search for *bitcoin pricing models*, for instance).

For an interesting (and years-long) discussion of a pricing model, starting in 2014 through the present day, see Trololo's Bitcointalk thread at `https://bitcointalk.org/index.php?topic=831547`. The curve looks pretty good, if not a bit more optimistic than it turned out.

Bitcoin Technical Analysis, Market Indicators, and Other Tea Leaves

The term *technical analysis* refers to the analysis of an investment's past price trends and patterns in trading activity, based on the belief that such information can help one identify *future* trends and patterns and then, of course, trade the asset based on those predictions. The technical analyst creates charts that show past trading activity, and often extrapolates into the future or provides buy or sell indicators.

Technical analysis is nothing new in the investing field. The concept goes back at least 400 years. And, of course, many people have applied technical analysis to the Bitcoin market.

TIP

You may — or may not — find these useful, but they are at least interesting. We suggest that you don't rely on any of these analyses without understanding them thoroughly first, and deciding yourself whether they make sense. Here are a few examples.

- **Mayer Multiple:** The Mayer Multiple, created by Trace Mayer, tracks the current price of Bitcoin in U.S. dollars, divided by the 200-day moving average price (a *moving average* is one that filters out short-term fluctuations). For example, if the price today is $12,000, and the price over the previous 200 days has been on average $6,000, then the Mayer Multiple is 2. This indicator gives a good relative signal as to when the market has spiked up in price or inversely crashed. Higher multiples are warning signs; lower multiples are suggestions that it may be a good time to buy. See `https://mayermultiple.info`.
- **NVT ratio:** The network value to transactions (NVT) ratio (also called the NVTr) tracks the dollar value of Bitcoin transactions compared to the relative total network value. It is calculated by dividing the daily average market capitalization (or total market value) in dollars by the number of daily transactions in dollars. In other words, it's a measure of what proportion of all the Bitcoin in existence is being traded on a particular day. See `https://charts.woobull.com/bitcoin-nvt-ratio`.
- **NVT signal:** The NVT signal is very similar to the NVT ratio. However, instead of taking the market value and dividing it by the daily transaction total, it is the 90-day average market value divided by the daily transaction value. See `https://charts.woobull.com/bitcoin-nvt-signal`.
- **Realized market capitalization:** A popular metric in the cryptocurrency space is market capitalization, which is calculated by multiplying the current market price of a cryptocurrency by the total amount of the cryptocurrency in circulation. The realized market capitalization (RMC), however, is calculated by adding up the market value of each coin at the time it was last spent as a transaction on

the blockchain. The purpose is to get to a more rational market capitalization number; for instance, it to some degree removes the effect of Bitcoin that has in fact been lost and can never be traded again. See `https://coinmetrics.io/realized-capitalization` for a great explanation of how the RMC metric works.

- **Market Value Realized Value ratio:** This ratio (MVRV for short) is calculated by taking the market capitalization and dividing it by the realized market capitalization. This indicator can help put the market value in perspective, and proponents believe it can be used to detect over- and under-valuations. See `https://charts.woobull.com/bitcoin-mvrv-ratio`.

Be careful with any model you happen across. A term used in Bitcoin circles — *moonmath* — refers to analysis that projects that the price of Bitcoin will "go to the moon!" So, you might ask yourself, "Is it math, or is it moonmath?"

Slow and Steady Wins the Race

Bitcoin is often mistaken for a get-rich-quick scheme, and admittedly it has been for some. But today it is more of a build-assets-slowly scheme. The old story of the tortoise and the hare might be handy here, with the moral of slow and steady winning the race.

Patience, Bitcoiners of the 2020s believe, is key, and hodling your position is key. Plenty of Bitcoiners regret selling their coin to pay off student loans or to buy that used commuter car (or to buy pizza). Hodling Bitcoin is a simple enough strategy but is often difficult to execute. Many folks would gladly sell their coins and take gains after an investment goes up 1,000 percent, but if you would have done that with Bitcoin over its lifetime, you may have missed out on 1,000,000 percent gains.

Saving in Bitcoin is ultimately a trade you're making with your future self. Consume frivolously today or squirrel value away for the future into a digital coin account. As the old saying goes, time in the market beats timing the market.

Tell Everyone, or Speak Softly?

Now that you've discovered the mathemagics of Bitcoin, do you shout about it from the mountaintops or keep your involvement with the network a secret?

One approach many owners of significant Bitcoin holdings have taken is to keep quiet about it! Many Bitcoin owners can't stop themselves telling everyone who will listen. They regard Bitcoin as a financial "fire escape" and want to save as many others as possible from what they regard as weak fiat currency that's constantly losing value due to inflation.

However, others accept survivors' guilt and keep Satoshi's secret to themselves for security reasons. Some folks have been targeted for robbery due to their involvement with the Bitcoin network. In Chapter 4, we talk about the *$5 dollar wrench attack,* assaults on Bitcoin owners by thieves who try to beat the information out of them. Investors with truly significant amounts of Bitcoin often devise intricate methods for distributing the information regarding their keys and seeds, so that it cannot be retrieved quickly. This includes spreading the information geographically. Perhaps your neighbors *don't* need to know about your Bitcoin riches!

Still, many Bitcoiners regard themselves as evangelists for the Bitcoin religion. With Bitcoin, the network is stronger, so the more the merrier, some think. What good is a digital Internet cash system if you cannot share it and enjoy it with other users? You'll have to decide for yourself.

documentaries, books, and guides

» Discovering block explorers and data aggregators

» Participating in Bitcoin forums

» Tracking Bitcoin's volatility

» Studying foundational documents, wikis, and data visualizations

Chapter 11
Ten Types of Bitcoin Resources

After more than a dozen years of Bitcoin, if anyone claims they completely understand the technology, they're most likely either fooling you or fooling themselves. Bitcoin is a humbling lesson in lifelong learning. This book can't possibly cover everything about Bitcoin, and likely missed many important details, but the resources in this chapter should help you drop down comfortably into the Bitcoin rabbit hole. As the Bitcoin saying goes, "Stay Humble, Stack Sats."

Bitcoin Documentaries

A number of interesting documentaries about Bitcoin and the cryptocurrency field provide some great background info:

- Banking on Bitcoin. `https://vimeo.com/226777744`
- The Trust Machine. `https://youtu.be/ZKwqNgG-Sv4`

- The Rise and Rise of Bitcoin. `http://bitcoindoc.com/`
- The Bitcoin Experiment. `https://www.amazon.com/Bitcoin-Experiment-Pal-Karleson/dp/B01JBA8HYK/`
- Hard Money. `https://www.hardmoneyfilm.com/`
- This Machine Greens. `https://www.youtube.com/watch?v=b-7dMVcVWgc`
- Bitcoin is Generational Wealth. `https://www.youtube.com/watch?v=3Rnqst5qCgA`

Bitcoin Books

The publishing industry isn't ignoring Bitcoin, of course. After all, you're reading a book about Bitcoin right now! Here are some additional useful and interesting books in case you want to dig deeper:

- Antonopoulos, A. M. *Mastering Bitcoin: Programming the Open Blockchain.* O'Reilly Media Inc., 2017.
- Ammous, S. *The Bitcoin Standard: The Decentralized Alternative to Central Banking.* Wiley, 2018.
- Song, J. *Programming Bitcoin: Learn How to Program Bitcoin from Scratch.* O'Reilly Media Inc., 2019.
- Rosenbaum, K. *Grokking Bitcoin*. Manning Publications, 2019.
- Yakes, E. *The 7th Property: Bitcoin and the Monetary Revolution*. Black Poodle Publishing, 2021.
- Antonopoulos, A. M., et al. *Mastering the Lightning Network: A Second Layer Blockchain Protocol for Instant Bitcoin Payments.* O'Reilly Media, Inc., 2021.
- Bitcoin and Bible Group, Breedlove, R., et al. *Thank God for Bitcoin: The Creation, Corruption and Redemption of Money.* Whispering Candle, 2020.

Bitcoin Guides and Walkthroughs

More educational resources for Bitcoin are available now than ever before, and it has become easier to become a basic Bitcoiner. Here are some of our favorite repositories of resources and learning tools.

- **Crypto Clear: Bitcoin & Cryptocurrency Made Simple (co-author Peter's own course):** https://www.CryptoOfCourse.com
- **Bitcoin Support (for Bitcoin wallets):** https://www.bitcoinsupport.com/
- **BTC Sessions (Bitcoin news and tutorials):** https://www.youtube.com/channel/UChzLnWVsl3puKQwc5PoO6Zg
- **The case for Bitcoin (Bitcoin news, including markets, stats, and rates):** https://www.casebitcoin.com/
- **21 Lectures (about Bitcoin for developers):** https://www.21lectures.com/
- **Bitcoin Lessons (earn Bitcoin while you learn):** https://www.bitcoinlessons.org/
- **Bitcoin EDU (learn Bitcoin remotely):** https://www.bitcoinedu.com/
- **Bitcoin is Hope (Bitcoin news, websites, and more):** https://www.hope.com/
- **Learn me a Bitcoin (Bitcoin lessons from beginner to advanced):** https://learnmeabitcoin.com/talks/
- **Teach Bitcoin (learn the Bitcoin protocol):** https://teachbitcoin.io/
- **Jameson Lopp (helping people control their Bitcoin):** www.lopp.net
- **Bitcoin for Everybody (an extensive Bitcoin course, divided into segments):** https://learn.saylor.org/course/view.php?id=468
- **The Bitcoin Standard Academy (exclusive/early access to Saifedean Ammous's books):** https://saifedean.com/academy/

Bitcoin Block Explorers

Blockchain explorers provide an easy way to audit blockchains directly from your web browser. They can search for blocks, transactions, and details of those transactions, hashes, and addresses. Here's a list of useful Bitcoin blockchain explorers.

- **Blockstream Explorer:** https://blockstream.info
- **Mempool.space:** https://mempool.space/
- **Blockchair:** https://blockchair.com
- **Blockchain.com:** www.blockchain.com/explorer
- **Blockcypher:** https://live.blockcypher.com/btc
- **cryptoID:** https://chainz.cryptoid.info/btc
- **OXT:** https://oxt.me
- **TradeBlock:** https://tradeblock.com/bitcoin

Bitcoin Data Aggregators

Cryptocurrency data, comparisons, and statistics websites can be very useful, helping you to compare cryptocurrencies. Here are several good cryptocurrency data aggregators.

- **Coin Metrics:** https://coinmetrics.io/charts
- **BitInfoCharts:** https://bitinfocharts.com/cryptocurrency-charts.html
- **Bitcoinity:** https://data.bitcoinity.org/markets/volume
- **CoinDesk:** www.coindesk.com/data
- **Bitcoin Visuals:** https://bitcoinvisuals.com
- **Coin Dance:** https://coin.dance
- **How Many Confirmations:** https://howmanyconfs.com
- **Crypto51 (51% Attack Cost Comparisons):** www.crypto51.app

Bitcoin Forums

The deeper you go into the rabbit hole, the more you're likely to want to engage, to talk with other Bitcoiners. Here are a few good places to do just that.

- **Reddit r/Bitcoin:** www.reddit.com/r/Bitcoin
- **Bitcoin Forum:** https://bitcointalk.org/
- **Stack Exchange:** https://bitcoin.stackexchange.com/
- **Bitcoin on Twitter:** https://twitter.com/search?q=bitcoin
- **Quora Bitcoin:** https://openblockchain.quora.com/

Bitcoin Volatility Charts

Throughout the book, we've touched on the volatility of Bitcoin — the price goes up and it goes down, all the time. These sites provide charts to help you track Bitcoin volatility.

- **Woobull Bitcoin Volatility:** A useful chart tracking 60-day Bitcoin volatility over the past decade, compared to dollars and euros. You can even add USD/EUR volatility, Bitcoin price, and a 200-day average Bitcoin price over the same period of time. Go to https://charts.woobull.com/bitcoin-volatility.
- **Bitcoin Volatility Index:** This volatility index provides percentage-based Bitcoin volatility over 30, 60, 120, and 252 days, measured against the U.S. dollar. Go to https://www.buybitcoinworldwide.com/volatility-index/.
- **Coin Metrics Volatility Charts:** These charts provide volatility figures for 30, 60, and 180 days for more than 30 different cryptocurrency assets, including Bitcoin, Litecoin, Ethereum, Dash, Zcash, Monero, Dogecoin, and many others. (Pick the volatility index you want from the drop-down menu and then select which cryptocurrencies to display on the option-button boxes at the bottom.) Go to https://coinmetrics.io/charts.

» **The Satochi.co Bitcoin Volatility Index:** This index tracks daily, 30-, and 60-day volatility estimates against the U.S. dollar. It also has volatility comparisons for gold, Ethereum, and many other currencies. Go to `www.satochi.co`.

» **Woobull Bitcoin Volatility Comparisons:** This chart allows you to compare 60-day Bitcoin volatility estimates against oil, U.S. stocks, gold, U.S. real estate, and other noteworthy assets. Go to `https://charts.woobull.com/bitcoin-volatility-vs-other-assets`.

Bitcoin Foundational Documents

The Bitcoin explosion of the last decade started with Satoshi Nakamoto's release of his idea to the Cypherpunk Mailing List (archives found at `http://mailing-list-archive.cryptoanarchy.wiki`), the Bitcoin base code, and an accompanying whitepaper. You can find his original whitepaper, outlining the concept, at `https://bitcoin.org/bitcoin.pdf`, but here are two other sites you can visit to read more documents that are foundational to Bitcoin.

» **The Satoshi Nakamoto Institute:** This site contains the entire known writings of Satoshi Nakamoto (whoever he/she/they is/are!; see Chapter 1), along with numerous other documents that "serve to contextualize Bitcoin into the broader story of cryptography and freedom." It's required reading and yet another great way for Bitcoin and cryptocurrency enthusiasts to go down the rabbit hole: `https://nakamotoinstitute.org/literature`.

» **The Cypherpunk Manifesto:** This foundational document, written by Eric Hughes in 1993, is one that many cryptographers and cryptocurrency users have read over the years. It's an interesting introduction to the politics behind the origins of cryptocurrency: `www.activism.net/cypherpunk/manifesto.html`.

Bitcoin Wikis

While Wikipedia.org has good pages for Bitcoin and Bitcoin history, these pages are often brief descriptions and not a deep-dive resource that can cover every aspect of a typical cryptocurrency. Not to worry, as other wikis go into much greater depth.

- **Bitcoin.it Wiki (thousands of Bitcoin- and cryptocurrency-related pages):** `https://en.bitcoin.it/`
- **Bitcoinwiki.org (and thousands more):** `https://en.bitcoinwiki.org`
- **The Wikipedia Bitcoin Page:** `https://en.wikipedia.org/wiki/Bitcoin`
- **Wikipedia's Simple-English Bitcoin Page (Bitcoin de-geeked):** `https://simple.wikipedia.org/wiki/Bitcoin`
- **Wikipedia's History of Bitcoin Page:** `https://en.wikipedia.org/wiki/History_of_bitcoin`

Bitcoin Data Visualizations

Blockchain explorers are good resources for finding information from the blockchain, but some creative individuals have taken this concept a step further, pulling data from the blockchain and creating interesting data visualizations for the Bitcoin and cryptocurrency space. Here are some of our favorites.

- **Bitcoin Big Bang:** `https://info.elliptic.co/hubfs/big-bang/bigbang-v1.html`
- **Market Value Visualizations:** `https://coin360.com`
- **Bitcoin Blocks:** `https://blocks.wizb.it`
- **Bitnodes:** `https://bitnodes.earn.com`
- **Bitbonkers.com:** `https://privacypros.io/tools/bitbonkers/`

- **Bitcoin Transaction Interactions:** http://bitcoin.interaqt.nl
- **OXT Landscapes:** https://oxt.me/landscapes
- **Bitcoin network graphs:** http://bitcoin.sipa.be
- **bitcointicker:** https://bitcointicker.co/networkstats
- **Statoshi.info:** https://statoshi.info

» Knowing what "Bitcoin is dead" means and why you'll hear it

» Finding out about the new Bitcoin network layers

» Looking at Bitcoin development and improvement proposals

» Exploring why Bitcoin *has* to get easier

Chapter 12

Ten (Plus One) Thoughts about the Future of Bitcoin

Bitcoin is not static. Like any young but booming technology, Bitcoin is evolving quickly. The Bitcoin true believers see a bright future for Bitcoin, but they have since the beginning. Nobody can say for sure what's going to happen to Bitcoin, but give credit where credit's due: *The true believers have certainly been right so far!* They're laughing all the way to the bank, in fact, or would be, if they kept their Bitcoin in a bank.

For years Bitcoin was ignored by most people in banking and finance. Then it was derided; it was, after all, "not real," or a scam. At the end of 2017, when the price crashed, many said, "See, we told you so," while the true believers said, "Just wait" (and, "It's a good time to buy!"). On a long-term chart, the crash of late 2017 looks like nothing more than a little blip. The price per Bitcoin dropped from a little over US$19,000 to a little under $8,000, and then dropped some more. But at the time of writing, the price hasn't been below $20,000 for more than a year and reached almost $70,000 at one point.

In this chapter, we look at a few developments in the Bitcoin field that may well be important, part of the evolution that will, perhaps, ensure its survival. If this chapter seems to be *too* optimistic, well, we're just giving you the true believers' point of view. Remember, they've been right so far!

Bitcoiners Love Lindy's Law

People in the Bitcoin field often cite something called the *Lindy Effect* or *Lindy's Law.* This principle suggests that the longer something has survived, the longer its life expectancy becomes; already long-lived things have a higher life expectancy than young things. (Okay, this doesn't work for people and animals; it's intended to apply to technology, organizations, and ideas.)

When Bitcoin was a week old, there was no reason to think it would live another week or another month. But over time, more and more people got involved, and as interest grew, its life expectancy grew. The more time that passes, the stronger Bitcoin will get, and thus the longer it is likely to survive. Combine this with the "network effect," which says that the larger a network, the more people working in the network, and thus the more useful the network becomes. (A telephone network with one hundred customers isn't terribly useful; one with one billion is incredibly powerful.)

A brand-new bank, for instance, is unlikely to survive. Most banks in the history of the world have gone out of business. The Bank of England, however, has been in business since 1694; it's unlikely to go out of business any time soon.

At the end of 2021, Bitcoin had been around for 13 years. That's still not particularly long, but long enough for it to have become worth hundreds of billions of dollars (with most of that growth in value occurring over the previous four-and-a-half years).

As time goes on and Bitcoin continues to function, and more people and institutions buy in to the idea, it becomes ever more likely that humanity will continue to contribute to and propagate the Bitcoin blockchain into the future. Indeed, many believe that folks will always require the freedom, liberty, and sovereignty that the system of Bitcoin offers.

However, let's just say that nothing is set in stone. Sometimes even long-lived institutions die, of course. The East India Company survived for 274 years — until it didn't. Consider also that although a number of academics have written about and developed the Lindy Effect, it was originally posited by comedians. *Lindy's* is a New York deli where comedians would gather and talk business. At some point, the group developed the idea that in order to last long in the comedy business, one should avoid overexposure. That's where the Lindy Effect started, though it's developed into a different concept, of course. So the Lindy Effect is not a law of nature; sometimes it doesn't work, but the basic principle — that, as institutions grow and endure over time, they become more capable of survival — is worth bearing in mind.

Bitcoin's Limited Supply Drives Price

One of the critical features of Bitcoin is the limited supply. There will never be more than 21 million coins in circulation. These 21 million coins are being issued in an extremely strict programmatic process every block — about every ten minutes. This supply issuance rate has been precise, predefined, and set in stone since the first block was mined. If a user were to change the rules and, say, change the issuance to 22 million coins, then objectively, that new system would not be Bitcoin; in fact, unless a node operates under the rules, it can't function in the network.

True, as Willem Buiter (an economic consultant and one-time Global Chief Economist at Citigroup) has said, "Anything that can be programmed can be reprogrammed." Technically that's correct, but it could not be reprogrammed without the support of the majority of the Bitcoin community.

The rules of Bitcoin, like the rules of checkers or baseball, are fixed. You can make more checkers pieces or a larger ball, but then you would simply be playing a new game: Chinese checkers or softball. So every node must adhere to this computational monetary policy or cease to operate on the Bitcoin network. This concept was baked into the Bitcoin by Satoshi Nakamoto to ensure that no single actor or group of actors can collude to cheat the system.

Nakamoto's *genesis block* (the first block of transactions in the Bitcoin blockchain) created 50 new Bitcoins, and every block after that created 50 more. The supply of new Bitcoin created is cut in half roughly every four years, though, in a process called the *halving* or *halvening*. With a 10-minute average block time, that's 210,000 blocks.

So when the 210,000th block of data was added to the blockchain, the number of new Bitcoins created in each block dropped to 25; four years later, it dropped to 12.5; at the time of writing, it's 6.25 Bitcoins per block. About 90 percent of the maximum Bitcoin supply has already been issued, and the rest will dribble out bit by bit, slower and slower, over the following decades, until around 2140, when everything will have been distributed. After that, the system will operate on transaction fee incentives alone.

In fact, the rate of issuance of Bitcoin is not merely halving every four years; it's being reduced every ten minutes. Each time new Bitcoin is issued, the supply of Bitcoin goes up slightly so that the next block's issuance is, of course, a smaller proportion of the total supply. It's a small drop daily, but a significant drop over the four-year period. At the current rate of 6.25 coins per 10-minute block period, 1,314,000 Bitcoins will enter circulation during that four-year period.

Bitcoin supply is rigidly defined; it has near perfect supply inelasticity. That is, the supply of Bitcoin will not increase with demand; rather, as demand goes up, price will go up. It doesn't matter how high — or low — the price demand for Bitcoin goes, the supply won't change in response. Inelastic supply is rare. Sure, the *Mona Lisa* has perfectly inelastic supply; as demand for the painting goes up, price goes up, because you can't create more *Mona Lisas*!

One could argue that even Manhattan real estate, a stereotypically scarce and arguably hot commodity, is not perfectly inelastic, for example. Developers can always expand the supply of New York real estate via density techniques such as vertical construction. The supply of Bitcoin is nearly perfectly inelastic and suffers no such supply shifts with an increase in demand. The supply of Bitcoin is so programmatically defined that it is more than digitally scarce; it is algorithmically supply inelastic.

This, Bitcoiners believe, suggests that Bitcoin price has to keep going up. Consider this recent headline from *Business Insider* (November 29, 2921): "Former bankers — including one who quit Goldman Sachs to play Axie Infinity — are reportedly launching a $1.5 billion crypto fund." As more and more people become interested in Bitcoin, the price *has* to go up, as supply won't increase in order to meet demand.

Bitcoin Adoption Coin Rush

Another thing Bitcoin true believers often point to is the speed of adoption of Bitcoin in comparison with other technologies. It took over fifty years for electricity to hit mass adoption; the telephone actually took a little longer. The Internet took around fifteen years, and social media only ten. Of course, we have to consider the "additive" nature of technological advancement: Social media had the Internet to build on, and the Internet had the electric grid to power its infrastructure and the phone system to connect through (as well as cable and satellite infrastructure). So new technologies can grow faster as they sit on top of earlier, widely adopted technologies.

Bitcoin has all these technology networks to use as a foundation to build on, and thus may see even quicker levels of advancement than the Internet or even social media. The Internet went from less than 10 million users in 1992 to 1 billion users in 2006 (15 years). Bitcoin went from less than 10 million users in 2016 to, according to some Bitcoin true believers, more than 100 million users in 2020 (5 years).

Some people (co-author Peter included) are skeptical about estimates of the number of Bitcoin "users," as some widely publicized surveys have been very badly designed, inflating the true numbers. Also, there's the question of what a Bitcoin "user" is. If you bought a little Bitcoin through an ATM (see Chapter 3), are you really engaged in the Bitcoin network?

Still, interest in Bitcoin is growing, and growing fast. More and more corporations and financial institutions are getting involved, and yes, more individuals are buying in. There's every reason to think that growth will continue.

Bitcoin Adoption by Corporations

Talking of Bitcoin adoption, it's not just individuals stampeding to buy Bitcoin; many large corporations have jumped in. Companies have been adopting Bitcoin as a "reserve asset" at a rapid pace; that is, instead of dropping excess cash into a bank account or other form of short-term investment, they're buying Bitcoin.

Consider the words of Michael Saylor, CEO of MicroStrategy (a $6 billion public software company), on his decision to buy hundreds of millions of dollars' worth of Bitcoin. The company had half a billion dollars in cash to store, but they also "had the awful realization that we were sitting on top of a $500 million ice cube that's melting," thanks to inflation. So, they dropped $425 million into Bitcoin (and then saw the value increase by 50 percent and then drop back down to a more modest 5 percent or so rise at the time of writing). "Bitcoin is a bank in cyberspace," said Saylor, "run by incorruptible software, offering a global, affordable, simple, and secure savings account to billions of people that don't have the option or desire to run their own hedge fund."

The idea that large corporations should drop their cash into Bitcoin took many Bitcoiners by surprise, but it bodes well for pricing. Another well-known corporate purchaser of Bitcoin is Tesla, which purchased 48,000 Bitcoins, and has seen the value rise by around $500 million since then. If you'd like to see a list of dozens of such companies, with holdings between a few dozen Bitcoin and tens of thousands, check out `https://bitcointreasuries.net/`.

Bitcoin Is Dead!

It's worth considering past claims and predictions when considering what may happen. One thing we can be sure of is that, just as in the past, claims that *Bitcoin is dead* will continue!

While Bitcoin continues its overall rise in price — yes, with disturbing drops, admittedly — claims and predictions of the demise of Bitcoin have been common, so much so that dedicated websites collect such claims:

- Bitcoin Is Dead, at `https://www.bitcoinisdead.org/`
- 99Bitcoins, at `https://99bitcoins.com/bitcoin-obituaries/`

The latter, for instance, claims that "Bitcoin has died 434 times." Actually, not all of the collected citations are of pundits claiming that Bitcoin *is* dead. Many are stating that it *will be* or *should be* dead; they are collections of Bitcoin skeptics.

We haven't seen the end of Bitcoin yet (and Bitcoin true believers would claim that we won't live long enough to see its end). So, while you'll run into plenty of skeptics — and from an investing standpoint, you might want to at least be aware of their arguments — the true believers are having the last laugh, at least for the moment.

Bitcoin Boom-and-Bust Cycles

The prices of many commodities, such as oil or precious metals, seem to go through boom-and-bust cycles. An oil-price chart for the last 75 years looks like an extreme roller coaster, for instance.

In the case of some commodities, this is generally due to supply and demand issues. Co-author Peter well recalls the bust in the oil business in the early 1980s, as supply increases caused a high of $133 in 1980 to crash to a low of $27 in 1986, which is when he lost his oil-business job! (That's not the worst, though; one day in 2020 the price actually went *negative!* You couldn't give oil away!)

Over time, the production of oil can grow dramatically, which causes these drops in pricing. With commodities such as gold and Bitcoin, though, pricing is essentially dependent on demand, on belief in the asset. If an asset has little or no *intrinsic* value — that is, it can't be used for anything but as a store-of-value asset — it's all about how people think about the stability of the asset.

REMEMBER

Gold, for instance, is not used for much beyond acting as a store of value, a subject we discuss later in this chapter. Bitcoin can't be used for *anything but* a store of value, and so its value is very sensitive to belief, and tends to be quite volatile.

This dependance on belief is a double-edged sword. It is *belief* that has led the price of Bitcoin to go from essentially nothing all the way up to $60,000 a coin, and it is *belief* that has led to gold being used as an asset for 6,000 years. But *belief* — or rather, a lack of belief or reduction in belief — can lead to a sudden drastic drop in price, and even (according to some economists) could lead to a complete crash of Bitcoin.

The Bitcoin true believer accepts this volatility, with the belief that over time, there's an upward curve. It may drop today, but hold on (or hodl on, as they'd say), it'll come back. Maybe tomorrow, maybe next month, or maybe next year, but it *will* (they believe) come back. If you want to invest in Bitcoin, that's a decision you'll have to make for yourself. One of the biggest questions in life is "Who do you believe?"

In short, the future of Bitcoin includes great volatility. In fact, Figure 12-1 shows what CoinMarketCap.com has to say about the volatility of Bitcoin, starting from when the public first started to take notice of Bitcoin in the summer of 2017.

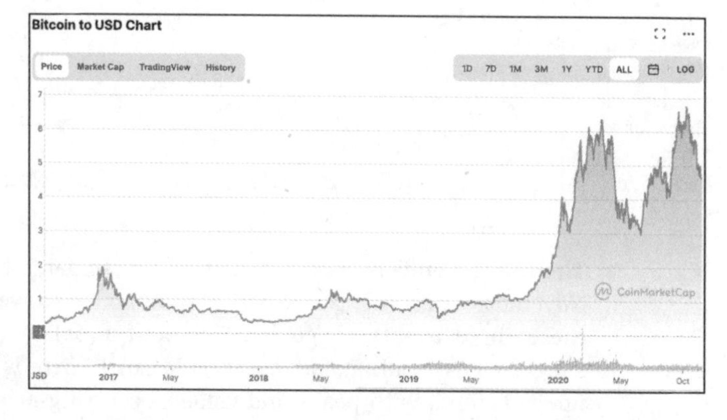

FIGURE 12-1: Bitcoin volatility — it's a wild ride!

The Halvening and Bitcoin Price

There is a belief among Bitcoiners that the price of Bitcoin is given a "boost" by the halvening event. As we discuss in the section, "Bitcoin's Limited Supply Drives Price," earlier in this chapter, every four years the number of Bitcoins issued for each block drops in half. Many Bitcoiners believe these halvening events line up with boom-and-bust cycles of Bitcoin. Are we going to see some effect due to future halvenings?

The theory in some quarters is that the price of Bitcoin rises just before and after the halvening events, and some posit there's somehow a relationship between the price and the fact that immediately after the halvening, miners will earn half as much Bitcoin. Another argument is that because the rate of increase slows, and demand keeps going up, price has to go up.

However, these theories have a few problems. (You can see the halvenings on the price chart in Figure 12-2, by the way.)

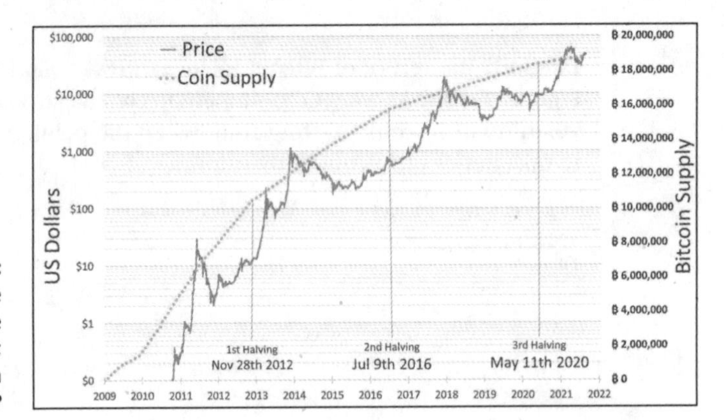

FIGURE 12-2: Bitcoin price and the halvenings; is there an association?

There have only been three halvenings so far, of course — November 2012, July 2016, and May 2020 — so we only have these three events to go by. The first problem is that the suggested association *does not seem to exist!* There is a constant upward trend, with peaks and valleys occurring now and then, but there doesn't seem to be a particular correlation between the actual day of the halvening and these peak prices and subsequent drop-offs. The peaks seem to occur at different times during the cycles, and there are, in fact, multiple peaks and drops during each cycle.

The second problem is that there has been no really good suggestion for *why* the halvening should have a rapid effect on pricing. Price, remember, is based on belief in Bitcoin, not the desires of the miners. As belief goes up, price goes up, and as the market starts to get a little scared, the price goes down.

A basic Bitcoiner belief posits that price is directly correlated with demand and supply. If supply goes down and demand remains the same, price goes up. If demand goes up and supply remains the same, price goes up. But what does that have to do with the halvening exactly? After each halvening, the supply has not only not declined but has actually continued increasing (by 900 new Bitcoins every day after the most recent event, which equates to about 30,000 Bitcoin a month); thus, the price is going up because demand has increased. And if the price is going up because demand is going up, then what *exactly* is the correlation between halvening and price, if anything? Nobody seems to be able to say much beyond, "halving Bitcoin issuance rates boosts prices."

(Here's a challenge. Create a chart showing world population over time, then mark the leap years on it. You'll see that after every leap year, the population of the world goes up!)

It's far more likely that price changes are associated with activities in the Bitcoin markets and the prognostications of pundits than they are related to the halvenings. Any possible effect caused by a slowing of the new supply is swamped by interested investors and institutions joining the Bitcoin network. Any association that an observer might *think* they can see is most likely a combination of coincidence and confirmation bias.

So, here's our prediction. After every halvening, the price of Bitcoin will go up — unless demand for Bitcoin drops!

New Bitcoin "Layers"

There's a big problem with the Bitcoin "base layer," the basic functioning of the network. There simply isn't enough capacity for Bitcoin to ever become a genuine currency managing tens of millions of transactions a day. There is quite simply not nearly enough capacity on the network to service the needs of all the folks who would want to use it if Bitcoin were a genuine currency. Bitcoin is often criticized, in fact, for low transaction capacity, too much energy usage, and slow transaction settlements.

For instance, the Visa network processes around 45,000 transactions per second, which is far beyond what the Bitcoin network can possibly do. (As we discuss in Chapter 3, it takes *minutes* for your transactions to be processed.) Because of this, many in the Bitcoin community have begun working on additional "layers" to scale the Bitcoin network and speed up the processing of large numbers of transactions (and also to add other capabilities to the network).

Bitcoin Lightning Network

The Bitcoin Lightning Network (see Chapter 4) has been in the works since early 2016. Check out the original proposal for yourself at `https://lightning.network/lightning-network-paper.pdf`. Since this paper was released, capacity on the Lightning Network has grown to over 2,200 Bitcoins across 10,000 nodes.

The Lightning Network allows Bitcoin owners to run transactions outside the Bitcoin network — on the Lightning Network — and have them periodically recorded in the Bitcoin blockchain. The Lightning Network will process the transactions very quickly and cheaply, and "settle up" with the Bitcoin network later. This is similar to the age-old bar tab (a hashed, time-locked bar tab).

The Lightning Network is many times more efficient, has a quicker final settlement, and holds more transaction capacity than even the most centralized network. It has been estimated that the Lightning Network would be able to process transactions far, far faster than the Visa network — in theory, exponentially faster. Transactions can be completed in milliseconds with almost zero energy usage at a rate of millions per second. The Lightning Network can handle micropayments, too.

You may have heard that in June 2021, El Salvador's Legislative Assembly voted to use Bitcoin as legal tender, based on the Lightning Network. The government even issued its own Lightning Network wallet (though citizens can use others if they want).

Bitcoin sidechains

A *sidechain* is a blockchain separate from, although dependent on, the Bitcoin blockchain. Additionally, it works in conjunction with the Bitcoin blockchain, uses Bitcoin as a currency, and can send transactions to and from the Bitcoin blockchain. (Other blockchains have sidechains, too; a sidechain is always dependent on its parent blockchain.)

Thus, sidechains can be created, and likely will be, for many different purposes. The idea has been around since at least 2012, though it has moved slowly. There are, however, a couple of functioning sidechains:

- RSK (https://www.rsk.co/) brings smart contracts to the Bitcoin network. Smart contracts essentially create smart money; transactions can be created that depend on the fulfillment of certain criteria in the contract.
- The Liquid Network (https://blockstream.com/liquid/) was designed to provide faster, cheaper transactions between traders and exchanges.

Bitcoin Will Get Easier

Bitcoiners believe Bitcoin is the future of money, but numerous changes are needed for that to happen. Bitcoin transactions have to be quick, easy, and ubiquitous. They're not, of course. Working with Bitcoin can be complicated and frustrating. In fact, Bitcoin true believers have two conflicting beliefs: 1) Bitcoin is the future of money, and 2) "not your keys, not your money" — if you own Bitcoin, you need to manage your private keys for yourself, not allow someone else to do so. Custodial (as in *custodial wallets*) is a dirty word for true believers.

The problem is that unless working with Bitcoin becomes easier, it can never become as widespread; it's quite simply too complicated. (Compare how easy it is to use your credit card with everything we teach in Chapters 3, 4, and 5, where you discover how to buy and sell Bitcoin and keep it safe.)

REMEMBER

Many Bitcoin movers and shakers already understand this and are working to make owning and using Bitcoin easier and safer. Yes, that means encouraging the use of custodial wallets, but provided by solid corporations following best practices to secure (and even insure) clients' assets. Today, most Bitcoin owners use custodial wallets. Some of those wallets are on exchanges that are probably *not* safe, but many are in a new generation of secure, well-run institutions.

Bitcoin Development and Bitcoin Improvement Proposals

We talk in this book about how the Bitcoin network has certain characteristics "backed into" the mathematics that are used to run the system. And that's true. As we discuss earlier in this chapter, the halvenings are pre-determined — baked in, if you will.

However, Bitcoin is an open-source system, meaning anyone can download the Bitcoin software and modify it. Many people have done this and started their own cryptocurrencies. More than 10,000 cryptocurrencies exist; many of them are based on the original Bitcoin source code. Some of these cryptocurrencies are even named after Bitcoin: Bitcoin Wrapped, Bitcoin Cash, Bitcoin BEP2, and so on.

REMEMBER

These are not the same as Bitcoin. This entire book is about the Bitcoin network, BTC. Today that network has a market capitalization of almost $900 billion and a coin price of over $47,000. The next closest Bitcoin-named "clone" is Wrapped Bitcoin, with a market capitalization of around $340 million, a tiny fraction of Bitcoin's value (though at the time of writing, the individual coins are worth about the same).

Anyway, because the Bitcoin network is open source, not only can anyone download and use the software, but anyone can also suggest changes to the software; these are known as *Bitcoin Improvement Proposals* (BIPs). Nobody can jump in and change the code, because in order to change the actual Bitcoin network, the entire network has to agree to and adopt the changes. Bitcoin was designed to be difficult to change, so that no individual group or organization can take control and push it in a direction that most Bitcoin community members would not approve of.

But the software *does* evolve. (You can actually see the evolution in action at `https://github.com/bitcoin`.) The Bitcoin network is sometimes accused of evolving too slowly, but many feel that limited and cautious system improvements are a good thing. The changes that have been made and proposals currently in the works include modifications such as these.

- **Schnorr Signatures — BIP 340:** Schnorr Signatures are a cryptographic digital signature tool (originally developed by Claus Schnorr). Some Bitcoin developers want to use these on the Bitcoin network because they provide a slightly more elegant, efficient, and capable signature implementation compared to the Elliptic Curve Digital Signature Algorithm (ECDSA) system in use today. Schnorr should actually reduce transaction fees a little.
- **Segwit BIP 84:** Segwit — Segregated witness — is an improvement in the way transaction messages are constructed, so that the signature is not included in the size calculations for block size considerations.
- **Dandelion BIP 156:** Dandelion is a transaction routing mechanism that would provide protection against user privacy attacks at the network level. Dandelion enhances user privacy by sending transactions through an anonymity layer before distributing them out to the network.
- **Simplicity:** Some Bitcoiners are calling for the integration of the *Simplicity* scripting language to be added to the Bitcoin network, allowing the development of special scripts that would add useful features to Bitcoin. For instance, Simplicity scripting could be used to build *vaults* into the Bitcoin blockchain — essentially locking one's Bitcoin into the blockchain — with built-in *devaulting periods*. After a transaction is sent to the network, the Bitcoin will not be transferred until after the end of the devaulting period, blocking someone who has wrongfully accessed a private key from quickly stealing the Bitcoin.
- **PSBT BIP 174:** This proposal is for partially signed Bitcoin transactions. They would allow for unique multi-signature applications, as well as offline signatures, and various other multi-party features.
- **RGB:** This is a suite of protocols for scalable and confidential smart contracts on the Bitcoin and Lightning Networks. We haven't discussed smart contracts in this book, because they're not a big Bitcoin feature, but are very important on the Ethereum network, the second-most important

cryptocurrency network. See *Cryptocurrency All-in-One For Dummies* (Wiley) for more about Ethereum and smart contracts. You can find more info at `https://rgb-org.github.io/`.

What *Is* the Future of Bitcoin?

As someone perhaps famous once said (nobody's quite sure who Niels Bohr, Samuel Goldwyn, Yogi Berra, or someone quite different), "It's difficult to make predictions, especially about the future." What, *exactly*, will happen to Bitcoin? Will it become the world's predominant currency, or will it disappear in a sudden collapse? Will it survive as a useful "store of value," as gold has but with little transactional use, or will it just fade away?

The Bank of England recently issued a warning. Sir Jon Cunliffe, the Bank's deputy governor, said that Bitcoin "could theoretically or practically drop to zero." (It's estimated, by the way, that a tenth of a percent of household wealth in the UK is stored in cryptocurrencies; not huge, but not nothing.)

The bank's financial policy committee said that at present, Bitcoin represented little threat to the stability of the UK's financial system, but that could change as cryptocurrencies become more embedded and interconnected to it. A bank blogpost stated that, "The problem is that, unlike traditional forms of money, Bitcoin isn't used to price things other than itself. As Bitcoiners themselves are fond of saying, 'one Bitcoin = one Bitcoin.' But a tautology does not a currency make."

The same blogpost stated that Bitcoin's scarcity, far from being a powerful feature, "may even, ultimately, render Bitcoin worthless. Simple game theory tells us that a process of backward induction [thinking through a process starting at the end point and moving back in time] should, really, at some point, induce the smart money to get out. And were that to happen, investors really should be prepared to lose everything. Eventually."

Or how about Nobel prize–winning economist Paul Krugman, who describes himself as a "crypto-skeptic." It's not a real currency, he says, and as we point out in this book, that's correct; there are much easier ways to buy coffee, groceries, and beer — the essentials — than using Bitcoin. Krugman understands that this is not necessarily a problem. As he points out, gold has held value even though it hasn't been used as a currency for a long time, and even large quantities of $50 and $100 bills are not being used as currency; the share of dollars held as cash has actually gone up over 30 years, at a time when cash transactions have been in decline.

However, Krugman's worry is that there is no direct "tether" between Bitcoin and the real economy. Gold, he says, has a weak tether to the real economy; while most just sits around storing value, at least some is used for electronics, jewelry, and gold teeth, another form of jewelry, really (and, in fact, the purpose of much of the world's jewelry — likely most — is actually as a household store of value with, when not locked away, the additional benefit of adornment).

This "provide[s] a weak but real tether to the real economy. Cryptocurrencies, by contrast, have no backstop, no tether to reality. Their value depends entirely on self-fulfilling expectations — which means that total collapse is a real possibility. If speculators were to have a collective moment of doubt, suddenly fearing that Bitcoins were worthless, well, Bitcoins would become worthless" (`https://www.nytimes.com/2018/07/31/opinion/transaction-costs-and-tethers-why-im-a-crypto-skeptic.html`).

REMEMBER

But the tether between gold and the real economy is *very* weak. At the time of writing, gold is $1,772 per ounce. What is the *intrinsic* value of gold? What would it be worth if everybody stopped using it as a store of value? Well, first, only around 2,900 tonnes (a tonne is a metric ton, which is a unit of mass equal to 1,000 kilograms) of gold are mined each year. But there are around 177,200 tonnes of existing gold stocks, virtually all of which are being used for a store of value, and the true consumption uses of gold seem to be around 400 tonnes a year. What if all that gold came on the market for no-store-of-value jewelry, electronics, and a few other purposes such as some medical applications?

That's hard to say, but gold's value would decrease — most estimates seem to be in the range of $10 to a few dozen dollars per ounce. Way back in 2014, the Global Chief Economist at Citigroup compared gold to Bitcoin, and described gold — thanks to the fact that it has very little intrinsic value — as a "six-thousand-year-old bubble" and effectively "shiny Bitcoin." He regards gold as an asset whose price is dependent on a financial bubble ("the longest-lasting bubble in human history"), but also believes that the "bubble may well be good for another 6,000 years." (This is a fascinating paper; check it out at `https://willembuiter.com/gold2.pdf`.)

Even crypto-skeptic economist Krugman has at times suggested that the intrinsic value of gold is so low that it *is* comparable to Bitcoin, and thus Bitcoin may well survive as a store of value, just as gold has.

So, let's finish with another quote about the future. As President Eisenhower once said, "The future lies before us." That's really the *only* thing we can say for sure.

Index

Numbers

2FA (two-factor authentication), 109, 154–158
51% attack, 234
401(k)s, 182–183

A

acquiring Bitcoin, 55–58. *See also* mining
  caution with exchanges, 88–90
  Coinbase
    finding best exchange rates, 56–57, 85–87
    overview, 75–79
    sending Bitcoin to another wallet, 79–84
    sending Bitcoin to Coinbase wallet, 84–85
  Coinme network
    custodial wallet, 65–67
    overview, 58–61
    purchase process, 61–65
    sending Bitcoin from Coinme wallet, 67–70
  credit and debit card programs, 90
  fees
    ATMs, 59, 60, 71
    exchanges, 85
    overview, 57
  financial institutions, 92–93
  as form of payment, 91–92
  other ATM networks, 58, 70–72
  other exchanges, 87–88
  person-to-person trading, 73–75
  pricing, 56–57
  retail Bitcoin, 72–73
addresses, 14–15, 19, 30, 41
  entries, 31–33
  keys and, 99
  public/private-key encryption, 46–50, 203
  wallets and, 41, 47, 99–100, 119–120
adoption, 211–212
  corporate, 212, 262–263
  governments
    El Salvador, 214–217
    overview, 212–214
    poorer nations, 219–221
    promotion by other nations, 217–219
    troubled nations, 221–224
  speed, 261–262
air-gapped wallets, 35, 104–105
anti-money-laundering (AML) regulations, 63–64
anti-virus software, 2, 150
Apple, 7–8
Apple Pay, 74, 90
arbitrage strategy, 180–181
assets
  Bitcoin as, 165–170
  stock-to-flow model, 170–173
ATMs
  Coinme network
    custodial wallet, 65–67
    overview, 58–61
    purchase process, 61–65
    sending Bitcoin from Coinme wallet, 67–70
  overview, 70–72
authenticator apps, 154–158
Azteco, 168

B

backdoor software, 108
backups, 2, 124–125, 144, 148
Bank of England, 218, 272
Bank of Lithuania, 217
bans, 212–214, 227–228
belief-based value, 18–19
  boom-bust cycles, 264–265
  Milton Friedman economic theory, 19–22
  money, 22–23
best practices. *See* security
Bing.com search, 56–57

BIPs (Bitcoin Improvement Proposals), 270–273
Bisq person-to-person trading, 74
Bitcoin, 1–4, 7–8
  addresses, 14–15, 19
  as asset
    overview, 165–170
    stock-to-flow model, 170–173
  banning of, 212–214, 227–228
  belief-based value, 22–23
  benefits
    overview, 23–27
    rise in value arguments, 167–168
    troubled nations, 221–224
  Chainalysis on adoption of, 211–212
  corporate adoption, 212, 262–263
  criticisms of
    cost/fees, 231–233
    electricity costs/energy usage, 169, 174, 184, 234–236
    government bans, 212–214, 227–228
    investment bubble, 168–169, 230–231
    overview, 225
    security risks, 233–234
    similar to Ponzi scheme, 229–230
  disadvantages, 93–95, 169–170
  durability, 25
  finalized settlement, 26
  financial institutions and, 92–93, 168
  future
    adoption speed, 261–262
    halvening events effects, 260, 265–267
    improvement proposals, 269–273
    layers, 267–269
    limited supply effects, 259–261
    Lindy Effect, 258–259
    overview, 257–258, 272–274
    possible end, 263
  genesis block, 12, 14, 260
  gold versus, 167–168, 173–175, 231
  governmental adoption of
    El Salvador, 214–217
    government bans, 212–214, 227–228
    poorer nations, 219–221
    promotion by other nations, 217–219
    regulation, 212–214
    troubled nations, 221–224
  halvening events, 14, 27, 171, 209
  importance of understanding, 13–17
  insurance, 89–90
  layers, 267–269
  lost/stolen
    2FA, 154–158
    Bitcoin value, 172
    in cases of death, 161–164
    creating powerful passwords, 145–147
    digital inheritance feature, 163–164
    insurance, 89–90
    multi-signature wallets, 162
    other considerations, 158–161
    overview, 55, 139–142
    password-management programs, 147–149
    phishing, 151–154
    protecting computer, 149–151
    recovering wallets, 125–127
    scheduling future transactions, 163–164
  market capitalization, 7, 167, 246–247
  maximum number, 17, 259–261
  origin, 8–12
  partial units, 16–17
  regulation, 213–214
  retail Bitcoin, 72–73
  selling, 75, 93–95
  stock-to-flow model, 170–173
  technical analysis, 245–247
  value versus fiat currencies, 212–213
Bitcoin ATMs
  Coinme network
    custodial wallet, 65–67
    overview, 58–61
    purchase process, 61–65
    sending Bitcoin from Coinme wallet, 67–70
  directory, 71
  other, 70–72
Bitcoin blockchain, 32, 37–40
Bitcoin exchanges, 41, 75
  caution with, 88–90
  Coinbase
    buying Bitcoin, 75–79
    sending Bitcoin to another wallet, 79–84
    sending Bitcoin to Coinbase wallet, 84–85

different types, 87–88
exchange rates, 56–57
finding best rates, 85–87
Bitcoin Improvement Proposals (BIPs), 270–273
Bitcoin ledger, 13–15, 40–41
addresses
entries, 31–33
overview, 41
public/private-key encryption, 46–50
immutability, 32, 37–40
Bitcoin network, 29–31, 195–196. *See also* nodes
addresses, 30, 46–50
Bitcoin blockchain
hashing, 37–40, 205
immutability, 32, 37–40
Bitcoin wallet, 30
transactions
change address, 202–203
encryption, 42–43
fees, 200–202
overview, 36–37, 200
verification, 203–204
"Bitcoin P2P e-cash paper" (Nakamoto), 10
bits, 218
blockchain, 8–12
addresses, 14–15, 19
distributed, 32–34
encrypted, 43
explorer, 41, 43, 66
messages to
fees, 200–202
message signing, 46–50, 100
blockchain explorer, 41, 43, 66, 252
blockchain-based cryptocurrencies, 8–11
BlueWallet software
checking addresses, 119–120
finding wallet via, 107–108
importing wallets, 125–127
increased security with fake account, 115–116
notifications, 118–119
Plausible Deniability option, 116
private keys and, 99
receiving Bitcoin, 100, 116–118
recovering wallets, 125–127
seeds
creating 24-word seed, 113–115
overview, 99, 106, 107, 112–113
sending Bitcoin, 120–123
setup, 110–113
UTXOs, 123–124
vault wallets
creating, 130–134
overview, 109, 129–130
sending Bitcoin from wallet, 134–135
wallet backups, 124–125
watch-only wallets, 127–128
boom-bust cycles, 264–265
brain wallets, 34–35, 101–102
Brazil, 219–221
Buiter, Willem, 260
Bukele, Nayib, 215

C

candidate block, 205, 208
Carmichael numbers, 44
cascading timeouts, 164
cash, 22–23, 31, 95, 213
Central Bank Digital Currencies (CBDC), 218
Chainalysis, 211–212, 219–221
change address, 202–203
Chaum, David, 9, 11
cheat sheet, 3
child keys, 114
China
Bitcoin ban, 213, 228
cryptocurrency use, 10, 219–221
digital currency, 218–219
Chivo wallet software, 215–216
civil disturbances, 221–224
Clear, Michael, 12
Coinbase
buying Bitcoin, 75–79
COIN exchange, 101, 181, 182–183
exchange rates, 56–57, 85–87
sending Bitcoin to another wallet, 79–84
sending Bitcoin to Coinbase wallet, 84–85
Coinme ATMs, 58–61
custodial wallet, 65–67
purchase process, 61–65
sending Bitcoin, 67–70

cold wallets, 34–35, 89, 100–101, 144
computers
  on Bitcoin network, 196–200
  caution with public, 159–160
  full nodes on
    Bitcoin network, 198–200
    overview, 35–36, 105–106
  protecting, 147–151
  security, 149–151
core wallets, 109
corporations, 212, 262–263
Craigslist transactions, 73
credit cards, 9, 10, 34, 90, 95, 221
criminal activity, 74, 169, 216–217
cryptocurrencies, 43, 94
  blockchain, 8–11
  in China, 10, 219–221
  Ethereum, 186, 188–189, 271–272
  investment strategies, 185–187
cryptography, 9, 41–43
  email, 34, 46, 156–157, 159
  public/private-key encryption
    message signing, 46–50, 100
    overview, 44–45, 203
    wallets, 50–51
  triangular arbitrage, 181
crypto-to-cash broker, 221
Cunliffe, Jon, 272
currencies, 17–18
  belief-based value, 30–31
  Bitcoin exchange rate between, 56
  Bitcoin value versus, 18–23
  digital, 8–10, 218–219
  roles played by, 23–24
  trading Bitcoin for, 74
currency debasement, 27
custodial wallets, 64–67, 71
  safety and, 144–145
  web wallets, 105
cybersquatters, 75–76
CypherWheel metal wallet, 103

D

data aggregators, 252
data visualizations, 255–256
databases, 32–33
dBTC (deci-Bitcoin), 16–17
DCA (dollar cost averaging) strategy, 177–178
death, 161–164
debit cards, 9, 90, 95
decentralized finance (defi), 186–187
deci-Bitcoin (dBTC), 16–17
dedicated full nodes, 35–36, 105–106
  Bitcoin network, 198–200
deposit accounts, 23, 213
digital currencies, 8–10, 218–219
digital gold comparison, 173–175
digital inheritance feature, 149, 163–164
Digital Transitional Action Plan, 217
digital-art market, 188–189
Dimon, Jamie, 169, 170
divisibility, 25
dollar cost averaging (DCA) strategy, 177–178
Dorsey, Jack, 167
Draper, Tim, 217
dry powder strategy, 242
durability, 25

E

e-gold cryptocurrency, 10
El Salvador, 17–18, 214–217
electricity costs, 234–236
Electrum server, 99, 118–119, 125–127
Elliptic Curve Digital Signature Algorithm (ECDSA), 271
email, 34, 46, 156–157, 159
encrypted blockchains, 43
encryption, 41–43
  email, 34, 46
  public/private-key
    message signing, 46–50, 100
    overview, 44–45, 203
    wallets, 50–51
  transactions
    overview, 42–43, 46
    public/private-key encryption, 46–50
energy usage, 234–236
e-Renminbi, 218–219
Ethereum cryptocurrency, 186, 188–189, 271–272
exchange brokers, 87–90
exchange rates, 56–57, 85–87

exchange traded funds (ETFs), 182, 212
exit scam, 144

F

Fair Labor Standards Act, 91–92
fake wallet accounts, 115–116
Fear Of Missing Out (FOMO), 176
Federal Reserve Bank of New York, 21, 218
fees, 57, 59, 60, 71, 85
  criticisms of, 231–233
  transaction messages, 200–202
fei stones, 19–22, 24, 172
fiat currencies, 15
  belief-based value of, 18–23
  Bitcoin value versus, 212–213
  roles played by, 23–24
  trading Bitcoin for, 74
51% attack, 234
finalized settlement, 26
financial institutions, 92–93, 168
financial technology (fintech), 186–187, 212
five dollar wrench attack, 116, 248
FOMO (Fear Of Missing Out), 176
401(k)s, 182–183
four-wallet groups, 162
Friedman, Milton, 19–22
fully validating nodes, 35–36, 105–106, 198–200
future transaction scheduling, 163–164

G

GameKyuubi, 98
genesis block, 12, 14, 260
Ghana, 219–221
Gibraltar, 218
Gnutella, 227–228
gold, 15, 185, 273–274
  belief-based value of, 264
  Bitcoin versus, 167–168, 173–175, 231
  stock-to-flow model, 170–173
Google Authenticator, 155
government bans, 212–214, 227–228
Great Britain, 15

H

hacking, 153
  of exchanges, 88–90, 93, 144
  passwords and, 145–149
  prevented by hashing, 37–40
  wallets and, 100–101
halvening events, 27, 171, 209
  Bitcoin price and, 260, 265–267
  overview, 14
Hanyecz, Laszlo, 95
Harari, Yuval Noah, 22, 30
hardware wallets, 35, 100, 104–105
hashing
  Bitcoin mining, 205
  exchanges, 82–83
  immutability, 32, 37–40
hierarchical deterministic (HD) wallets, 109, 113–115
hodling strategy, 95, 176–177, 184–185
  defined, 98
  tips
    conducting research, 239–240
    dry powder strategy, 242
    getting off zero, 240–241
    lowering cost basis, 241
    patient investing, 247
    price-prediction models, 244–245
    running Bitcoin-node software, 242–243
    securing keys and seeds, 243–244
    silence, 248
    technical analysis, 245–247
hot wallets, 35, 99–100, 107–108, 144
Human Freedom Index, 222

I

implicit bans, 213
inflation, 18–19, 223
insurance, 89–90
International Energy Agency (IEA), 235
international reply coupons (IRCs), 229
Internet
  blockchain-based cryptocurrencies and, 8–12
  cryptography, 41–43
  domain name system, 153

intrinsic value, 168, 170, 273–274
investment bubble
  Bitcoin, 168–169, 230–231
  boom-bust cycles, 264–265
  NFTs, 190–192
investment firms, 212
investment strategies, 165–167, 175–176. *See also* hodling strategy; volatility
  arbitrage, 180–181
  Bitcoin fall in value arguments, 169–170
  Bitcoin rise in value arguments, 167–168
  boom-bust cycles, 264–265
  DCA strategy, 177–178
  halvening events effects, 260, 265–267
  NFTs, 187–192
  other cryptocurrencies, 185–187
  other investment vehicles, 181–182
  retirement savings, 182–183
  stock-to-flow model, 170–173
  timing the market, 179–180
IRAs, 182–183
IRCs (international reply coupons), 229

K

Kenya, 219–221
keystroke logger software, 150, 159–160
Kleiman, David, 13
Know Your Client (KYC) regulations, 25, 26, 63–64
Kraken exchange, 85, 88, 181
Krugman, Paul, 15, 167, 169, 273–274

L

large corporations, 212, 262–263
ledger, 13–15, 40–41
  addresses
    entries, 31–33
    overview, 41
    public/private-key encryption, 46–50
  immutability, 32, 37–40
leetspeak, 153
libertarianism, 27, 211, 213
Lightning Network, 9, 17, 136–137, 267–268
lightweight nodes, 199
Lindy Effect, 258–259
listening nodes, 36, 198

M

M0 money supplies, 22–23, 31
M1 money supplies, 23, 31
M2 money supplies, 31, 213
Madoff, Bernie, 229
malware, 150
Market Value Realized Value (MVRV) ratio, 247
master passwords, 149
McCook, Hass, 235
memory pool (mempool), 204
metal wallets, 35, 102–103, 105
micro-Bitcoin, 16–17
MicroStrategy, 212
microtransactions, 9–10, 136–137, 267–268
milli-Bitcoin (millibit), 16–17
milliSatoshi, 17
mining, 14, 92, 195–196
  electricity costs
    criticisms, 234–236
    overview, 169, 174, 184
  mining contests, 204–208
  presets, 209–210
  winning Bitcoin, 208–209
mining rigs, 198, 206
money, 17–19
  belief-based value, 22–23
  Bitcoin exchange rate between, 56
  boom-bust cycles, 264–265
  cryptocurrencies versus, 94
  Milton Friedman economic theory, 19–22
  roles played by, 23–24
  trading Bitcoin for, 74
money service businesses (MSBs), 74
MoneyGram, 72
multi-signature wallets, 109, 129–130
  creating, 130–134
  for security, 162
  sending Bitcoin from, 134–135
Musk, Elon, 12, 167
MVRV (Market Value Realized Value) ratio, 247

N

Nakamoto, Dorian Prentice Satoshi, 12
Nakamoto, Satoshi, 2, 10–13, 14, 173, 184, 227, 260
Napster, 227–228

network value to transactions (NVT) ratio, 246
networks, 33–34. *See also specific networks*
NFTs (non-fungible tokens), 187–192
nodes, 34–36, 196–197. *See also* wallets
full
Bitcoin network, 198–200
overview, 35–36, 105–106
lightweight, 199
listening/super, 36, 198
nonlistening, 198
running own, 242–243
trustless system and, 199
non-fungible tokens (NFTs), 187–192
nonlistening nodes, 198
not your keys, not your coins maxim
caution with exchanges, 88–90
hodling strategy, 243–244
wallets and, 141, 144
NVT (network value to transactions) ratio, 246

O

O'Keefe, David, 172
Okung, Russell, 91
operating systems, 108–109

P

P2P networks. *See* peer-to-peer networks
Pakistan, 219–221
paper wallets, 34–35, 102
partially signed Bitcoin transactions (PSBTs), 271
passwords
for all devices, 150–151
creating powerful, 145–147
management programs
overview, 2
private keys/seeds, 113, 142, 144
safety plan, 147–149
PayPal, 9, 10, 74, 92
peer-to-peer networks
decentralization, 10–12
functionality, 33–36
immutability, 32, 37–40
remittances, 220, 223
personal computers. *See* computers
person-to-person trading, 73–74, 75
Philippines, 219–221
phishing, 151–154
picks-and-shovels investing, 181–183
Ponzi scheme, 229–230
poor nations, 219–221
portability, 24
port-out scam, 157–158
Portugal, 217
PoW (proof of work), 20, 205–206
Prasad, Eswar, 170
price-prediction models, 244–245
private keys
addresses and, 99
encryption, 44–45
message signing, 46–50, 100
protecting
hodling strategy, 243–244
overview, 140–144
wallets, 50–51
public keys and, 99, 203
wallets, 50–51, 98–99
private wallets, 144–145
proof of work (PoW), 20, 205–206
PSBTs (partially signed Bitcoin transactions), 271
public computers, 159–160
public keys, 44–45
addresses and, 99
encryption, 203
message signing, 46–50, 100
private keys and, 99, 203
wallets, 50–51
public Wi-Fi, 159
pump and dump schemes, 187
Punycode system, 153

Q

QR codes, 63, 100
quantum computing, 234

R

rai stones, 19–22, 24, 172
Rainbow Chart, 179–180
Raspberry Pi, 105, 106, 197
realized market capitalization (RMC), 246–247
remittances, 220, 223

resources
  blockchain explorers, 252
  books, 250
  data aggregators, 252
  data visualizations, 255–256
  documentaries, 249–250
  forums, 253
  foundational documents, 254
  guides, 251
  volatility charts, 253–254
  wikis, 255
retail Bitcoin, 72–73
retirement savings, 182–183
RGB protocols, 271–272
RMC (realized market capitalization), 246–247
Russian Federation, 219–221

S

safe deposit boxes, 143, 161, 162
safety. *See* scams; security
Satoshi clock, 17
Satoshis (sats), 16–17, 25, 60, 201
savings accounts, 23, 35, 213
Saylor, Michael, 167, 262–263
scams, 55–56, 73, 75–76
  backdoor software, 108
  exit, 144
  port-out, 157–158
  pump and dump schemes, 187
  seed, 73, 104–105
Schnorr Signatures, 271
security, 139–142
  addresses, 30
  backdoor software, 108
  backups, 144
  Bitcoin wallet backups, 124–125
  concerns over risks to, 233–234
  custodial wallets, 144–145
  losing Bitcoin, 140–142
  new addresses for receiving Bitcoin, 100
  planning for
    2FA, 154–158
    in cases of death, 161–164
    creating powerful passwords, 145–147
    digital inheritance feature, 163–164
    multi-signature wallets, 162
    other considerations, 158–161
    password-management programs, 147–149
    password-protection for all devices, 150–151
    phishing, 151–154
    protecting computer, 149–151
    scheduling future transactions, 163–164
    SIM swaps, 157–158
  private key protection, 140–144
  private wallets, 144–145
  protecting seeds
    hodling strategy, 243–244
    overview, 112–113, 142–144
    software wallets, 99, 106, 107, 112–113
  recovering wallets, 125–127
  wallets and, 100–103, 105
seeds
  creating 24-word, 113–115
  HD wallets and, 109, 113–115
  protecting
    hodling strategy, 243–244
    overview, 112–113, 142–144
    software wallets, 99, 106, 107, 112–113
  scams, 73, 104–105
  wallets, 99, 106, 107, 112–113
segregated witness (Segwit), 271
self-directed retirement accounts, 182–183
selling Bitcoin, 75, 93–95
silver, 15, 171
SIM (subscriber identity module) swaps, 157–158
simjacking, 157–158
Simple Payment Verification (SPV), 199
Simplicity scripting language, 271
smart contracts, 269
smartphones
  authenticator apps, 155, 156
  cryptocurrency wallets, 35, 98, 221
  hardware wallets, 105
  lightweight nodes, 199
  passwords, 148, 151
  QR codes, 63, 100
  security, 157
social engineering, 151–154
software wallets, 35
  addresses and, 99–100, 119–120
  backups, 124–125

considerations when acquiring, 108–109
creating 24-word seed, 113–115
fake account increased security, 115–116
finding, 107–108
importing wallets, 125–127
Lightning Network, 136–137
multi-sig
creating, 130–134
overview, 109, 129–130
sending Bitcoin from wallet, 134–135
notifications, 118–119
receiving Bitcoin, 100, 116–118
recovering wallets, 125–127
seeds, 99, 106, 107, 112–113
sending Bitcoin, 120–123
setup, 110–113
UTXOs, 123–124
watch-only wallets, 127–128
solo retirement accounts, 182–183
South Africa, 219–221
South Korea, 219
specialized dedicated Bitcoin node hardware, 197
SPV (Simple Payment Verification), 199
stacking sats. *See* hodling strategy
stock-to-flow model, 170–173
store of value, 166–168
Bitcoin versus gold as, 173–175, 231
stock-to-flow model, 170–173
subscriber identity module (SIM) swaps, 157–158
super nodes, 36, 198
Szabo, Nick, 12

T

tablets, 35, 98, 105
Tesla, 94, 167, 212, 263
Thailand, 219–221
time deposits, 213
tokens, 187–192
Tor, 227–228
trading platforms, 87–90
transactions, 36–37, 200
Bitcoin blockchain
hashing, 37–40, 205
overview, 36–37
change address, 202–203
encryption, 42–43
fees, 200–202
messages
fees, 200–202
message signing, 46–50, 100
overview, 43, 50–51
nodes and, 34
verification, 203–204
triangular arbitrage, 168, 181
Trojan Horses, 150
troubled nations, 221–224
trustless systems, 10–11, 32, 199
Tulipmania, 190–192
Tunisia, 213
Turkey, 168, 222
two-factor authentication (2FA), 109, 154–158

U

Ukraine, 217, 219–221
Umbrel software, 106, 197
United States, 15, 217, 219–221
University of Cambridge Bitcoin Electricity Consumption Index, 235
unspent transaction outputs (UTXOs), 123–124

V

Valereum, 218
Venezuela, 168, 219–221, 222
Venmo, 9
Vietnam, 219–221
viruses, 150
volatility, 7, 24
argument against investment, 94, 169–170, 226–227
boom-bust cycles, 264–265
volatility charts, 253–254
Vries, Alex de, 236

W

Wallet Import Format (WIF), 126, 127
wallet programs, 196, 202–203
wallet seeds, 99, 106, 107, 112–113, 113–115

wallets, 97–98. *See also specific wallets*
- addresses and, 41, 47, 99–100
- Bitcoin
  - checking addresses, 119–120
  - creating 24-word seed, 113–115
  - importing wallets, 125–127
  - increased security with fake account, 115–116
  - notifications, 118–119
  - receiving Bitcoin, 100, 116–118
  - recovering wallets, 125–127
  - seeds, 99, 106, 107, 112–113
  - sending Bitcoin to wallet, 120–123
  - setup, 110–113
  - UTXOs, 123–124
  - wallet backups, 124–125
  - watch-only wallets, 127–128
- change address, 202–203
- core, 109
- dedicated full nodes, 35–36, 105–106
- finding, 107–109
- Lightning Network, 136–137
- private keys and, 50–51, 98–99
- safety with, 89, 144–145, 162
- software
  - considerations when acquiring, 108–109
  - finding, 107–108
  - overview, 35
  - tasks performed, 99–101
- transaction messages
  - fees, 200–202
  - message signing, 46–50, 100
  - overview, 43, 50–51
- web, 105

Walmart2Walmart transfers, 74
watch-only wallets, 127–128
web wallets, 105
Western Union, 220–221
WIF (Wallet Import Format), 126, 127
Wi-Fi, 159
Wikileaks, 13

Y

Yap islands, 19–22, 172

Z

Zelle, 74
Zimbabwe, 19, 168

About the Authors

Peter Kent and **Tyler Bain** are the co-authors of *Cryptocurrency Mining For Dummies*. For decades, Peter has been explaining complicated technical subjects to regular people; he knows how to explain technology in a way that you can understand. He's the author of around 60 technology books — including *SEO For Dummies* and the *Complete Idiot's Guide to the Internet*. Since the 1980s, Peter has been teaching and explaining to readers and consulting clients — even attorneys, judges, and juries (he serves as an expert witness in litigation related to Internet technology). He also worked with a research institute visiting legislative offices in the United States Congress to help them understand the new world of cryptocurrency.

As for Tyler, he's been in the cryptocurrency mining trenches gaining experience in the ecosystem for a few years. He's also a professional engineer registered in the state of Colorado and studied engineering with an electrical specialty at the Colorado School of Mines, a university originally founded to support Colorado's mining industry and still one of the world's top mining schools (and no, they don't teach cryptocurrency mining. . . yet). Tyler is an active member of the Institute of Electrical and Electronics Engineers (IEEE) and the Rocky Mountain Electrical League (RMEL) and has advised the Electric Power Research Institute (EPRI). His passions include financial and transportation electrification, peer-to-peer systems, and the electrical grid.

Dedication

Tyler: For Satoshi, whoever that may be.

Peter: For Monique, once again. Now this is over, let's get out and ski!

Authors' Acknowledgments

Thanks to Steve Hayes and Chrissy Guthrie at Wiley for their patience and flexibility; they needed it for this one! Also to Margot Hutchison at Waterside for her assistance, and, of course, to the rest of the Wiley team who clean, polish, and produce the *Dummies* books.

Publisher's Acknowledgments

Executive Editor: Steven Hayes

Project Manager: Christina N. Guthrie

Development Editor: Nicole Sholly

Managing Editor: Kristie Pyles

Copy Editor: Marylouise Wiack

Technical Editor: Mark Hemmings

Production Editor: Saikarthick Kumarasamy

Cover Photos: © derrek/Getty Images

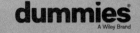

Small books for big imaginations

9781119177173
USA $9.99
CAN $9.99
UK £8.99

9781119177272
USA $9.99
CAN $9.99
UK £8.99

9781119177241
USA $9.99
CAN $9.99
UK £8.99

9781119177210
USA $9.99
CAN $9.99
UK £8.99

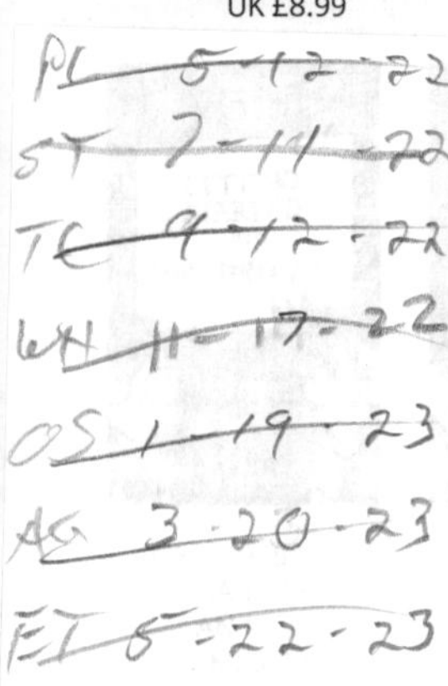

EXPERIMENTING WITH
Science
Think, Test, and Learn!

9781119291336
USA $9.99
CAN $9.99
UK £6.99

9781119233527
USA $9.99
CAN $9.99
UK £6.99

9781119291220
USA $9.99
CAN $9.99
UK £6.99

9781119177302
USA $9.99
CAN $9.99
UK £8.99

Unleash Their Creativity

...om

dummies
A Wiley Brand